W9-DCW-689

DOING
WHAT
HAD
TO BE
DONE

The Life Narrative of Dora Yum Kim

In the series *Asian American History and Culture*
edited by Sucheng Chan, David Palumbo-Liu, and Michael Omi

DOING
WHAT
HAD
TO BE
DONE

The Life Narrative of
Dora Yum Kim

Soo-Young Chin

Temple University Press PHILADELPHIA

Temple University Press, Philadelphia 19122
Copyright © 1999 by Temple University
All rights reserved
Published 1999
Printed in the United States of America

Text design by Dennis Anderson

⊗ The paper used in this publication meets the requirements of
American National Standard for Information Sciences—Permanence
of Paper for Printed Library Materials, ANSI Z39.48-1984

Library of Congress Cataloging-in-Publication Data

Chin, Soo-Young.
    Doing what had to be done : the life narrative of Dora Yum Kim / Soo-Young Chin.
        p.   cm.
    ISBN 1–56639–693–X (cloth : alk. paper). — ISBN 1–56639–694–8 (pbk. : alk.
paper)
        1. Korean American women Biography.   2. San Francisco (Calif.) Biography.
3. Women social workers—California—San Francisco Biography.   4. Korean Americans—Services for—California—San Francisco.   I. Kim, Dora Yum, 1921–   .
II. Title.
        E184.K6C468   1999
        305.48′8957073—dc21
                                                                    99–20104
                                                                        CIP

For Dora Yum and Young Ja Kim,

Mothers of the Female Lineage,

and my Father, Ki Bok Chin

CONTENTS

Preface   ix

Introduction   1

Part One: Chinatown, San Francisco   17

Descendants of Man Suk Yum
and Hang Shin Kim:
A Korean American Family Tree   24

1   American Origins   27
2   Coming of Age   41
3   A Mother's Devotion   62

Part Two: Dewey Boulevard   73

4   Leaving Chinatown   77
5   The Influx   91
6   Centering Service   112
A Family Gallery *following page*   138

Part Three: A Room of Her Own   139

7   Hidden Costs   143
8   On Her Own   149
9   *Hwan'gap*   163

Conclusion: Doing What Had to Be Done   169
Epilogue: Loose Ends   193
Chronology   201
Notes   207
Index   225

PREFACE

IT has been ten years since I started working with older Korean Americans and five years since I started this life story in order to more fully understand the meaning of one Korean late life ritual. Over the last ten years, although Koreans continue to immigrate to the United States, Korean America has changed. In 1992, after the civil unrest that wreaked havoc in the Los Angeles Korean American community following the Rodney King decision, a surprising number of immigrant Koreans simply packed up and returned to Korea. However, the majority remained, determined to take a stand in the only place that feels like home. The establishment of the Korean American Museum in Los Angeles reflects that determination.

When I moved to Los Angeles in January of 1995, to take a position at the University of Southern California, I was asked join the Program Committee at the Korean American Museum (KAM). Still just a start-up, the Museum had two staff members and a committee group of volunteers who did all the planning and installation. When I first started attending the meetings I was uncomfortable. As an anthropologist, I analyze the process of cultural reproduction and its impact on consumers, but as a member of the Program Committee I would be participating in cultural production and legitimation. Ambivalent as I was, I threw myself into the task, attending meetings to hammer out a five-year plan of exhibitions and educational programs. Unexpectedly, I became more involved in KAM's administration; within a short time I was asked to become chair of the Program Committee as well as chair of the committee planning an exhibition based on family stories, scheduled to open in July 1996. I suggested that the exhibit focus on life stories of pioneer families (in part because I wanted to continue my work on Dora Yum Kim's life), and museum personnel of staff and volunteers, all post-1965 immigrants, were enthusiastic. This exhibition allowed me to write the conclusion to Dora's life narrative at the same time that it gave me perspective on pioneer Korean families.

The story of the museum and the exhibition marks a significant shift for Korean America. Before the civil unrest of 1992, there were few public projects that captured the imagination of Korean Americans, and even fewer inspired community volunteers. Just three years later I found myself working with a team of volunteers of all ages who were committed to publicly claiming their place in America. Despite a unified goal, the museum is not an easy place to volunteer, as it is a challenge to satisfy the often divergent visions of Korean America held by various constituents. However, it can also be extremely rewarding and, in Dora's words, I "do what has to be done" there. I know it was my involvement with her that precipitated my enmeshment with the museum, and I both curse and thank her for getting me involved with "those Koreans."

Books are rarely written in isolation. There are numerous people who have directly assisted me in this project, people without whom this book would not have taken the form it has. I would like to thank my dissertation advisor, Christie Kiefer, without whose encouragement I might not have pursued Korean late life rituals. The seeds for this book on Dora were planted in a discussion with him when he asked, "What does Dora's life exemplify?" I would also like to acknowledge Mary L. Doi, as many ideas about the sixtieth-birthday ritual emerged from conversations with her. Preliminary research for this book was done as part of my dissertation—"A Comparative Study of Korean Late Life Ritual: Seoul and San Francisco." That research was funded by a University of California Regents Fellowship, a Three-Year National Institute on Aging Training Grant, and the University of California President's Doctoral Dissertation Award.

I would like to acknowledge Karl Lueck for his careful trancription of the last seven audiotaped conversations with Dora. Funding for trancription of these tapes was provided by San Jose State University's Faculty Research Grant. The NIMH Post-doctoral Fellowship in Culture and Mental Health at the University of Chicago gave me a year to work on the first draft of the manuscript. I would like to thank the participants of the Culture and Mental Health Seminar for their thoughtful feedback on the Conclusion. Adam Rose's careful reading of an early draft of that chapter is also much appreciated. Conversations with Rick Shweder and Jon Haidt were important for understanding the structure of Dora's narrative. Gil Herdt's input about life themes was helpful for developing the notion of resistance as a life orientation developed in the Conclusion.

I would like to acknowledge those involved in the Korean American Museum life story exhibition. I would like to thank Ralph Ahn, Howard Halm, Yin Kim, Colonel Young Kim, Dora Yum Kim, Carrie Kwon, and Mary Shon, the narrators of U.S. mainland-based pioneer family stories. With the ceaseless efforts of the museum staff Sunhee Ahn, Shih-ching Chiu, Myung Lee, Jung Jae Lee, Susan Park, and Mike Reinschmidt, along with the tireless work of volunteers Joseph Cha, Anna Chee, Yoon Cho, Pensri Ho, Eugene Kim, Susan Yang, and too many more to name, the project placed Dora's life story within the context of other mainland pioneer families, providing me new perspectives on her life.

I am grateful to Ellen Lewin for her invaluable comments on an early draft of the Introduction and her tireless support, which helped me through some dark moments of the project. Geyla Frank's insightful comments on an early version of the Introduction were extremely helpful, as was Sharon Suh's reading of a later draft. My gratitude goes to Greg Gottainer for proofreading the Introduction and Chapter 1 of the manuscript. I am also grateful to Anne Chee for her careful reading of the manuscript. I would like to thank my sister Suhl-Young Chin, ever the grammarian, for reading an early version of Part 1 of the manuscript and assuring me that the project was worthy. My thanks to Joseph Cha for reading and commenting on the manuscript without the Conclusion. I am thankful for discussions on feminism, resistance, and marginalization with Jay Hasbrouck, as these conversations influenced the direction of the book's Conclusion. I also appreciate the thoughtful comments from Sean Roberts on the Introduction and the Conclusion, and for urging me to reconsider issues of resistance and hegemony.

Comments from James M. Freeman and Melanie Han, the reviewers for the manuscript who let themselves be known to me, were of tremendous assistance. Suggestions from Michael Omi, the series editor at Temple University, were also invaluable. My deepest appreciation goes to Lon Y. Kurashige, whom I called too many times to discuss ideas related to the project, for reading a completed draft of the manuscript. I would also like to thank Janet Francendese, the editor at Temple University Press, for all her helpful suggestions, Alexa Selph for her careful copyediting, and Jay Hasbrouck for assisting me with the final proofing and indexing. Finally, I would like to thank Dora for her patience and support throughout the entire process.

DOING
WHAT
HAD
TO BE
DONE

The Life Narrative of Dora Yum Kim

INTRODUCTION

March 1986

ON *my first day as a volunteer at the Senior Meal Program at the Korean Community Center, an unassuming, seemingly ordinary, older woman who was filling glasses with barley tea introduced herself by saying, "Hi, I'm Dora. Why don't you help me serve lunch?" Although I knew that this woman was Dora Kim, it didn't sink in that this was the Dora Kim who was so highly regarded as a community leader. Given my own preconceptions of eminent Koreans, I expected someone more formal and authoritative. Instead, she handed me an apron and continued, "Why don't you ladle the rice onto the plates and pass them to me. Then I can finish serving the meal and bring it out to the seniors." I did as she asked, and for a little over two years I served lunch twice a week at the Korean Community Center, with and without Dora. Unlike most older Koreans I had met, Dora was obviously not a recent immigrant. While fluent in Korean, she spoke with an accent unfamiliar to me—not only did her Korean sound studied and non-native, there was also a regional dialect that I could not immediately place.*

In the months that followed, I started volunteering at Korean senior citizens' groups and attending churches that attracted older Korean immigrants. My interest in Korean seniors had to do with aging and community ritual life, focusing on the hwan'gap *celebration, a Korean rite of passage into old age conventionally marked at age sixty. When I started asking seniors about the* hwan'gap, *the number of people who spontaneously referred me back to Dora Kim's* hwan'gap *surprised me. Many described it as "amazing," and volunteered detailed descriptions of the event. In May, while I was attending the second of many* hwan'gap *celebrations I studied, the General[1] took me aside and told me, "I have noticed that you're observing many community celebrations. That's good*

1

because they're important. But you were absent from Dora's hwan'gap *celebration. Until you learn about Dora Kim's* hwan'gap, *you will not really fully understand the practice in the United States." The celebration of "a life well-lived" by community members is the affirmation of the kind of life that contributes to community development, and the emergence of a virtuous life model to which others can point.*

TERMS OF THE TELLING

I lost touch with Dora in 1989 when I went to Korea to do comparative fieldwork on late-life ritual, and I did not reconnect with her until the spring of 1992, when I ran into her at the Annual Conference of the Association of Asian American Studies in San Jose.

Dora and I met for lunch a week later, and I eventually asked about the life story that she had been considering when I last saw her. Around the time of her hwan'gap *in 1986, many people in the Korean American community had encouraged Dora to write her life story. Recent immigrants were eager to learn more about the history of Koreans in America. The old-timers, mostly descendants of Koreans who had immigrated at the turn of the century, had urged her to write her own story to resist the appropriation of her story by recent immigrants. Given Dora's involvement and allegiance to both groups, I was curious to see how she would negotiate the telling of her life.*

It had been my understanding that several people had approached her about working with her on her story, but either other commitments or Dora's reservations about how her story would be used had stalled the project. We talked about the various obstacles for a while when suddenly the direction of this conversation became clear to me. After a long pause I asked, "Would you like me to work with you on your life story?"

Dora replied, "I think that would be a pretty good idea." But before making a commitment, she wanted to call several people who were hoping to start such a project with her at some future date. "I'll call you and let you know in a few days."

And with that conversation we started negotiating this life story project.

Born in 1921 to Korean Christian immigrant parents, Dora Yum Kim was only one of about a hundred Koreans living in San Francisco's Chinatown. Situated as a minority within a minority, Dora, like other second-generation Korean children of her age, developed creative strategies to manage her "difference" in ways that would appease her Korean parents, permit her to get along with her Chinese and Japanese American peers, and manage the often hostile Euro-American society. People who succeed at such cultural crossings develop a variety of culturally appropriate self-presentations. This adaptive skill shows up in behaviors that express resilience among the American-born children of Koreans who immigrated at the turn of the century. This distinguishes them from their second-generation Chinese and Japanese American peers[2] who had ethnic age-mates with whom they could associate and commiserate. The particular ways in which she utilized her survival skills throughout her life also distinguish Dora from other Korean American women of her generational cohort.

Dora Yum Kim is now a prominent figure in Korean America as well as in the larger San Francisco community. Between 1965 and 1977, when she worked for the California State Department of Employment, Dora placed over three thousand Korean immigrants in their first jobs. In 1977 she took early retirement so that she could focus on the first Korean community center in the United States, which she cofounded in 1976. Ten years later, at age sixty-five, Dora retired from her position as coordinator of the Senior Center at the Korean Community Center; the Korean community gave her a hwan'gap celebration of grand proportions that is still unsurpassed in the San Francisco Korean community. While Dora does not officially work with any Korean service group, she still works as a medical interpreter for Korean immigrants. Dora Yum Kim is viewed by many community members as a heroine because of her activism on behalf of the Korean immigrant community.

Dora, however, does not see her life as singularly focused on the immigrant community nor exemplary in any way. She sees herself as someone who, throughout her life, "did what had to be done" to overcome the race and gender limitations that she and other Asian Americans faced. In the concluding section of this book, "Doing What Has to Be Done," the overarching logic Dora invokes to make sense of her life is the discourse of moral action, of making ethical choices. While the idea of overcoming the inequities of social and cultural constructions of race and gender is embedded in the Western notion of individual rights,[3] Dora's sense of corrective moral action, "doing what has to be done," is tied to the ethics of her social location.[4] "Chinatown, San Francisco," where she lived until age thirty-seven, highlights issues of duty, status, hierarchy, and interdependence engendered by her family and the situation of racial minorities in the United States. Dewey Boulevard, where she resided between the ages of thirty-seven and sixty-one, is couched within the American ethics of autonomy. "A Room of Her Own," which she has maintained since age sixty-two, is cast within a higher moral order in terms of right and wrong, merits and faults, sanctity and sin,[5] and reflects Dora's mind-set at the time of the telling. Dora was seventy when we started the life story project, and she had just rehabilitated from a stroke. Acutely aware of her own mortality, Dora sat in judgment of her life, seeking assurance that the choices that she had made were the appropriate ethical options, given her circumstances.

Despite the differences in orientation in the various self-designated stages of her life, "doing what has to be done" is the theme that links the three life locations. "Doing what has to be done" refers to actions inextricably tied to social circumstances: her position in the broader social milieu, as well as the specific relationships within which actions transpired. While Dora generally framed her stories within the moral context of her self-location at the time of the event, she also offered alternative interpretations.[6] She often repeated stories: her first version would generally reflect the way she remembered experiencing an event, while subsequent renderings would reflect her sense of increased autonomy in middle adulthood as well as the freedom that older people take in retrospection.

I have often wondered to what extent Dora's choice of a collaborator was simply timing and how much of it was my fitness for the task. I know that both factors played into Dora's decision.

Dora mentioned, "I am at an age when I have to just do what I want to or live with the fact that I may never do it."

Like Dora's other potential collaborators, I am of Korean descent. Dora likes to evoke Koreanness by way of explanation. She often comments on incidents by simply saying, "It's so typically Korean."

She leaves me to try to clarify her meanings by asking, "Do you mean unequal? Do you mean male-dominated? Do you mean status-conscious?" I know that Dora enjoyed the fact that I was willing to work for her story.

But I believe there were other reasons I may have been a good fit for Dora. She classifies Korean Americans into three categories: old-timers descended from Koreans who came to the United States between 1902 to 1924; the interim immigrants who came as students, professionals, servicemen's wives, and adoptees; and post-1965 immigrants. Although I am of Korean descent and came to the United States after 1965, Dora does not regard me as a regular post-1965 immigrant. There is a safe distance because I do not fit into Dora's scheme of Korean America. Having grown up in Southeast Asia, I am not easily traceable to parents or relatives who live in the United States or in Korea. As such it is difficult to locate me in any social ordering of Koreans or tie me to any of the many factions that exist within Korean and Korean American communities. Dora extended my liminal position in the community to my house, which she treated as a deterritorialized site where she could rail against the Korean or Korean American communities if she pleased.

Dora chose to come to my house to work on the narrative, saying, "I could not talk like this if I were at home. Someone might overhear, or interrupt. There is just too much interference, and I would not have been able to do it." Disconnected from her daily life, she could focus on her narrative, reconsidering her lifelong social ties, roles, and obligations.

Additionally, Dora, like other Korean women who shared parts of their lives with me for my dissertation research, feels that I am adult in a way that very *few Korean women are. If you are single, the older Korean woman's obligation is to protect you from the potential pitfalls of marriage so that you can move toward that institution. If you are married, the older woman's role is to encourage you to comply with conventional standards of marriage. I am neither. I placed myself outside conventional Korean standards years ago when I was divorced. As such, Dora felt free to discuss issues of an "adult nature," such as the difficulties of being female, marriage, and childbirth. Such topics are considered unwomanly to discuss and are mentioned in hushed tones under a code of silence. This code plays itself out in most interactions between women unless some "unfortunate" circumstance short-circuits the unspoken rules.*

Finally, although I am part of the academy and the vehicle for publishing her life story, Dora sees me as belonging to the academy in the abstract. She does not consider me a part of the academy with which she is familiar. Dora's rendering of Koreans in the academy is not flattering. She feels it is comprised of a group of status-conscious people, mostly men, who meet once a month at a "Ph.D. Club." These are men who will not deign to speak to another without academic credentials.

But Whose Life Is It?

A life story elicits and records a person's remembered and thus subjective past.[7] The anthropological study of lives and the critical use of life story as an ethnographic genre is one way to study culture through individual experience.[8] The usefulness of such a study has been thought to hinge on the selection of a "typical" subject who was somehow representative of her social group.[9] The interpretive turn of the social sciences has rendered the very notion of finding a "representative subject" or a "typical life" problematic, since the production of a life story reflects not only the ethnographer's questions, but also the models of biography within which those are framed.[10] In the current debates about interpretation, questions arise around the criteria for the typical or normative, as well as the ethnographic authority to speak of and for an informant.[11] Calls for "ethnographies of the particular" and "clinical ethnography"[12] have resulted in a shift in the genre of life writing. Works such as Crapanzano's Tuhami: Portrait of a Moroccan,[13] *Kendall's* Life and Hard Times of a Korean Shaman,[14] *and Behar's* Translated Woman[15] *attempt to reflect the cooperative process of eliciting and writing a life text. They recognize the reciprocal relationship between the telling and the stories themselves, giving equal significance to the telling and life narrative developed within the telling.[16]*

The focus of more recent life stories, as with ethnographies of the particular or clinical ethnographies, is the unique way in which subject and anthropologist jointly make sense of a lived life. While this calls for a reconsideration of the ways in which social facts are remembered, constructed, and reconstructed, it does not extract the teeth from anthropological life writing. Life stories reveal important subjective information, such as the narrator's understanding of her own life and her perceptions about the range of possibilities that were culturally appropriate, as well as the relationship between the subject and her culture.

The life story has moved well beyond the disciplinary boundary of anthropology and become particularly relevant to emergent scholarship that focuses on the examination of life patterns outside "normative" or male Eurocentric perspectives. Mapping a range of "alternative" experiences, these findings have served as a foundation for interdisciplinary fields such as Women's Studies, Ethnic Studies, as well as Gay and Lesbian Studies. In Asian American Studies several books have presented multiple life narratives.[17] While these texts are particularly effective in illustrating the multiple, layered, and nonequivalent experiences of men and women from various Asian ethnic groups, they do not capture the complex, often contradictory aspects of single lives. At this time there are no book-length English-language accounts of American-born women of Asian ancestry that span the entire life cycle.[18] Dora Yum Kim's life story is the first.

METHODOLOGICAL CONSIDERATIONS

The collection of a life story is a collaborative effort that emerges for various reasons. In discussing the need for collaboration in writing her life story, Dora commented, "You know I had a stroke a couple of years ago. I don't think I can wait any longer to write my life story and I can't write it alone. I think we can write my life story together." For Dora, it is not just health issues that prevent her from writing an autobiography; to write about herself is not in the realm of acceptable behavior. The autobiographical tradition emerged in the West, firmly rooted in the value placed on the individual, "with the confessionals of the Renaissance period. No comparable tradition arose in the Asian countries and autobiography writing . . . [was] not in the tradition of the Asian cultures that produced the first immigrants."[19] In China and Korea, the written form was the province of the elite, the educated, landed gentry—members of a class that was least likely to emigrate. The literati "traditionally confined themselves to poetry and classical essay. Autobiography was virtually unknown, since for a scholar [man] to write a book about himself would have been deemed egotistical in the extreme."[20] In Korea the only use of autobiographical form was for political purposes, although not many did so.[21] It has only been in recent years that prominent Koreans who spent time in the West have begun to engage in autobiographical endeavors.

Autobiographical form requires the presentation of a Western ego who is "a bounded, unique, more or less integrated motivational and cognitive universe, a dynamic center of awareness, emotion, judgment, and action organized into a distinctive whole and set contrastively both against other such wholes and against a social and natural background." [22] *This is in sharp contrast to many non-Western cultures that view humans as fundamentally connected to each other. According to Markus and Kitayama, in such cultures "experiencing interdependence entails seeing oneself as part of an encompassing social relationship and recognizing that one's behavior is determined, contingent on, and to a large extent organized by what the actor perceives to be the thoughts, feelings and actions of others in the relationship."* [23] *Since meaning rests within relational frames with social contexts mediating behavior, the person is not a bounded whole. The notion of a relational self defies the Western idea of an immutable ego, leading to a different construction of the basic social body. Power and control are generally contingent on position within social structures, not individual determination. And within the literary tradition the thematic concerns focus on performance of social roles rather than individual feelings or desires.* [24]

The implications of culture-of-origin notions of socially appropriate self-presentation and construction are significant for East Asian Americans, particularly for those who have maintained home country values and lifeways. Yet a relatively large body of Asian American autobiographical fiction and nonfiction emerged as early as 1909. [25] *This literary tradition, embedded in the Western tradition, is a new form adopted by Asian Americans. Asian American autobiography breaks from traditional Asian notions of writing and was adopted by immigrants and their descendants not steeped in Asian literary form. Still relatively few by or about women emerged until the mid-1930s.* [26] *The emergence of this literary form, particularly among immigrant women who came to the United States as adults, is quite remarkable. It speaks to the power of environment, the mutability of cultural sensibilities, and the rate at which notions of self change in relation to context. The ability to accept autobiography as a legitimate form speaks to the rapid transformation of the sense of self from one diffused in the collective body to an ego with individual agency; that is, the ability to write autobiography requires a relatively Western construction of self, family, and community.*

Asian Americans who adopt the autobiographical form speak or write about individual lives or life patterns that are distinct from group experience. However, both writers and audiences often impose the notion of a "collective self." Since audiences understand autobiographic materials as somehow the "truth" about the specific group or about Asian Americans as a racialized category, some writers feel pressured to write representatively. [27] *The audience to which I refer is not limited to readers outside the author's racialized or ethnic group. Audiences who share the author's background have also come to expect writers to be accountable to the group for the messages they may purposely or inadvertently convey. This phenomenon is not unique to Asian American autobiographies. It permeates the writing genre considered ethnic by virtue of the topic or authors' heritage. The notion of a "collective self" in autobiography, put forth by Brian Niiya, is key to understanding the Asian American autobiographical tradition:*

> Such autobiographies are published and read presumably because they tell us something not only about the individual author, but also about some group to which the author belongs. . . . [They] are written with the knowledge that people are reading to get insight about a group and they consciously speak not only for the author but for that group. . . . The collective self is often employed by members of a minority or alien group writing to members of a majority or ruling group.[28]

While the self-conscious rendering of a collective self is a strategy employed in ethnic autobiography or life story, there are other reasons that Dora utilized the collective agent. In the telling, Dora often used the collective "we" for many different voices. The use of the "we" may be embedded in the Christian tradition of the ecclesiastical "we" that, for the most part, describes the religious affiliation of the majority of Korean Americans. This tendency can also be traced to the Korean language, in which the term uri *(our) is the preferred and proper possessive pronoun used as a referent.[29] While there are many possible referents of the term* uri, *the primary "we" in Korean is the family. However, Dora's use of "we" is more mutable;[30] she uses it to allude to multiple referents, ranging from Koreans or Korean Americans in general, pre-1924 Koreans, women writ large, Korean women, her family of nativity, her nuclear family, to the two of us engaged in this life story project.*

When Dora uses "we" to include family and friends, it reflects people and individuals with whom she feels affinity, or chong.[31] *However, her more generalized use of the "we" to refer to entire groups such as the Koreans or Korean Americans reveals a conflation between family and community that occurred in childhood. The San Francisco Korean community remained stable at around a hundred people until after the 1965 immigration law, which opened up Asian immigration. According to Dora, the small Korean American community was "like a family. I don't think anyone from San Francisco in my generation married each other. That felt funny, like marrying your brother or something."*

Dora is second-generation Korean American, and she conceives of individuals as separate from their families and communities. Nonetheless, Korean social values that construct autobiography as self-absorbed and inappropriate do influence her. While the life story is a variant of the autobiographical form, its structure differs. Life stories are conveyed within relational frames, within the context of a giver and a solicitor of the story. This important feature allows many who would otherwise be uncomfortable talking about themselves to share their lives. When Dora agreed to tell her story to me, the telling of her life story was structured within the context of my solicitation, one of many requests for her life story.[32] *When we discussed the issue of joint authorship, Dora stated, "It's my life story, but you're the one who's going to have to work to get it out. Besides, don't you need single authorship for your job? As long as my name is on the cover, as part of the title, I think you should be the single author. After all, people will know it's my life story anyway."*

While it is true that Dora is concerned about the way this project will affect my career, that I would ultimately author her life story also subverts any potential allegations of acting in self-service, since I ultimately bear the responsibility for what goes into the text. Hence, life story emerges as a compromise between autobiography and biography.

Notwithstanding single authorship, the construction of a life story meant for publication is a joint production between investigator and informant. However, Dora's status in the San Francisco Korean American community complicates her life story. As a community heroine, Dora has a reputation to contend with, a reputation that includes a version of her life story that differs from the one constructed for publication. The large hwan'gap celebration that the community awarded Dora at her retirement is significant.[33] The purpose of the hwan'gap is to reify Korean notions of a life well lived, and to alert community members of the respect awarded an elder. In marking such a transition, the cumulative effect of a person's life work and relationships are reaffirmed in the planning and preparations for the event, as well as commemorated in the event itself.[34] As part of Dora's hwan'gap celebration, the local Korean newspapers and Korean language television publicized one version of her life story. Reaching scores of Koreans in the community, this heroic life narrative is now accepted as part of community lore.

The version of Dora's life story that the Korean media picked up was the biographical sketch that was included in the program of Dora's hwan'gap. It was recounted in Korean by the post-1965 immigrant Korean emcee and embellished upon in English and Korean by participants who came to give testimonials about Dora. While Dora had some input into the official text, it was her son, the director and cofounder of the Korean Community Center, and other post-1965 members of the Korean Community Center who wrote the copy. This public version of Dora's life celebrates her unwavering concern for "helping Koreans adjust to life in America." Dora's devotion and duty to the Korean community emphasize the subordination of self to the group, a virtue that supports the ethics of community.

Constructed around historical facts, the public version of Dora's life story that was crafted by the predominantly post-1965 Korean media was fashioned to reach both the minority of pre-1965 Koreans who are American-born, as well as those who have immigrated more recently. The primary focus of the public version of Dora's life was on her activism in the face of the barriers she faced as a

Korean and a woman. Her father's encouragement, however, was duly noted, and her accomplishments were couched in terms of her father's influence. This implicitly links Dora to male lineage, a Korean index of status that has been reaffirmed by more recent Korean immigrants. And while Korean American genealogies do not have the temporal depth of Korean lineage charts, the immigrants who pioneered the Korean American community at the turn of the century were, by and large, freedom fighters for the Korean Independence Movement. The Independence Movement is the most widely supported and continuously sustained social movement among Koreans in the twentieth century, and any contribution to this cause is considered to be of historical note. This movement also links Koreans in the United States to their contemporaries in Korea.[35] While it is a remote link for younger Korean Americans, for their elders, evoking this common effort joins recent immigrants with Korean Americans in a "community of memory," a sense of being constituted by the same past.[36] Hence, Dora's father's participation in the hungsa dan, *an organization established by well-known freedom fighter Ahn Ch'ang Ho to oppose Japanese occupation, further legitimates claims of Dora's Koreanness beyond Korean America.*

While being a Korean female certainly shaped her, Dora's personal narrative also focuses on the impact of social constructions of race and ethnicity on her life. Unlike the public narrative that focuses on her father's influence, the personal narrative specifically points to her mother as the primary source of encouragement. Additionally, although Dora actively worked with Koreans after she retired from the State Department of Employment, she reports that she fell into social work by chance, not by design. Given her language ability and the timing of the Korean influx to San Francisco, she was well situated for work with Korean immigrants.

The two versions of Dora's life have contrasting purposes. For public purposes, the life narrative is appropriated to foster a sense of cultural continuity and community. The construction of a personal life narrative is a way for the subject to look at her life retrospectively and create meaning out of accidental, incidental, and intentional incidents in her life. While purposes vary, both the public and the personal constructions grapple with issues of morality—how virtue is constituted in a life. Even though the differences between the public and personal versions of Dora's life story were never in question, the public version often interfered with the production of the personal narrative. As a well-known figure in the community, Dora felt that her life was not her own, and she was initially hesitant to diverge too much from the publicly known account of her life. Public figures are public property, and members of the Korean American community have made claims on her life story as somehow part of their story. Consequently, Dora felt obligated to recount parts of her life for them. For ex-

ample, in a relatively recent controversy about designating the first Korean church in San Francisco as an historical landmark, supporters asked Dora to give testimony from her life on the church's significance for the early Korean American community.

Over the course of the telling Dora became much more comfortable in revising the public account. This revisioning is, in part, a kind of culturally accepted license awarded to Korean elders. The liberties associated with old age are particularly powerful for women, because old age is a time when women become free from the social proscriptions they faced in earlier life stages. While it is unlikely that Korean cultural notions are the sole standard to which she subscribes, it is interesting that at age sixty-two Dora set up a studio apartment, "a room of her own," to which she could escape when "family stuff got to be too much." She felt that this was the time for her to overcome her lifelong impulse to ch'ama, to endure, restrain and hold back, and finally speak her mind. While it is an American sensibility that permits her to take on the project of making her personal narrative public, the construction was not easy. For much of her life Dora was a woman bound by notions of filial duty, obligation, and loyalty, and both Dora and I wrestled with issues of privacy and disclosure. Although Dora wanted "to tell it like it was," she sometimes worried about the discrepancy between the two versions of her life story and what community members might say if they read this book. However, we finally came to an understanding that to smooth out all her particulars would be at odds with the intent of the project.

Dora is burdened by the stories she remembers. As one of the few surviving members of the San Francisco Chinatown Korean community, and part of a small cohort of native second-generation Korean elders, she feels responsible for passing on her stories. According to Dora, "I have so many stories that will go with me to my grave untold unless I can include them in the life story." It offends her sense of morality and society that these stories might be lost, and the telling was the corrective measure. But to me, many of these tales sometimes seemed disconnected from the life story project or the hwan'gap. Once I recognized that despite my Asian ancestry, my model for a life was embedded within the Western autobiographical tradition and that Dora was committed to including particular stories, I struggled to make them fit. But I did not understand her sense of person and story until about six months into the project.

I said to Dora, in frustration, "So far you've told me stories about everyone you remember—family, family friends, acquaintances, clients. . . . You've included everyone. But you never really talk about yourself. Who exactly are you? How do you think about yourself?"

Dora paused before responding, "That's a really hard question. I don't have an answer to that. I don't really know how I think about myself. I know kids these days seem to be concerned about 'who they are,' but I don't think we thought about things like that when I was growing up. Who am I?"

After another long pause she said, "I just don't think of myself like that. I'm telling you about my life, and that should tell you something about me. I don't know what else to tell you. If it's really important to you, maybe you'll get a better sense of it as we continue the life story."

I have come to appreciate that Dora's life narrative, made up of other people's stories as much as her own, reflects Dora's sense of herself. She sees herself in relation to others; as a situationally defined person, and there is no life story without the people with whom she has shared life space. Dora includes other people's stories because they are essential to conveying the social whole created in interaction. She does not present a stable ego that is influenced by the changing environment. Instead, Dora offers and integrates numerous stories and often contradictory versions of self and social life that depend on her relationship with the social other; told within relational frames of familial and ethnic ties, Dora's life story is an account of the ways in which Dora's relationships with her social world changed.

Since Dora believes that a chronological presentation is most accessible, I attempted to record the narrative that way. Since I already had information about her life, she asked me to prepare guidelines of topics so that we could cover various periods of her life in the sessions. While this served to keep the narrative from wandering too far toward tangential topics, it also reinforced Dora's position as the giver and mine as the solicitor. This relationship was essential to the telling, and on many occasions I had to persist to get Dora to speak about her well-known achievements. Although she responded to direct questions, she would frequently qualify her account with comments such as, "If I say what I did, it is boasting or bragging. I don't want to do that. I think we should be modest and humble. I don't think that anyone told us to be like that, but it was implied, so we [Dora's second-generation Korean peers] all grew up that way. In terms of things that I've done, I only did what had to be done."

Despite our plan, Dora's narrative often leaped through time to follow up the themes about which she started speaking. About a month into the interviews, Dora asked to review the transcripts. Dora did not like the sequential breaks. While the transcripts from the first month revealed the continuity of themes throughout her life and much more about the way she thinks, she felt that this rendering broke the flow of the narrative. I then created a time line on a sheet of drawing paper and continued to fill it in for her to use as a reference. Dora was pleased with this arrangement and assumed the responsibility for filling the gaps for me.

As soon as we ordered the first month of transcripts chronologically, Dora *and I went through them for content. Reviewing the text for meaning was not easy. With red pen in hand, Dora would delete portions that she felt were too personal and correct the text, often commenting, "You need to 'fix' the transcripts for the book. I may have said this, but it doesn't make sense when you read it." Another problem that we both had with the life narrative was Dora's free-floating use of the relational referent "we." After we struggled through some two hundred of pages of transcripts to clarify the "we's," I asked Dora if she could, in future interviews, locate herself more explicitly. Dora concurred, commenting, "It would probably be a lot easier if I could be more specific in the future." Yet she still lapsed into the unfixed "we" unless I reminded her. In everyday speech, Dora uses the "I" only to refer to personal memory, as in "I remember . . ." or "I recall . . ." type statements and statements she felt were her own versions of cultural conventions. While it is controversial to impose structure on a subject, both Dora and I agreed it was necessary because the referential slippage in Dora's generalized use of the "we" created difficulties in understanding.*

As an academic anthropologist, I am somewhat troubled with the implied inequity in the relationship between the anthropologist and the subject. In academic anthropology the written form is privileged over the oral, and ultimately creates the expert. While it is the writer who must synthesize and analyze the words of informants, this process generally advances the position of the writer, not the informant. In this type of enterprise, the researcher can more easily study subjects who are of unequal status in terms of education, class, and race than establish rapport with people of equal or higher status. Once one has established expertise by writing, informants rarely have access to the work or to a platform from which to raise issues about the work. Additionally, while those of us engaged in such study often believe that we honor subjects simply by selecting them, they do not necessarily share that view.

The ethnographic relationship is often based on the willingness of informants to disclose information that interacts with the rough template that the anthropologist brings to the situation. While anthropologists do address investigator bias, it is difficult to get around the fact that compliance and complicity invariably influence informant selection. Like all human relationships, the ethnographic tie is reciprocal by its very nature, and a delicate balance between giving and taking is maintained. As anthropologists, we often privilege the informant with attention and tokens of gratitude in exchange for information or stories. My association with Dora, however, does not resemble the conventional ethnographic relationship. Not only does Dora have access to the life story, she came to me as an informant who shares my views about written work. She believes that written work is more enduring than oral storytelling and wants to leave a written record of her life. There was a complicitous element as we both undertook this endeavor to "elevate" her story beyond the oral form. Additionally, Dora is more privileged than I in the practice of life. Materially and experientially, she is light-years ahead of me and possesses the cultural cachet of influence.

Initially Dora came to my house two or three times a week, in the late afternoon after she finished work. We tape-recorded her narrative for several hours until we got hungry. At the end of each session she would say, "Let's go eat." She never let me cook for her, as that would not be appropriate. "Don't bother," she would say. "We're professional women, and we can afford to go out to eat." Dora would then insist on paying for dinner since I was just at the beginning of my career. Over time, I did manage to pay for a pitiful few of the numerous meals that we shared. Dora would also bring me gifts—like souvenirs from her travels to St. Petersburg or Seoul—more often than I gave her gifts. The currency of exchange was my time for her story. The explicit agreement we struck was that she would tell me her life story and I would structure and contextualize this life story.

At the outset, Dora assured me that she would not interfere with the text, but the nature of our relationship concerned me, and I worried about the text. The telling was to be a collaborative process, but I worried that her generosity could influence me to craft the text to her specification. I was uncomfortable with the idea of being accountable to Dora as much as I was troubled with the idea of appropriating someone else's life to serve the academy. My vision of the process was that I would collect the life narrative, then alone fashion my own text. I did, in fact, isolate myself with my computer to craft the text, and I realized that my notion of intellectual "freedom" was untenable. In working with the text we had constructed together, Dora's voice was always in the back of my mind. I had no freedom from her, and it became evident that my task was to thread Dora's life themes throughout the narrative as accurately as I could. In retrospect I am embarrassed by the doubts that plagued me. I have since discovered that Dora's vision of her life story is conceptually bolder than mine. Dora is also more accepting of alternative interpretations than I am, and she pushed me to be imaginative with the text.

When she started the project, Dora had already read most of the autobiographies and life stories about Asian American women. In deciding how to structure the life story, we started by discussing them.[37] Dissatisfied with the possibilities they presented, Dora asked for a reading list of life stories by anthropologists to get a sense of the range of possibilities. After reading a rather hefty list of titles,[38] she decided that Behar's Translated Woman was the most compelling. Dora was pleased to have found an "honest" book that framed the life story so that the informant's voice, the context of her life story, and the author's position were clearly delineated. However, she felt that the contrast between the lives of the two women made the last chapter seem patronizing.

"Ruth is so clearly more privileged than Esperanza," she commented. "I'm not sure how you will write the book since it is, ultimately, your decision. However, I think our situations are more similar than theirs, so I'm sure it [our project] won't seem as contrived."

Dora was not familiar with the anthropological literature regarding the transformation of narrative to text. She was, however, well versed in the practice of distilling meaning out of living and applied her understanding of that process to our collaborative project. In our many discussions about the collaboration, one of the first points that Dora brought up was the issue of voice and authority.

She said, "This is really two life stories, since you're going to write it."

I asked, "How do you see that?"

"Well, whenever I read a book, whether it's fiction or nonfiction, I want to know about the author. Then you know how to read the book."

"What do you mean?"

"Well, if you are reading a life story, there are two stories. First you have the author, her experiences, and her reasons for working on the book. Once you know that, you can figure out what the experience of the person whose life story it is. Do you know what I mean? So I think this book should be a dual life story."

There is precedent for this notion of "dual stories" in the life story literature. Gelya Frank writes of the investigator's "shadow biography," [39] and taking her cue from Frank, the last chapter in Behar's Translated Woman is entitled "The Biography in the Shadow." However, this type of self-reflection is controversial. [40] While the production of life stories is contingent on the relationship between the storyteller and the writer, as well as the author's understanding of the life, the two perspectives have to be balanced so they do not compete. I am also uneasy about self-revelation and am uncertain that there is much that I, a middle-aged woman, can add to her life. Nevertheless, in keeping with Dora's wishes, I have written the book in three distinct voices, demarcated by the use of different typefaces. There is Dora's voice, the voice of the investigator framing her narrative, and I have included my voice in the form of reflections on my own life as I listened to her narrative.

I appreciate Dora's approach to the project, and her ability to discuss the text and open up new possibilities without interposing her will on the text. At this juncture I deliver one rendition of Dora's life and hope that this account suffices in making her life narrative accessible to others.

1 *Chinatown, San Francisco*

I GREW up with discrimination. Discrimination affected every aspect of my life. You're not born with it. It's a learned thing. But when you grow up with it, it's just part of life. When I was growing up, I just took it for granted and did what I could.

Someone recently asked me, "How come you lived in Chinatown, in the ghetto?"

And I replied, "I never thought of Chinatown as a ghetto. We just couldn't live anywhere else."

Growing up, we really didn't go out of Chinatown. Since we couldn't even rent a place outside Chinatown, why would we want to go beyond it? And it never bothered us. There was injustice and discrimination, and we just took it for granted. Chinatown had its distinct boundaries. Broadway marked one edge of Chinatown, and it seemed like there was an iron curtain dividing the Chinese on one side and the Italians on the other. North Beach was on the other side of Broadway. Although it was just across the street, it seemed far away because we didn't cross over. After all, we couldn't even rent a place there, even in North Beach. When the fellas, the Asian boys, would cross Broadway, they were beaten up by the Italian boys. Kearny and Bush marked the downtown borders of Chinatown. Powell marked the incline up to the exclusive Nob Hill neighborhoods.

We grew up in Chinatown, quite literally. When we were growing up, I thought we had a pretty good life. I still think it was pretty good. We never knew about the hardships because my parents never talked about it. We lived through the depression and we did okay. We were lucky because we were never hungry. Maybe that's because we had a restaurant.

Others were not so lucky. I remember in our restaurant we always had Chinese cooks. One Chinese cook had a son. I guess he was about six years old. Have you seen those round-tiered Chinese lunch boxes? Well, this child used to go around to all the restaurants picking up the leftovers for dinner. Now that's hardship.

Most of my earliest memories are about living in Chinatown. We weren't exactly immersed in the Korean community because there were so few Koreans around us. Korean activities were limited to the Independence Movement and other church-related activities once a week or so. So growing up, our parents had to drill into us that we were Korean.

But living in Chinatown—my memory of things Korean are kind of dim. I can remember the seasonal celebrations like Chinese New Year and All Soul's Day in Chinatown much more vividly. I remember how much we looked forward to it every year.

I actually have more memories of what happened in Chinatown rather than in the Korean community. I suppose it's because most of the things that the second-generation Koreans, like me, did were with second-generation Chinese. We joined in all the Chinese activities because there weren't enough Koreans to do anything just Korean. We knew we were Korean, and knew all the Koreans around. Yet when we [she and her brothers] were growing up, we compared ourselves to other people in our world—other Orientals. I don't know that my parents did, but we [the children] did. We didn't think about the world beyond Chinatown because it just wasn't accessible to us.

What I didn't understand was that it would be my Korean heritage that really shaped both my personal and professional life.

Part 1 is constructed from seven interviews: two conducted during the summer of 1987 and five during the summer of 1992. It chronicles the first thirty-seven years of Dora Yum Kim's life in San Francisco's Chinatown. While Dora and her brothers were integrated into non-Korean activities in Chinatown, this did not blur the ethnic boundaries that existed between her and her Chinese peers. While she acknowledges the importance of Chinatown, her larger social setting, Dora presents a selective shading of the past, focusing on the formation and maintenance of a Korean sensibility. The impact of minority status on Dora's self-construction is evident in her narrative, which focuses on her position as a Korean in Chinatown and as an Oriental of Korean descent in the broader social context.

Dora was born at a time when racial segregation was socially acceptable and legally supported. Most outsiders attributed similar characteristics to all Asians, and the social construction of Asians was of a homogeneous racial group of mongoloids, or Orientals.[1] Often restricted to ethnic enclaves, Asian immigrants did not think of themselves as Oriental or as nationally identified when they first arrived in the United States. As with other immigrant groups, Koreans' initial reference group consisted of their compatriots, especially people from their particular province or city.[2] Although Asian immigrants were also forced to engage with the Oriental construct in interactions with members of the dominant society and flatten their construction of themselves to fit this social category, they also were mindful of the differences among the groups who lived next to each other in Chinatown. Despite the commerce across ethnic lines and the sense of a shared situation as Orientals in America, language differences as well as ignorance of one another's cultural practices unquestionably promoted the maintenance of separate social spheres.

Faced with a new land of strange history, different cultural practices, and a hostile society, Koreans—perhaps more emphatically than other Asian immigrant groups—evoked a strong love for their homeland and its people. Perhaps the hostile social climate reminded immigrants of Korea's embattled history and her struggle to keep a Korean heritage alive in the face of alien elements. Nationalist consciousness was certainly fueled by Japanese aggression toward, and eventual occupation of, Korea. In 1905 the American government changed Korean immigrants' status to Japanese subjects when Japan took control of Korean foreign affairs. Korean immigrants objected to this policy, which would subject them to the same treaties and legislation as Japanese immigrants. Korean immigrants also protested against U.S. recognition of Korea's annexation by Japan in 1910, but again without success.

While Korean migrants faced the same social discrimination as other Asians, they viewed the Japanese, not Americans, as their oppressors. Hence, while many Chinese and Japanese immigrants bristled at anti-Asian sentiments directed toward them, Koreans endured because they considered the American government a potentially powerful ally in their struggle against Japanese occupation. Some Koreans compared their situation in United States to those of American Christian missionaries in Korea who had overcome the initial hostility they encountered in Korea; perhaps Korean migrants could overcome American hostility if they demonstrated their worth through good work.[3]

Dora, like other American-born children of Korean immigrants, understood that her immigrant parents' sole focus was on homeland politics and the perpetuation of Korean heritage, but her own attention was grounded both materially and ideologically in America. The economic and social marginalization that Orientals faced sharply contradicted the ideology of equality that she learned at school. So while Dora uses Koreanness to frame her life story, she recalls a childhood in Chinatown where Asians of diverse backgrounds, particularly the American-born generation of her age, forged an enclave community in response to the larger anti-Asian legal and social climate.[4]

Dora begins her life story with her American origins, in which she collapses the story of her parents' voyage to America with her own "myth of creation."[5] *Not herself an immigrant, Dora sees immigration as the essential formative experience that defines Americanness, an identity that is critical to her life narrative. This reconstruction is difficult since Dora knows little about her parents' lives in Korea or the circumstances of their immigration;*

she composes an origins tale from bits and pieces of information, creating possible scenarios about her parents' circumstances and motivations. The narrative takes on the quality of a quest, a journey of discovery in which some elements will never be known. For this reason, the first chapter is a speculative tale, replete with conjecture, misinterpretation, and contradiction.[6]

What we do know is that her father, Man Suk Yum, arrived in 1904, which places him in the first wave of Korean immigrants—a small number of diplomats, students, and merchants (e.g., ginseng salesmen)[7] who came to the continental United States from the late 1800s to the turn of the century. Most Koreans who came to the continent came via Hawaii, after their contracts on Hawaiian sugar plantations had expired, but Dora asserts that her father migrated directly to the Pacific coast.

Beginning with the missionary involvement in recruiting workers to Hawaii, the church played an instrumental role in establishing Korean American communities, and over time, community churches became centers for social and political activity. In 1898 Horace N. Allen, the medical missionary turned American minister to Korea, began working with the Hawaiian Sugar Planters' Association (HSPA) to recruit Korean workers to relocate to Hawaii to fill the gap in labor on the plantations when Chinese and Japanese labor became problematic. Relying on Allen's missionary networks to recruit laborers, the HSPA brought the first group of Korean laborers over in December 1902. However, the total number of Korean immigrants to Hawaii in this initial influx numbered just over seven thousand.[8] Most of these persons were male laborers, although there were a few with business backgrounds, and approximately six hundred were women. Korean migration to Hawaii halted in May 1905, when Japan took over Korea's foreign affairs and restricted migration to Hawaii and the United States.[9]

Missionary involvement in this migration and the church's role in political and social resistance in Korea helped to make the church the most important institution in Korean communities established in the United States. Forty percent of immigrants were Christian before they immigrated, and many worked hard to convert their compatriots. In the first two decades of the century over a dozen churches were established in the United States, in large measure as a platform from which to speak out against the Japanese occupation of Korea,[10] *and their Korean ministers who were often the political leaders of the community. In Northern California the first church was established in San Francisco in 1905.*

Between 1904 and 1907 about a thousand Koreans entered the mainland from Hawaii through San Francisco. At the turn of the century, when the first Koreans arrived in San Francisco's Chinatown, Ahn Ch'ang Ho, an expatriate intellectual and anti-Japanese patriot who arrived in San Francisco in 1899, based himself in Chinatown and established the Chinmok Hoe *[Friendship Society] in 1903. The* Kongnip Hyop Hoe *[Mutual Assistance Society], the first Korean language newspaper, established in 1905, was also located in San Francisco's Chinatown. While San Francisco served as the port of entry, many Koreans left the city, scattering along the Pacific Coast, primarily doing farm work, although there were also dozens of Koreans who worked as wage laborers in mining companies and as section hands on the railroad in Oregon, Washington, Montana, and Utah.*[11] *The variety of crops grown along the Pacific Coast allowed for something to be harvested year-round, so farm workers were mobile, following the crops from region to region. Because their numbers were small, Korean workers saved and pooled wages and resources to lease land.*

Most of the Korean tenant farmers in Northern California worked in the Sacramento–San Joaquin Valley around the towns of Reedley and Dinuba, as Man Suk Yum had. In the two decades after migration was halted, the practice of sending for picture brides became common for Korean men.[12] *About a thousand picture brides arrived in Hawaii before 1924, and about a hundred arrived on the Pacific coast.*[13] *Dora's mother, Hang Shin Kim, was a picture bride from northern Korea who arrived in San Francisco in 1920.*

After the Japanese occupation of Korea in 1910, Korean immigrants in America regarded themselves as exiles—a passion that united Koreans in a single cause. Even those who were not political refugees had relatives who suffered under the Japanese occupation of Korea, and still others had to abandon plans to return home. Japanese occupation riveted immigrant Koreans'

*attention to news of conditions in the homeland and filled them with such a
sense of loss that many did not engage fully with their situation in America.*[14]
*In fact, for some, preoccupation with the Independence Movement served as
an effective way to deny the difficulties of the new context; instead of focusing
on their material and historical location in America, these immigrant Koreans remained focused on conditions in the homeland.*

*In small businesses, family life was not separate from business, and the
labor contributions of wives and children were critical.*[15] *As the younger generation aged and had families of their own, the American social landscape
changed dramatically. World War II brought tremendous change for Asians
in Chinatown; housing covenants were struck down, and there was an out-
flow of Asians from Chinatown over the next twenty years. Part 1 of this
book, Chinatown, San Francisco, begins with "American Origins" and spans
the fifty-four years from Dora's father's entry to the United States in 1904
and the Yum family's settling in San Francisco's Chinatown in the 1920s to
Dora and her husband's decision to move out of Chinatown after the death
of her last surviving parent in 1958.*

Descendants of Man Suk Yum and Hang Shin Kim:
A Korean American Family Tree

1st Generation

2nd Generation

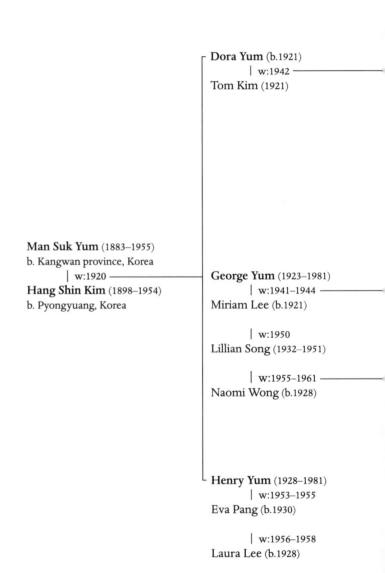

Dora Yum (b.1921)
| w:1942 ───────
Tom Kim (1921)

Man Suk Yum (1883–1955)
b. Kangwan province, Korea
| w:1920 ───────────
Hang Shin Kim (1898–1954)
b. Pyongyuang, Korea

George Yum (1923–1981)
| w:1941–1944 ───────
Miriam Lee (b.1921)

| w:1950
Lillian Song (1932–1951)

| w:1955–1961 ───────
Naomi Wong (b.1928)

Henry Yum (1928–1981)
| w:1953–1955
Eva Pang (b.1930)

| w:1956–1958
Laura Lee (b.1928)

3rd Generation   4th Generation   5th Generation

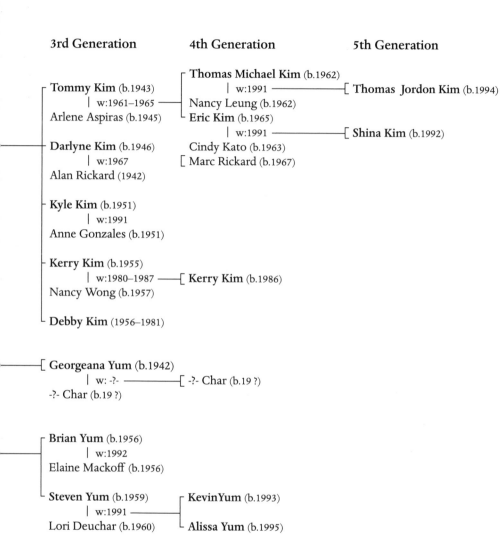

Tommy Kim (b.1943)
| w:1961–1965
Arlene Aspiras (b.1945)

Thomas Michael Kim (b.1962)
| w:1991 ——————⌈ Thomas Jordon Kim (b.1994)
Nancy Leung (b.1962)
Eric Kim (b.1965)
| w:1991 ——————⌈ Shina Kim (b.1992)

Darlyne Kim (b.1946)
| w:1967
Alan Rickard (1942)

Cindy Kato (b.1963)
⌈ Marc Rickard (b.1967)

Kyle Kim (b.1951)
| w:1991
Anne Gonzales (b.1951)

Kerry Kim (b.1955)
| w:1980–1987 ———⌈ Kerry Kim (b.1986)
Nancy Wong (b.1957)

Debby Kim (1956–1981)

Georgeana Yum (b.1942)
| w: -?- ——————⌈ -?- Char (b.19 ?)
-?- Char (b.19 ?)

Brian Yum (b.1956)
| w:1992
Elaine Mackoff (b.1956)

Steven Yum (b.1959)   ⌈ Kevin Yum (b.1993)
| w:1991 ———
Lori Deuchar (b.1960)   ⌊ Alissa Yum (b.1995)

ONE

American Origins

June 1992

       ONCE Dora had cleared the way for us to collaborate on her life history, we decided that we should tape-record our sessions and do the work at my place. Although Dora had not told me her life story in any chronological or directed fashion, over the five years I had known her, I had conducted two interviews with her and gathered fragments from other conversations. I was also aware of the life narrative that was released publicly around her hwan'gap celebration. But this was to be her version of her life, and I asked her to think about how she would like to begin her story before our first session. In preparation for our interview, I had cleared the kitchen table so that we might work there. When she arrived, I met her at the door, which opened into the kitchen. Dora looked around and, without hesitation, walked straight into the living room, where she settled on the couch and started telling me about her day while I set up the tape recorder. When the tape machine was ready, she began:

I'm an American. A native-born Californian of Korean heritage. When I was growing up, there weren't more than a hundred Koreans, total population, in San Francisco. With so few Koreans around, being of Korean heritage was something we were told about more than experienced. The Korean community was more like a big family than an ethnic group, and that's the way it was for a long time. The immigration laws weren't changed until 1965,[1] and that's what caused the influx, and I mean *influx* of Koreans into the United States. And even though the immigration laws were changed in 1965, they didn't really start coming over until the early 1970s. Apparently it took that length of time to process papers or whatever. And now, if you take the Korean population in San Francisco, there are almost as many Koreans as there are Japanese. I didn't really think

27

about being a native Californian of Korean heritage before the influx. I suppose I assumed that our little community was somehow representative of Koreans. But as I started meeting more and more Korean immigrants, I started noticing the differences between us native Korean Californians and the immigrant Koreans. We might share the same Korean heritage, but there are some real differences as well. I can see more similarities between the new immigrants and my parents, although there are differences there as well.

So how do you want to start your story?

Since the majority of Koreans here are immigrants, most Koreans' stories are around immigration and adjustment to America. I never thought that being born and raised here would set me apart. But in terms of the Korean community, it has. My parents made the journey here, and I was born American. So my life story is an American story. American stories, with the exception of the American Indians, begin with how we happen to be here. Not everyone who came to America came with the intention of immigrating, especially not the old-time Asians who came for contract labor. But we Asians ended up here anyway. So in explaining how we happened to be here, my story starts with my father.

My father came over in 1904. That's when the first Koreans came over as contract laborers. But very few came over to the U.S. mainland. The majority went to Hawaii, evidently to work in the Hawaiian plantations. My father was one of the few who came directly to the mainland. He worked building the railroad.

How do you know that?

I remember there was a Union Pacific Railroad card among his possessions when he died. He worked up in Washington State, across the United States to the central areas. I think he came over with the Chinese. Otherwise why would he have worked on the railroad?

My father was born in 1883, so he came over when he was twenty-one. I'm not clear on the details, but he was working on the railroad, and when the work was over in 1906, the government said you didn't have to go back. There were all these single men after the railroads were built here. I'm not exactly sure what my father did after that. I recall that my father was a foreman in the country. Although he was a good farmer, he talked about working as a foreman. I also remember him mentioning being in Vacaville and then being up in Dinuba, Reedley, Delano, out there. There were some Koreans there, and my father was fooling around with the *insam* [ginseng] the Korean *sam,* selling it up and down the coast.[2] I can try to recreate my father's life from the comments he made in passing, but in those days our parents never talked about their past.[3]

I don't know why my parents never talked about the past, but they never did. Maybe it's because they didn't have any opportunities and didn't want to talk about the bad times. It was just discrimination and hardships they endured. And they really endured some. Maybe they thought it wasn't right to tell their children about the difficulties they faced. I really don't know. But there's so much I don't know about my parents, about the past. I don't even know if my father went to school or how much schooling he had. Maybe he was a self-taught man. I do know that every night he read the American newspaper, the Chinese newspaper, and the Korean newspaper. I was really impressed with that. So I figure he's got to have been educated. In those days there really weren't that many learned men, and my father was learned. But I don't know how he learned all that he knew because I assume that my father came over as a contract laborer. And once he got here, of course, he delved into the community, the independence movement, and the *hungsadan* [Corps for the Advancement of Individuals] with Ahn Ch'ang Ho and all that.[4]

Can you tell me what you know about your mother's passage to California?

My mother was a picture bride. In those days, after the contract work, some Koreans came down here to San Francisco, some went further down into the country, they went all over. There were no women here, and so what they did was send for picture brides. In other words, they all exchanged pictures. My father had a friend who had a sister in Peyang[5] [Pyongyang] and another who had a sister or a female relative somewhere else, or knew of someone who knew some woman somewhere else. They all exchanged pictures. And somehow my mother picked my father and came over. My parents were married at the Korean Methodist Church on Oak Street on May 1, 1920, shortly after my mother came over from Korea. My mother was twenty-two years old at the time, and my father was thirty-seven. At that time almost every man was at least fifteen years older than his bride.[6] That's about how long it took the men to save the money for the passage fare. I know of one man who was *forty* years older than the wife.[7] When I think about my mother and father, and the way they met, I figure they were pretty closely matched. My father had the acumen for business, but he wouldn't act on anything until my mother approved his decisions. If she said no, that was the final word. And so, I think they got along in that way.

I don't know how they felt about their marriage. I think all of the picture brides, including my mother, were resigned to their fate. I remember the stories the ladies told when they used to get together. I wish I could remember all their stories and put them down. They were really something, about how they grew up and what they went through in Korea and coming here, and how some of the picture brides didn't even get here because they got so seasick that they committed suicide, just jumped overboard. Those are the "loser stories" that no one hears about. And then there were the personal recollections when the ladies got together.

One story that stuck with me is the story about the most beautiful woman among the group of picture brides with whom my mother came over. She had a picture of a good-looking guy coming over on the ship. They all came over by ship; we didn't have planes. It took them twenty-three days steerage class, where they kept the cattle, and she said, "All of a sudden I saw an old man hobbling up to me with a cane and I realized that he had sent me a picture taken of himself when he was young. And what could I do? I burst out crying."

What could she do? She couldn't go back. Nobody had the money. The guys barely had fare for them to come over, and that was it. But when I heard these stories, I often wondered, "How can they marry and have children like that?" But they did.

And even then I used to think, "Gee, after these people go, there will be nobody to pass these stories on for posterity." They were important stories of struggle and survival.

I think my mother had less opportunity than my father. My mother was born in 1898, and she grew up as an only child. That was unusual in Korea in those days. I don't know the events which led to my mother's coming over as a picture bride, but the promise of life here must have been a better choice than living in Korea. I know my mother could read and write Korean because she always read the Korean paper. I guess someone must have taught her when she was in Korea. But at that time people believed that girls did not need to be educated. I believe my mother came from a pretty good family because we have pictures of her and her *singmo* [servant] from her childhood. If you have a *singmo*, that indicates higher class standing. When she got here though, she was just a subservient woman—just cooking and cleaning and taking care of the family.

After my parents married, they lived in Dinuba for a while. I guess my father was farming there. They decided to move up to San Francisco after about a year. My father had a Model T Ford when my parents got married in 1920 so it was easier for them to move. On the drive up they stopped to see the Moons, another Korean farming family in Manteca. During that visit with the Moons, I was born. I was born in a hospital on March 16, 1921. That's what my birth certificate shows. But there was a woman named Mrs. Lee, a woman who had twelve children of her own, who gave me my first bath in Manteca.

And soon after I was born, my parents continued up to San Francisco, and I've lived here ever since. So even though I wasn't actually born in San Francisco, I've lived here all my life.

When my parents moved to San Francisco, my father opened a cigar stand at the corner of Jackson and Kearny. I think my mother must have helped mind the shop because my father traveled quite a bit to sell *insam*. He would sometimes go down as far as Monterey because that's how scattered the Koreans were. But then, being in Chinatown, he sold a lot of it to the Chinese. The Chinese were really gung ho on Korean *insam*.[8]

At that time there were only a handful of Koreans in San Francisco, in Chinatown. I remember the first places in which Koreans lived. Do you know the alleys in Chinatown? It was off Jackson Street between Grant and Stockton where there are a bunch of alleys where three Korean families lived in one room, windowless basement rentals. I remember that. A midwife came to that alley apartment when my brother George was born.

It was a pretty basic place. There was a toilet but no bathtub in that place. We took baths in one of those big aluminum pots or pans. Other people who didn't have bathrooms went to bathhouses. There was one on Stockton Street, between Jackson and Pacific, run by Mr. and Mrs. Chun that had individual bathtubs for people who didn't have them at home. We had a gas burner at home, but no refrigerator. The lack of refrigeration was a big issue when we were growing up. I remember when a couple of Korean babies died they said it was because of the spoiled milk. In those days there was no way to keep it fresh.

After my brother was born in 1923, my father opened a restaurant with Charles Lee, a Korean man who owned a restaurant on Kearny and Jackson next to the cigar stand. The restaurant was called Lee's Lunch. My father also ran the pool hall on the other side of the restaurant.

Some time in there, I guess it was around 1928, our family moved to Oakland for about a year. When we were living in Oakland, my parents ran a grocery store. My father stopped working in the restaurant and the pool hall. However, he kept the cigar stand. I remember that my father used to commute to San Francisco to check on the cigar stand.

It was also in Oakland that my youngest brother Henry was born, in the house we lived. A midwife came to assist in the birth.

I think it must have been easier to live in San Francisco because we moved back shortly thereafter, and my parents were working at the restaurant again. We moved back into Chinatown, into an apartment on Jackson Street. It was a two-bedroom apartment, but we didn't use it that way. When we moved there I remember having my own room because I was a girl; my mother and my brother Henry slept together in another room because he was little; and my father and brother George shared a room.

Sometime in the 1920s Koreans opened a couple of cleaning shops, a bathhouse, one shoe repair store, three restaurants, and two barber shops in San Francisco's Chinatown. And by the 1930s all the Korean families in Chinatown had a business. We also had one Korean church, which, by then, had moved to Powell Street, a block down from where we lived. The church was at 1053 Oak Street before that, which is where my parents got married. It was started in 1906 by Lee Dae Wi. I even have a picture of it. It was just an old building in the Western Addition. I don't know how we happened to have a church there, but *all* the Koreans went there before it moved to Powell Street.[9]

I remember the church on Powell Street. It was really much more than a church. It was a social center. It was the only place that the Koreans could get together—for support or socializing or whatever you want to call it. At church there seemed to be two topics of conversation. People talked about each other—who was doing what and that sort of thing, and people told stories about Japanese oppression. And every March first we had a large gathering at the church to mark the Korean Independence Movement.[10]

What stories of Japanese oppression did you hear?

I remember the stories my mother and her friends used to tell me. They told stories about how the Japanese kidnapped and killed the beautiful Korean girls[11] and tried to eliminate the language. Once I remember giving a talk somewhere and I remember telling them that the Koreans are stubborn like the Irish and that's how they all kept their language.[12] It's amazing. They tell me that the Koreans that are here now that lived under the Japanese rule speak better Japanese than the Japanese themselves. And yet they can still speak Korean fluently. You were killed by the Japanese if you dared speak Korean. I remember the stories of what the Koreans went through during Japanese rule. So even if I wasn't there, it was drummed into me.

You mention yearly March First celebrations. What did March First stand for?

I don't know how other Koreans saw it. But I can tell you how I understood March First as a child who had never lived in Korea. What it meant was that in Korea, when all the Koreans were planning a fight for Korean independence, the Japanese oppressors somehow found out about it and they came with the bayonets and chopped off all the hands. You know, when they were shouting *mansei* [cheers or hurrah] and raising their arms, they would chop the hands off.[13]

So March First was a big deal. On March First, Mr. Yang—you know the man who recently died, the one who lived to be a hundred—would cry out, *"Dae han dongnib mansei! Dongnib mansei! Dongnib mansei!"* (Long live Korean independence) three times, just like that. I never forgot that.

Nationalism was so important to that early Korean community. By the time I was born, there were two Korean National Associations, the Kungmin Hoe and Syngman Rhee's Tongji Hoe [Comrades Society].[14] My father was the president of the Kungmin Hoe in San Francisco for many years. They built their own building in Los Angeles, on Jefferson. And I remember all of us going down for the opening there. All the Koreans in California really supported each other, because there weren't too many to begin with and, I guess, because of the commonality in language, customs, culture, traditions—whatever you want to call it.

Nobody had much money then, but all the Koreans were sending money to Korea. There were a few bachelors that weren't able to bring picture brides over. They worked in these wealthy homes, and on the one day they had off each week they would come to the Korean gatherings at church. I don't know how much money they made, but it probably wasn't much. Even they gave money toward the Korean Independence Movement. I remember how gung ho everybody was. When I was young, I guess what impressed me was I know that we didn't have the money, and people would all give money to that. I think the Korean Independence Movement was the main focus when the Koreans got together.

Ahn Ch'ang Ho was also here. When he died in 1938 in Korea, we had a memorial service for him at the Methodist Church here. Nowadays people are pushing Ahn Ch'ang Ho, only Ahn Ch'ang Ho, as the Korean Independence Movement activist in the United States. I didn't know him personally, but we all knew about him because our parents talked about him. But he wasn't the only activist. He was a great patriot, but he wasn't the only one. You can't do anything alone. You have to have people sup-porting you. My father was the delegate from Kangwando. Ahn Ch'ang Ho may have headed it up, but they had delegates from each of the prov-inces in Korea.

My parents were very nationalistic. And they always said that they wanted to go back to Korea to die. I supposed they hoped that Korea would be restored and they could go back. But at that time there was no way of going back. There was no Korea to go back to.

Earlier you talk about what your father did to support the family. Then, when your family moved to Oakland, your language changed. You started talking in terms of "my parents." Could you talk about that shift?

I actually don't have too many memories of Lee's Lunch before we moved to Oakland. But I do remember that, unlike the cigar stand or the pool hall that my father managed, the grocery store was a family busi-ness—my mother worked alongside my father. I didn't work because I was too young, but since we [she and her brother George] were too young to be left alone, my mother took us along to the grocery store.

Then in 1929, when we moved back to San Francisco, my father bought the restaurant from Charles Lee. That was also a family-run busi-ness. We owned that restaurant until 1942. Actually Orientals, as we were referred to, couldn't own land in those days, so we all rented. There was no such thing as a lease—everything was rented month to month. So although the business was ours, the restaurant was rented, as was our apartment.

When did you start working at the restaurant?

I don't know exactly when I started helping out at the restaurant. I recall starting to work in the restaurant around the time my mother got the piano. My mother got me a piano that she bought with a hundred dollars she had saved from her household budget when I was ten years old, so I must have been around ten when I started working in the restaurant.

That piano—that's the piano that's in our house. My mother had such dreams for me. I wonder if she felt bad when she had to enlist me to help out at the restaurant. I don't know, but I know my mother wanted me to have more than she had. She wanted me to take piano lessons, maybe become a recital pianist. I don't know where she got that idea, but that's what she wanted. So I took lessons at the San Francisco Conservatory of Music, which was a little shack on Sacramento Street at that time. I played in recitals and continued to take lessons until I was in high school. I remember my music teacher in high school, Miss McClade, really encouraged me. But I quit when I was sixteen or seventeen, when I realized that my fingers were too short. I could barely clear an octave with my hands.[15] I really enjoyed playing so I continued to play. I started playing the piano at church when I was sixteen. I played the piano at the church for at least ten years, when Hwang Sa Sun was the reverend.

But we were talking about the restaurant. When we weren't in school, studying or taking class of some sort, we worked at the restaurant. Our restaurant was open twenty-four hours a day. My parents would be there all day, for sixteen hours, but the night shift was run by two Chinese. We hired two Chinese, one as a chef and the other as a dishwasher and waiter. So we were open twenty-four hours.[16]

We had a lot of customers. A lot of the people who ate there were Filipino. There were a lot of Oriental bachelors too, but there were more Filipinos.[17] There were an awful lot of Filipino bachelors.[18] And they all lived in those residential hotels. They just had a room in the hotel. So they ate all their meals at our restaurant. In addition to Filipinos, we had Japanese, Chinese, some Koreans, just all different bachelors.[19] Even though there were differences in who we considered to be Asian, in those days, in Chinatown you never thought about nationality. What nationality is this guy, what nationality is that guy? We were all Orientals to Americans, and we were all just there together. In those days Caucasians were referred to as Americans, and we were Orientals.

My mother felt sorry for all those bachelors who used to eat at our restaurant. They were our customers, but the place also used to be a hangout for them. It was a corner hangout where the Asian seamen used to hang out, and they were mostly from Hawaii, you know. And they were young boys, maybe eighteen years old. Having two sons of her own, my mother used to say, "Gee, what if my son . . . ," and "What if they were away from home like that?" So in many ways, my mother used to feed those boys and love them just like her own. And when my brothers left home, somehow everywhere they went there was some kind woman who took care of them. Sometimes you just get back what you give. And I never realized how much my mother was loved by those boys. I used to think, "She was my mother, mother of my brothers, but not the mother of all those boys." I used to think it was impossible to love somebody else's mother, but that's not true.[20]

Actually, everybody ate at our restaurant, even the Bank of America manager and president. The main branch of the Bank of America used to be on Montgomery and Clay. And so even they used to come and eat. It was American food, and for twenty-five cents you could get soup, salad, steak, dessert, coffee. And it was good. We didn't serve Korean food, but my mother would sometimes make *yangyom koki,* marinated beef, and people would ask, "Oh can I try some?" and she would let them. People really loved it, and as a result we ended up putting that on the menu. I used to type the menus there every day. We called it "chopped steak," I think.

My mother would work there waiting on tables, serving, dish washing, cashiering, managing. When I was there, I would fill in as needed. I would cashier, wait on tables, and do whatever was necessary. But my mother usually worked sixteen hours a day at that restaurant.

Sometimes I wonder about my mother's life. She never spoke about her feelings. She just did her dutiful roles. She worked at the restaurant, climbed up and down those hills on her errands, and also did everything around the house, including cleaning and laundry. In those days we didn't have machines, so she did everything by hand. And the next day it was the same thing. The only enjoyment she would have was at the end of the day. Sometimes we'd go to eat at a Chinese restaurant, or my mother and I would take long walks. Occasionally my father came along. That was the only enjoyment my parents had. I know it sounds like nothing, but they really enjoyed that. I remember the walks with my mother. It would be about eight o'clock at night when our shift was over, and my mother and I would take walks from Jackson Street all the way down to Market Street on Grant Avenue. That was our exercise. Sometimes my father or her friends who lived across the street from us would come along. I can still remember looking down on the Ferry Building all lit up from Commercial Street. That was the most beautiful sight to me. That was the tallest building in San Francisco at that time. And that was in the 1920s and 1930s. That was over fifty years ago, and still that Ferry Building never fails to amaze me. We'd always stop and look at it, then walk all the way down to Market and back home.

Other than that it was the same old routine, mostly work. And it got pretty hectic at the restaurant. Sometimes we would leave the cigar stand empty, especially if things were busy at the restaurant. If someone came to buy a pack of cigarettes or a cigar, we'd go outside and go into the stand and sell the cigars, and then return to the restaurant. And then we [the children] also used to steal a lot of candy from there, of course. There were only two Korean girls even close to my age in Chinatown. They were slightly older than me. I really wanted to play with them, but since they were older than me I guess they didn't really want me to hang around. So I would steal candy and give it to them so they would be my friends. In retrospect, it was childhood extortion—candy for friendship. I still feel a little guilty about taking the candy.

We used to watch the corner from the restaurant. There was a lot of action outside because it was a taxi stand. The taxis would stay here to look for business. It was a busy corner. During that time gambling was rampant in Chinatown as well as across the bay, in Emeryville. A car would stop across the street and pick all the guys up that wanted to go across the bay to go gambling. That went on every day. There was also a policeman who patrolled Chinatown who we saw regularly. He was well regarded by people in Chinatown, but apparently he also took payoffs from the gambling house. That was the reason the gambling continued. That's what our customers said, anyway. The people who worked in gambling houses were our customers, and we got to know them pretty well. There used to be runners, like keno runners, in Chinatown, who would come and eat at our restaurant or buy things at the cigar stand.

Earlier you mentioned your father's business acumen. Were you referring to his success in finding and operating a viable family business?

That's part of it, but it I was actually referring to his foresight in investing his money. He really knew how to invest. While my father had the restaurant, he started investing in real estate. That was in the thirties, and we [Dora and her siblings] didn't realize that when he went to buy real estate, people [of European extraction] wouldn't sell it to him because he was Oriental. He couldn't become a citizen, and he couldn't buy real estate.[21] Since I was born here, it would have been convenient if he could have bought it under my name, but there was a law which stated that you had to be twenty-one in order to own property.[22] So the first building he bought he bought in the name of the minister's son. He thought the minister's son would do since I was not of age. And one day the minister took their cousin and somebody around, and he said, "Oh, *igo uri jib e'da,*" that the house was his. And then this woman came back and told my father that. My father was a perfect gentleman. Instead of confronting the minister or anything, he just quietly sold the building. And I give him credit for that.

The Koreans didn't always wish him the best. When he first tried to buy the building on Mason Street, it wasn't considered part of Chinatown. It was one block above Chinatown at that time. And people like Mrs. Noh [pseudonym] would say, "Oh, *mang handa*" (They're going to be ruined). She was just one of the Koreans who were jealous of his abilities, but it didn't faze him. He just went ahead with his plans. In 1937 my father finally bought the four-unit building on Mason Street. That was a big deal. After the incident with the minister my father didn't want to buy it in anyone else's name, so he bought in the name of our Italian real estate broker. The title was in trust for me until I turned twenty-one. And in 1942, when I became twenty-one, we had a Jewish lawyer, Aaron Cohen, who deeded the property to me in my name. My father wasn't American, so technically he couldn't buy it. Orientals could not become citizens until after the war, and noncitizens couldn't buy property.[23] My father was the first Korean to buy property outside of Chinatown, in a "restricted area."[24] And even then, we couldn't rent anyplace outside of Chinatown, let alone buy a place outside of Chinatown. My father was an intelligent, brave man.

We moved to Mason Street just before I finished high school. We rented the empty apartments out. I remember there was a sewing factory that rented from us. You know, there's a lot of talk about exploitation and things like that. I remember the sewing factory. The women worked in their slippers. They took their kids to school and then came to work. When it was time, they would leave to pick their kids up from school and bring the kids to the shop to play in there. The factory owner hired a cook for the shop, and all the women and their children were fed. I used to watch the cooks make lunch and wished that I could have some of the food. The food looked so good. In retrospect, I suppose the women were working for minimum wage or below, but the women never wanted to become unionized. It was an acceptable situation for most of the women because they could tend to their children while they worked. At that time women who worked didn't have that option. There have been many efforts to unionize the garment workers in Chinatown, but to date, they have not succeeded. For many uneducated, non-English-speaking women, the garment factories in Chinatown serve their needs.

My father was a good entrepreneur, and he figured out how to get around the discriminatory laws. But there was also another side of him that I never fully appreciated. He was a real comic. He used to make everybody laugh; he was a natural public speaker. Whenever he got up there in front of the community to speak as the president of the National Korean Association—he would make speeches for March First celebrations, funerals, eulogies, and things like that—he would ad-lib. He was so good at that. I used to envy him because I was petrified of speaking in public. But then when he acted like a comedian, my brother and I used to just hide under the table, behind the chair or something. We were so embarrassed. I suppose that's because it seemed strange to us since he never joked around with us. When I think about it now, it was nothing to be embarrassed about. Now I realize it was actually something to be proud of. Whenever there was a social gathering, he used to get up and tell jokes and people would just roll over the sides. But most of the time he was a stoic, quiet gentleman.

Reflections

Dora's tale of American origins causes me to ponder the differences between us. Dora and I are at different life stages and grew up in different cultural and social contexts. My American education often obfuscates my background. No, I am not an American-born Korean. Nor do I fit the profile of the post-1965 Korean immigrant. Instead, I am best described as a "new wave" immigrant. I was born in Korea and grew up in Southeast Asia. While my father did emigrate from Korea to find a better life, he settled in Thailand. And although he faced obstacles, he did not have to struggle against anti-Asian or anti-immigrant sentiments there. My father was able to achieve a level of economic and social mobility to which I cannot even aspire. While I have worked hard in my pursuits, I know that my parents' efforts positioned us children to take advantage of the educational opportunities that were available to us in the United States.

The medium of my education was always English, and in the turbulent aftermath of the violent student revolt in Thailand in 1973, it seemed logical that my parents would send my younger brother and me to English-language boarding schools. In 1975, when the political situation took a downturn, we joined our older siblings who were going to college on the East Coast of the United States. My three siblings and I all went to private universities in the Northeast, made our respective visits to the ancestral home one summer while we were still in college, and reluctantly returned to Thailand after graduation to try and make our ways in the country that had become our adopted home. We all speak Korean, Thai, and English, and also learned a "foreign language" (meaning a European language other than English), which we were required to study since second grade.

I believe that Dora brings me photos and documents about her life to bridge the difference between us. But this is not the only reason that Dora brings out materials for me to examine. We are both aware that Dora's story of the San Francisco Korean immigrant community diverges from what scholars say, and that is why she has brought materials as proof. I am amazed at the evidence she has kept.

And despite our differences, I begin to see similarities between Dora's life and my own. The stories Dora has heard, of things Korean, remind me of the way Korean culture was presented to me. Having grown up in Southeast Asia where there were few Koreans with whom to socialize or mark public occasions, I acquired only a fragmented sense of what was Korean from the stories my parents told—stories often packaged to make some point. Like Dora, I experience Korean culture secondhand.

And even if our families were positioned differently within our respective adopted countries, I see similarities in our families, particularly between our parents. My mother, like Dora's, rarely speaks about her feelings. She dismisses my queries about life goals that might have conflicted with her obligations and duties as a wife and mother. She seems to have accepted her choices without self-reproach. I, like Dora, am continually surprised at my mother's devotion to us, her children, and her commitment to maintaining a harmonious family.

Dora's father also reminds me of my own. My father was one of the first Koreans to start his own business in Thailand and managed to get around laws that prohibited foreigners from doing business or owning land. My father also served as the chairman of the Korean residents' association in Bangkok for over ten years. However, unlike the members of the San Francisco Korean community who settled here permanently, our Korean community consisted of families associated with the diplomatic corps and Korean corporations and businesses stationed in Bangkok for only a few years. We were one of a few Korean families who settled with long-term investments in Thailand.

TWO

Coming of Age

AS Dora recalls her childhood and youth, she focuses on the
role of her education as it shaped her sense of her place in society, her expanding
social world during her adolescence, and her courtship, marriage, and the birth
of her first son.

At the time that Dora started going to school, educational segregation was
the norm for children of Chinese descent, and "Oriental Schools" had been established since 1885 to serve the Chinese.[1] Japanese and Korean students, however, attended American public schools at the turn of the century. In 1905 objec-
tions were raised by San Francisco's Board of Education, and Japanese and
Korean students in the public schools were ordered to go to the "Oriental School"
serving the Chinese. Wary of offending Japan, an emerging world power, and
aware of the outcry it caused in Tokyo, President Roosevelt sent his secretary to
investigate this matter. When the secretary discovered that Japanese and Korean
students were few in number (a total of ninety-three Japanese and Korean students in 1905), the children were permitted to continue attending public schools.[2]
Nevertheless, the majority of Asians lived in or around Chinatown, and even
after schools were desegregated, the majority of the children in San Francisco's
Chinatown attended public grammar schools where 95 percent of the enrollment
was Chinese.

The three public grammar schools that children from Chinatown attended
were Jean Parker, the school Dora and her brothers attended, Commodore Stockton, and Spring Valley. In addition to public schools, Asian ethnic communities
established language schools for their own communities. In Chinatown in the
1920s and 1930s there were at least ten daily Chinese language schools and one
weekly Korean language school in Chinatown. It is estimated that 35 percent of
Chinatown elementary school students attended these language schools.[3]

41

Dora's formal education was a key aspect of her development, but the completion of her education did not, in and of itself, denote entry into adulthood. Rather, adulthood was a kind of social status achieved through marriage and the birth of her first child, when Dora became privy to the world of adult Korean women.

I started going to school at Lincoln Grammar School in Oakland. Then we moved back to San Francisco when I was in second grade, where I started going to the Jean Parker School. When I started going to school, my mother told us that she had tried to take English lessons. She had gone to the ESL classes they had at a Chinese church located a block down from where we lived. But she said it just wouldn't go into her head, and so, . . . I knew I was on my own. I ended up translating for my mother. . . . I don't remember how old I was, but I think by the time I was in second or third grade I was writing notes for my mother excusing me from school when I and, later, my brothers were sick.

When I was in grammar school, my mother had two Korean friends who spoke good English. And this one woman was just beautiful. This family owned a cleaning shop, and she sewed, so she dressed up her four daughters just beautifully. And her English . . . I think I used to envy the girls because their mothers would come to the PTA meetings and talk with the teachers. My mother couldn't do that. She was so busy at the business that she probably couldn't have come anyway. But even if she did come, she couldn't communicate with anybody. In fact, most of the parents from Chinatown couldn't speak English and were fully engaged in minding their businesses. And I remember envying these girls because their mothers spoke English. When I was older, I learned that they spoke such good English because they were raised in Christian orphanages in Korea. But I didn't know that as a child. All I felt was the envy. . . .

What did going to school teach you about where you fit in America?

Going to school was a real eye-opener. When I was young, before I went to school, I never thought about what I was or anything like that. But when I started going to school in Oakland, I realized I was different from most of the other kids at school—I was Oriental. But they never taught us about Orientals in America. I suppose by the time I was in second grade I already knew not to expect that. But what they did teach us about was China and Japan. I came to realize that there was no mention of Korea in geography or history. I couldn't find out anything about my background. So as a Korean I was invisible outside the small Chinatown Korean community. At that time the Koreans in the area were so actively involved in events in Korea, yet there was no mention of it in school.

I was really curious about my heritage, so I started cutting out anything I read in newspapers or magazines that had anything to do with Korea. These articles are where I learned how to talk about Korea and being Korean. I recall one picture of two Korean girls standing, instead of sitting, on a seesaw. I showed it to my mother, and she said, "I used to be real good at this. I could jump really high."

The caption read, "Public Education for Girls in Korea."

I look at it now and think, "What a joke." For centuries Korean women have been virtual slaves. This would be a good article for the feminists, you know, in terms of the irony. Education of any kind used to be an extraordinary innovation for the ordinary Korean girl.

I'm confused. Why did you rely on newspaper and magazine articles? I thought you said that your parents taught you about Korean heritage.

My parents did teach us about Korea. I think they did a pretty good job of it. When I was growing up, I wanted to visit Korea because I felt proud to be Korean. But I wasn't quite sure what being Korean meant because we were different from our parents. Our parents' ideas of being Korean had to do with their experiences growing up and living in Korea. But we American-born Koreans didn't have that experience; all we had was secondhand information about it. Since I am Korean and not Chinese or Japanese, I found myself having to explain what I was at a young age. When I was in grammar school, it was hard for me to explain where Korea was and what the people were like. The articles and clippings I saved in my scrapbook helped me explain these things in English to my classmates.

There are other differences between my parents' perspectives and mine. They were anti-Japanese because of the situation at home, but for the children it was different. It's different to be American. You know that your parents hate the Japanese, and that it's a sore point with them, but if your own experience doesn't support the hatred, it's all hearsay. Your parents tell you that in Japan the Japanese hate the Koreans and they still fingerprint them even though they have Japanese names and all that. But within the community of people we knew, we had a Japanese doctor, Dr. Clifford Uyeda, who went to Japan to try to fight against that. It didn't do any good, but as Americans we have different feelings than we're supposed to have. You can't tell what people believe based on appearance.

I also had close Japanese girlfriends. But as far as having Japanese friends, I was restricted. I couldn't bring a Japanese friend home. And I understood, and I just didn't bring them home. But I associated with lots of Japanese people.

I know you can read and write Korean. When did you learn that?

By the time I was in second grade, I could read and write Korean even though I couldn't understand everything I read. I don't actually remember learning to read and write, but I think my parents must have initially taught me. You know, from 1924 to 1965, when immigration laws were relaxed, no Koreans could come over except missionaries or students.[4] The missionaries or students who did come over didn't have any money. So when they came to the restaurant, my parents felt so sorry for them and fed them. Anyway, I guess my dad must've made a deal with them. "Hey I'll feed you free if you'll teach my children Korean." So that's where I got some additional training in Korean. A few of them did come by to say hello after they got their Ph.D.'s.

I also remember going to Korean school with other Korean children. There were only about half a dozen kids of school age at any given time since there were no more than half a dozen total families here. I used to think that it was pretty terrible that the children would always cut classes. You would think that since we knew each other and their families they wouldn't just cut classes like that. . . . We had what they call *kuko hakyo* [Korean language school] at the church. The class was actually an organized tutorial. We tried to have that during summer vacations and other breaks. I don't remember studying very hard, but I remember all my Korean. In fact, even now I run into people who used to teach there. Not so long ago I ran into this man, and when we were introduced to each other, this guy says, "I taught her Korean." I remember reciting *kakya kokyo koekyoe ku kyu keu ki* [literally, the manner in which children recite the vowels with the first consonant (k/g) of the Korean alphabet] and all the other basics. I'm glad it stuck with me because I can read the Korean paper now and get the gist of it.

Can you tell me more about going to school?

In Chinatown we all went to the same grammar school, Jean Parker school. It was on Broadway. We had the same teachers. I remember all the old maid teachers: Miss Miller, the principal, Miss Guinasso, Miss Crowley, and all the other Misses. They were all old maid teachers in those days. We saw them as rather mean women who were strict and meted out punishment when you were bad. If you did something really bad, you were sent to Miss Miller. And we thought she was really mean! She would ask you to put out your hand and hit you with a ruler.

Actually, they were all nice when I think about it now. There was this Italian girl and myself who were Miss Valsangiacomo's pets. We used to clean up after school and we used to get a nickel and we all looked forward to that just for that nickel. It was amazing how much that nickel bought in those days. We used to run to a candy store called Splendid's, where you got five of this for a penny, five of that for a penny, and for a nickel you got a whole bunch of candy. Those were fun days.

At the Jean Parker school one student was always chosen to be captain of the traffic patrol they had at school, and one year my brother George was chosen to be the captain. He was the first Asian captain ever. You know, things like that are important. So many people today say, "What's so big about that?" It was a big deal. At that time they didn't hire Orientals even if you were born here, and our parents couldn't even buy property. Even in the schools, honors like valedictorian, which are supposed to go to the top student, weren't given to Asians. If you were an Oriental, you couldn't be a top student at that time. Forget it. Valedictorian? Are you kidding?

The Jean Parker school was the only school the kids from Chinatown could go to, and despite the limitations we faced as Oriental children, we had good teachers. When my three older children were in grammar school, they had all my teachers. Can you imagine? By then some of the teachers had gotten married, but they still remembered me. They taught my three kids before we moved out of Chinatown.

What did you do after school and weekends other than work?

Growing up in Chinatown, most of my girlfriends were Chinese, and they had to go to Chinese school after school. All the Chinese kids went to the Hip Wo school after school. So there wasn't really time to play with them. I have wondered if it's because they had to go to Chinese school every day that many of the Chinese who were born here still had accents. I actually think it's because the Chinese kids went to Chinese school that many of them really didn't have much time to study for American school.

In terms of the Korean girls, there were very few, and I was the youngest of the girls around my age. Often they wouldn't bother with me because I was younger than they were. So I didn't play with them much either. There were just a few girls who were younger, but they were much too young for me to play with.

So when I was growing up, I lived in the library. None of my girlfriends really used the library because they didn't have the time. But I would sometimes go twice a day. I'd read one book, bring it back, bring another book home. I was drawn to books. I enjoyed reading about other people's lives because I would get so absorbed when I read that I lived the parts. I still do. I remember being Jo in Louisa May Alcott's *Little Women*. Maybe it was because there was nothing else to do in Chinatown in those days. The library was right down on Powell Street, where it still is. I used to like Nancy Drew books, the whole set, then the Five Peppers. I remember reading all of those. That's what I did after school when I didn't go down to my parents' restaurant.

I was also the only girl in the family. Other girls had sisters to do things with. My best girlfriend was also an only girl, but she had to go out and work at her brother's place on Saturdays so we didn't have too much time together. So I learned how to be independent. I used to love to read about the few women who were accomplished. They were the closest thing to role models that I had. I also think that's why I wore glasses. My parents didn't wear glasses so I think it's because I read under the covers that I developed bad eyes. The lighting was poor. Since I was the only girl, I had my own room. But I wasn't allowed to have the lights on after a certain time. So I just read with a flashlight until I got too tired to do it anymore.

My brother Henry wasn't like me at all. He didn't like to do things alone. He wanted to be in the middle of everything, and I think he felt left out after school. He wanted to spend more time with his friends after school so he went to Chinese school. And every time we went to a Chinese restaurant, he would order in Chinese and everybody took it for granted we were all Chinese. It was great.

Did you also go to junior high and high school around Chinatown with your Chinese friends?

No, I didn't. I went to Girls' School for junior high and high school, which was a predominantly white high school. I decided on an all-girls school because it had the highest scholastic standing at the time. The graduates of Girls' School are very successful. The first woman judge in San Francisco graduated from there. In fact, most of the female city officials and professionals in the early days graduated from Girls' High School. Some of them remained old maids, and some of them married. But once you got married, that was it. Your career stopped, and you couldn't go any further. Many of the career women married late in life because once they married they would then live the part of the wife and mother. Maybe it was because it was an all-girls school that Girls' School had such a high scholastic standing. I'm sure other girls' schools are probably still the same; it's because there were no boys to distract us that we were so motivated.

What I didn't know when I started Girls' School was that despite the advantages that it provided, few of the Asian girls who attended would have the chance to use their educations. I basically lost touch with most of the Asian girls from Girls' School, so until we had our fiftieth high school reunion in 1988, I assumed that a lot of us went on to college and careers. Well, there were about ten of us Asian girls at that reunion, and we talked about our friends from school and what happened to our classmates. I believe only one of us passed away. We also found out that a couple of the Asian girls, two Japanese girls, had become nuns. One is in Japan, and the other is in New York. But what surprised me was that I was the only one who had gone ahead to college *and* worked professionally. I guess I had hoped that the other Asian girls from Girls' School would have lives like mine. I suppose that I believed that being Asian meant that we didn't have to stop working because we had children. But all of them stopped working when they became parents. So since most of us were parents and grandparents, that's what we talked about at the reunion.

Can you tell me what it was like going to Girls' School?

It was in Girls' School that I started becoming aware of the boy-girl stuff. That was also when I started menstruating. One morning I saw blood on my pants, and I told my mother, "Hey, there's blood on my pants." She didn't say one word. Apparently she was menstruating too, so she handed me this pad and just said, "Put this on." That was it. There was no explanation or anything. So it was from my friends and classmates that I learned about the girl stuff.

And it was after I got to Girls' School I found out that going to an all-girls school wasn't all that great. Going around with different groups of girls made a difference, but we were at the age when we needed coeducation. Once I was there, it was too late. I couldn't get out. Anyway, where was I going to go? Although nobody complained about it, we all felt stuck there until we graduated. There was a group of us who used to go out together, and we used to envy the girls at the other high schools who had boyfriends. None of us had a boyfriend, and no one chased after us. We used to say, "It's because we're in a girls' school and so all we could do is study and do the best you can." Perhaps it was for the best, because even if we did have boyfriends, our parents wouldn't have let us go out with them.

So who did you socialize with in junior high?

I still continued to hang around with the girls from Chinatown when I was a teenager. And on Saturday night the Chinese girls would all play mahjong. It was part of their culture, and they really enjoyed it. But I couldn't see playing mahjong, so I would study in the corner while they played. I think part of the reason I studied instead of playing with the girls is that I had this thing about finishing school before I turned eighteen. Normally you start kindergarten when you're five, but I didn't start until I was six. I don't know how come. So I really wanted to graduate when I was seventeen, like everyone else. It was kind of crazy but that's what motivated me to get out of school really quickly.

I did get out a year earlier. Girls' School went from seventh to twelfth grade—six years. And I got out of there in five. I found out you only needed so many credits to graduate. So I finagled my classes so I got just enough credits to graduate. I've forgotten which grade I skipped. High nine, I think. And I just barely made it, but I graduated just before my eighteenth birthday.

As a result of skipping a year, when I was in high school I felt closer to my class, which was a whole year behind me. Making friends was difficult for me because I was a very timid and naive person. When I was in high school, I couldn't even get in front of the class to speak. I got up to speak in front of the class and my knees shook. There was nothing I could do. I just shook. A girl I knew couldn't help but laugh at me, and she got sent out of the room for laughing. But it was my fault. I just couldn't do it. Still, somehow I made some friends with the girls in my class—a Chinese girl and a Japanese girl. With so few Asians there, we had to stick together.

I started doing a lot of things outside school with a Chinese girl who also went to Girls' School. We used to live on the third floor, and when she came around the house, she'd call up from the street, "Dora!" Then we'd run for the cable car and run for the bus. And in those days we could jump on the cable car, or the streetcar. Today you can't because they're all closed up. We'd barely make it to school every day cause the Girls' School was on the southeast corner of Scott and Geary.[5]

During high school it wasn't just the lack of coeducation that was difficult. My social life was also affected by discrimination. When I was at Girls' High School, there were dances. The girls used to be invited to dances at all boys' high schools. So my Chinese girlfriend and I decided to attend one of these dances just to see what it would be like. We talked about the fact that nobody was going to ask us to dance, but we decided to go just to see. Sure enough, every white girl was asked to dance, but this girl and I were never asked.

I didn't feel inferior or anything like that. I knew that not being asked to dance was part of discrimination and that it was a learned thing. And

I knew that all those white boys were not going to have anything to do with Asians. I mean, my girlfriend and I were disgusted. I'm really glad I went with my girlfriend because imagine how I would have felt if I had gone there alone as the only Asian girl, being ostracized like that. It also could have been worse if we didn't know that we would be hurt. But we knew. We just went to see what it would be like anyway. And it hurt anyway. Back then I didn't think too long on being hurt. I thought it was just a part of life. We knew that we were Asians, and we couldn't do the things Caucasians did. We accepted that fact. And we were sheltered from the worst of the discrimination in Chinatown. But now I often think about these kinds of incidents that we had growing up when I read about the different effects of discrimination. When you grow up with it, it stays with you.

I didn't go to any more Girls' School functions. Instead, we went to the Chinese dances every Saturday night. I used to go around with a Chinese girl. All the high schools like Galileo High School, George Washington High School, Lowell High School, Commerce High School, Balboa High School, Polytechnic [a couple of those are no longer in existence] had a Chinese club with all Chinese members. And each week one club would give a dance with a live band. They, Chinatown, had a good band that played at the dances, and everybody [all the Asian teenagers] would look forward to that. It was mostly Chinese, and all the Koreans went, what few there were. Then toward the end of high school all the Japanese started to come because they didn't have anything like that. I would dance with any of the boys who would ask me — Chinese, Korean, Japanese.

That was the social thing. We all went to school five days a week, but you can't study all your life. You've got to have your relaxation, your social life. We all looked forward to that Saturday night. No matter how tired you are, a night of dancing rejuvenates you for the rest of the week. It is really different today. I feel sorry for my kids [that] they didn't have the things that I had, like the dances we had on Saturday night. That was good clean fun. We enjoyed dancing and going out for *jook* [rice porridge] afterwards. And I think that dance is the reason that we didn't have as many youth problems. And even though it was once a week, all the teenagers looked forward to it. It's like you're rejuvenated for the following week. You forget everything, all your woes and things. That was our only recreation, and it was fun.

When I started going to dances, I was glad I had my brother George. It's not that I minded looking after my two brothers, but I didn't know that having a brother was going to be such an advantage. Our parents were very strict, and because I was a girl they wouldn't let me go out at night unless I was with my brother. So when I wanted to go out to dances or anything I would take him with me. George was always sort of mature for his age and good-looking, and at the dances he would dance with me. And even when I had a boyfriend, I couldn't go out. The boy couldn't pick me up or take me home so I would go to the dance with my brother George, and then once we got there, we split. He had his friends, and I had mine. Then we'd meet at the end, and we'd either go out to eat together or else we'd meet some place and we'd go home together. Looked innocent, you know.

But our parents wouldn't let us stay out late at night. I remember the times when our parents would lock the door on us because we were late. That was it—we were stuck outside all night. But it wasn't so bad because we'd just go to the restaurant and work or just hang around there until morning.

The social scene for teenagers in Chinatown sounds great. How did your social life fit in with your studies?

It didn't. My social life was really pretty separate from my school life. It was very disjointed, and I didn't like that. I think that's another reason I wanted to get out of high school as soon as I could. So it was a good thing that I did pretty well in school.

When I was in high school, one of my teachers said to me, "You have a photographic memory."

That's because she asked questions on the exam that weren't in the textbook but in her lectures, and I was the only one in class who got those questions right. I don't remember how I got them right because I didn't write them in my notes or anything. I just remembered the things she said. I suppose that's why she told me that I must have a photographic memory. I had a good memory, but I don't think it's that good now.

At my high school graduation my parents were sitting in the front, and I thought they would beam proudness because I got a scholarship to go to college. But there was no expression. They expected me to do well. At one point I wondered what would have happened if I didn't do well. I wondered if anything would have been different or if they would have said anything. But I don't even think they would have said anything even if I didn't do well because I knew they loved me.

When we were growing up, we knew our parents loved us, and though they never said "I love you," we took it for granted they loved us. Today kids say, "Gee, my parents never said they love me. They don't even love me." And you know, their feelings are hurt. But in those days we never worried about feelings being hurt like that. It's different. It's common to talk about things like relationships today, but not in those days. People thought about very different things then.

So did you go to college on scholarship?

Not immediately. I took a little less than a year off after I graduated from high school then went to CAL [University of California at Berkeley]. I know both of my parents wanted us to go to college and make something of ourselves, like all Korean parents do.

They always used to say, "If the three of you will go to college, we'll support you till the end."

You know how the Koreans are as far as education is concerned. They think if the opportunity is there and you don't take it, you're nuts. They were willing to work sixteen hours a day to put us through school.

I think part of it was my mother's influence. She never had the opportunity I did, and when I finished high school, she really encouraged me to take advantage of the opportunities that were available for women only in America. But I was still kind of timid, and couldn't see going to college by myself.

Then about a half a year after graduation a girlfriend Lillian called me. Lillian was a really sharp Japanese girl I'd known since seventh grade. She had just graduated from Girls' School a half a year ahead of schedule. She basically said, "I want to go to CAL," and asked if I wouldn't apply as well. So I agreed to apply, and that's how I happen to go to CAL. She was the one who encouraged me to go. We used go to school together—taking a train and a bus to get to CAL. I haven't forgotten her, but I lost track of her after she left for [internment] camp.

When I first went to U.C. in 1939, I noticed the discrimination right away. There were very few Asians, and as an Asian girl I discovered that the white boys wouldn't speak to me. So I joined the Chinese Students' Club at International House. There were so few Koreans that there was no Korean Students' Club. There were only two Korean girls at CAL—me and Mabel. Mabel was the first Korean girl to graduate from Berkeley. She eventually married a Chinese guy she met at CAL. There were so few Korean boys, and then they didn't really want girlfriends or wives who might have more education than them so it's not surprising that Mabel married a Chinese guy. Then she disappeared from the community like most of the kids who married out.

When I was going to Berkeley, I used to go straight home after classes to the restaurant to help. As in high school, while I was at CAL, my social life was pretty much outside the school. In 1940 the World's Fair opened at Treasure Island, and my Chinese girlfriends and I got really caught up going to the fair and hanging around with guys. It was just a little too much. In those days, it seemed like everyone I knew wanted to get married and have kids. That's what people did. I never even thought otherwise. There just wasn't enough time to have a social life and spend the time that I needed to on school. So I thought, "If I can't get all A's it's no use." So I quit. My parents were very disappointed when I stopped going to school. We were one of the few Korean families that could afford to send the children to college, especially a daughter, and they thought it was a pity. But they understood, because at that time dropping out of school to focus on getting married was considered pretty normal. So I dropped out thinking that my school days were over. But it turned out that wasn't the end of my formal education. Just a break.

Dora's parents put considerable pressure on their children to remain within the Korean cultural orbit, particularly in terms of finding spouses; for the most part, out-marriage constituted an almost irreparable break from the Korean community. That only small numbers of Koreans had immigrated to the American mainland at the turn of the century severely limited their children's marriage choices. However, despite the difficulties, the majority of second-generation Koreans of Dora's age managed to find Korean spouses.

Can you tell me how you happened to meet and marry your husband?

I fell in love. Falling in love is an interesting thing. First of all, you have to realize that my father was adamant that I marry a Korean. That was impressed on me when I was in high school. My father heard that I danced with a Japanese boy once.

He didn't tell me, but he told my mother, "If Dora ever marries a Japanese boy—I'm going to kill her and kill myself." And to them, if you danced with somebody, you were getting married to him. Well, my mother relayed that to me, and that's when I realized how strong his sentiments were.

And I thought, "Gee, he came here in 1904. And this is the 1930s. And he still feels that way?" I didn't understand at that time, and I still don't feel that way because I'm American. But I felt that my father really meant it. It didn't take long for me to see that it wasn't just Japanese boys that were off-limits for marriage. If I married anyone who was not Korean, he would have reacted just as negatively. I felt I was limited in terms of choices. And there really wasn't much interracial mixing until after World War II. At that time the only interracial marriages I knew were a couple of Korean boys who married Chinese girls.[6] Since most of the Koreans grew up around Chinatown, it wasn't surprising. One of them worked it so that in the summer the Korean boy worked as a houseboy down the peninsula, where this Chinese girl's father was a cook. And they got married. But once they married out, we never saw them again.

When I came "of age," they got a letter from a friend which pretty much said that they had a son who might be suitable for me. It wasn't uncommon for families to try matchmaking in those days. You know, the *chungmae*.

And when families start looking for daughters-in-law, I remember my mother saying, "They always look at the families first. If the mother's okay—they figure that the daughter is okay. If the mother doesn't have a good reputation, they don't want the daughter."

Although my parents wanted me to marry Korean, they allowed me some choices around marriage. They talked to me about it, but I didn't even know this guy so I couldn't very well say yes.

And so my father decided, "No, we're in America. We won't force her to marry anyone she doesn't know. She won't have an arranged marriage."

So that was it. It turns out this boy became a doctor and is doing really well. Now I think I would have been financially better off with him, but you just don't know about the other things.

In those days we respected our parents' wishes, but not to the point where we were willing to marry someone we didn't want to. Most of my generation of Korean Americans married other Koreans. We chose our own spouses although we respected our parents enough so that many of us chose our partners with our parents' blessing. What I thought was interesting was that there was only one couple where both the husband and the wife were from San Francisco. The half a dozen Korean families in San Francisco really stuck together. We all got together at the Korean Methodist church for social reasons, and stuck together because it was the only way to survive. But because we were all so close, it didn't even occur to us to marry one another. I think you tend not to marry someone you grew up with. It felt like we were one big family, and it would have been like marrying your brother or sister.

In keeping with my parents' wishes, I tried going around with one of the Korean guys who moved into San Francisco. But there were obstacles there too. The first Korean guy I went around with worked in a meat market. I never knew that Koreans looked down upon butchers. He was the nicest guy, but my parents objected. When they objected, I knew I couldn't get too serious.

So how did you meet Tom?

I met Tom, who became my husband, in 1940. Tom is from Honolulu. He was sent to Korea as a young child to be educated in Korean. When his mother died at age thirty-seven, he returned to Hawaii. I don't think his family fared too well during the depression. There were no jobs, and from what I understood from his older brother, the only opportunity, if you could call it that, was shipping out. Tom's older brother, Ray, started to do that, and then recruited his brother into that business. That's how they happened to come to San Francisco.

Now the corner outside the restaurant was a hangout for seamen. One day Ray, his oldest brother, was in the restaurant and said to me, "See that fella out there? That's my kid brother."

And I looked out there, and I didn't think anything of it. It didn't mean anything to me. He was a merchant marine, and he came to the restaurant to eat every day like all the other fellas did. We got to know each other casually, and eventually started hanging around together although we weren't really going together. I was with Tom when we found out about Pearl Harbor on December 7. I remember the headlines read "JAPAN BOMBS PEARL HARBOR!" I remember the look of shock on Tom's face. But as far as *really* meeting Tom, my husband, it was at a dance—during the war.

The war was also really terrible. All the Japanese were shipped out, and we lost touch with a lot of childhood friends because of that. It was really bad. And because we were in Chinatown, we didn't know about it until they were already gone. It happened so quickly. There were other repercussions from the anti-Japanese sentiment. I remember once when my father was walking outside Chinatown he nearly got beaten up by some people because they thought he was Japanese. After that he never went out of Chinatown again until after the war. And both my brothers, they were supposed to go to college. But then the war came and my brothers went into the service. You can plan your life one way, but things happen another way. What would you call war? A natural disaster?

Is the war somehow relevant to meeting Tom?

The war was a significant event in everybody's life, and it really changed our lives. I met Tom at a dance during the war. Well, before the war there were no such things as dances that we could go to. Nightclubs and dance places were pretty much limited to Americans. But things changed during the war.

Our social lives really opened up. It's a terrible thing to say, but in spite of it all, we had fun during the war. We were just looking toward the end of the depression when Japan bombed Pearl Harbor, and we entered World War II. The war brought prosperity. Everybody had money then. I remember going out practically every night, nightclubbing with whom-ever happened to be in town. There were always people coming in and out. Korean kids from Los Angeles who had joined the army came to San Francisco just for fun. And we'd meet them and take them out. By then a lot of the nightclubs in San Francisco had become accepting of Asians, blacks, Mexicans, and whatever, and a lot of Asians opened successful nightclubs in Chinatown.

I remember during the war there was the 365 Club, it used to be at 365 Market Street, and it was open all night. And then there was a place on O'Farrell Street, I don't remember the name of it, but it was open all night. It was one of those secret places where you knocked on a certain door to go in. You heard about Forbidden City, the first Chinese night-club. We used to hang out there, because we knew a couple of the girls who danced. One girl was Korean and one girl was Japanese, but they had to say they were Chinese, because they advertised as an all-Chinese nightclub act. So they passed as Chinese chorus girls.

There were other Koreans who passed as Chinese. Sunny Roh, Sun was his Korean name, he was a singer at a place called Skyroom at the top of the building on Grant Avenue on the corner of Pine Street. You took the elevator to the top, like going to the Top of the Mark.[7] The Chinese "Top of the Mark." The Skyroom had a bar and a dance floor and all-Asian floor shows. My mother and I went up there once just to see this Korean singer. He took the name of Sun Low to make it sound like Chinese, but he was one hundred percent Korean, and we were proud of that. He was the vocalist, and they had four chorus girls, and they were beautiful. I went to high school with one of the chorus girls. Another girl came from Honolulu. The girl from Hawaii eventually be-came a fan dancer—you know, a dancer who took her clothes off.

There was also a place called Chinese Village on Grant and Sacra-mento. I knew the owner, Joe,[8] and he did quite well. At one point he hired this Chinese boy from Honolulu as a singer. Joe introduced us, and I went out with him a couple times. And that was fun. And what we did during the war when we went out was go out to a show, dance, and then down to Chinatown to eat at the *jook* houses like Li Po or Sam Wo that had become really popular during the war.

I enjoyed dancing. We used to dance a lot—ballroom dances: waltzes, four-step. My two brothers were really good dancers. My brother Henry and I even won waltz contests together. And my brother George was known as the King of Jitterbug. It was the jitterbug at that time, the forties. I also jitterbugged. At that time I expected to marry a man who was a good dancer. I love the smooth ball—I used to dream that I had a home that looked like a palace, like Yul Brynner in *The King and I*, the big room where the two of them danced.

The war was terrible, but it also brought opportunity. With the war, not only did people have more money, but there was a lot more assimilation of people as well as neighborhoods. In 1941 my father sold two of the four units on Mason street and was able to buy a six unit building— 1549 Jones Street. Still, when we bought that apartment building on Jones Street, we got a letter from the Nob Hill Association because Jones Street was considered part of that area. It was a "welcome to the neighborhood" type of letter. I don't think they knew that Yum was a Korean name, because there weren't many Yums at that time. The message of the letter was something like, "Welcome to Nob Hill. We'd like you to join us and help us fight to keep the Chinamen out." This was when the Chinese had started to expand out of Chinatown. That was really something. I should have kept that letter. We didn't pay any attention to it. How could we? We just went on because we couldn't do anything about it anyway. In 1943 he sold that building and doubled the profit. My father bought a fourteen-unit building on the southeast corner of Broadway and Jones with the proceeds. We had that building for many years.

And it was during this time, during the war, that I started going with Tom. If it hadn't been for the war, we wouldn't have had anywhere to go at night, and I might not have really met Tom. I was actually with someone else—I went with this Chinese boy for a while. Of course, my father was never happy about that. . . . One night my Chinese friend got really drunk at the Shanghai Low, one of the clubs we used to go to. Tom happened to be there with his Japanese friend, and he asked me, "Do you want me to take you home?" And I said, "Would you?" and that's how we started going together. On the way home, when Tom took my arm, I felt a tingle go up me. And somehow it didn't matter that much that Tom didn't dance, although it was a bit disappointing.

I fell in love with Tom, but I didn't fall madly in love. In those days courtship was different. We kissed, but that's as far as it went. We believed that if the chemistry matched, then love would grow on you after you got married. But when you got married, you did it because you were "in love." And when you fall "in love," you think you have so many things in common. When I was younger, I really believed the idea that "opposites attract." It's a myth that encourages you to ignore differences, even if you know they're there. It's only after you're married for some time that you realize how important it is to have certain basic things in common. It's only then that you understand that those differences that you dismissed do matter. It can be upsetting, and it requires a lot of patience and understanding to keep love growing. Marriage is hard.

But when I was younger, I didn't know any of that. I also didn't have many choices. When Tom asked me to marry him, I thought, "Well, there are so few Korean guys, and he might be the last one—I'd better do it while the getting is good." So I jumped at the chance. My father objected to him at first because he was working on a ship. I didn't realize how badly Koreans looked down upon seamen. Then one day my mother gave one of her dinners for the community. There was a man from the Korean National Association, a delegate from Hawaii, at the dinner.

While we were having dinner, Tom walked in, and the delegate said, "I know him. He was an altar boy at his church." That indicated that he must be okay.

Then the delegate continued to say, "He comes from a good family." That was what mattered the most in those days, that you came from a good family. So since Tom was a churchgoer and from a good family, my father didn't object anymore.

Tom and I got married in 1942, during the war. After we got married, we moved into one of the units in the Mason Street building. My parents lived upstairs from us. That arrangement worked very well for me. I think it was important for me to have my mother close by because Tom was a seaman who was out at sea so much of the time. I didn't see Tom very often so it was pretty special when he came home. Tom also got along really well with my mother. It's amazing how close Tom became with my mother. My mother treated him just like her own. I think the reason was my mother was the most compassionate person I know. When she knew Tom was coming in from sea, she would go down to Chinatown and buy all his favorite foods. Her Korean friend, Mrs. Kim, used to say to her, "Are you crazy? He's not even your son."

It was the war that changed Tom's career. That terrible war brought so many opportunities that had never existed for most Orientals. They opened the Maritime Academy in Alameda. It was the officers' training school when the war started. Officers' training used to be limited to white men, but in 1942, given the war and the need to fill positions, they opened up admission to everyone. My brother George was the one who wanted to go. And so my husband decided to go along with him to Alameda.

When they got to the academy, Tom was persuaded to apply as well. Apparently you had to take an eye test. My brother's eyes were not as good as Tom's, so George flunked the eye test and didn't get accepted to the academy. However, they accepted Tom. Given his background, Tom went there, and he graduated as a second lieutenant in the Maritime Service. So he was a ship's officer for twenty years, and he retired as a marine engineer.

So 1942 was a big year for you.

1942 was also a big year for Koreans in California. That was the first time that we participated in the American Day Parade as Koreans. It was a big deal. It was public recognition for the first time. We were asked to march in the parade, and we had a float and people marching. But planning it was hard. I don't remember how it happened, but we wanted to have a bunch of girls walking as a group in the parade. We didn't have enough girls in San Francisco so we got Korean girls from all over California. Girls from L.A., as well as girls from the country, all came to San Francisco to march. I must have been chosen to lead the girls because I was from San Francisco and knew the route.

Did getting married in any way change your standing in the Korean community?

It's funny you should ask that. As soon as I got married, I started being included in "adult" conversations that Korean women had. I learned things about the community I had never known. It wasn't as if I had not been involved with the Korean community up till that point. When I stopped taking piano lessons at age sixteen, I started playing the piano at church and played for at least ten years. And being the church pianist you naturally know everyone in the congregation pretty well. But once I got married, the older women started talking to me about topics I hadn't even thought about. I was really shocked to hear that the small staid Korean community I grew up in had a completely different side to it.

Apparently the Korean community wasn't without scandal. Men and women had affairs outside marriage. I was pretty shocked when I first heard about things like that. But if you think about the way that people got married in those days, it's not really surprising. I often wondered if this person or that person knew who his father really was. . . . It wasn't that unusual for married people to have children from affairs, and for children to be sent to live far away in New York, Hawaii, or somewhere else.

There was also one Korean prostitute in the community. She was one of the few Koreans who spoke English because she had been raised in an orphanage. That was another scandal in the community. And apparently all the adults knew about it. That's when I realized that everybody knew everyone else's business. I think it was because the community was so small. It really was like family.

When did you start having children?

I started having children shortly after I got married. My first son, Tommy, was born in 1943 at the St. Francis Hospital—a couple of my children are war babies. The war was a special time, a time of abundance. I was at the hospital for ten days because in those days that's what they did. It was almost like a vacation because the nurses took care of you. You didn't have to do anything for ten days. But after ten days in bed, I thought, I'm ready to go home. I thought I could just get up and walk out of there, but you can't walk after staying in bed for ten days.

While I was in the hospital, a lot of people came to see me. I remember some of my girlfriends were working at the shipyards and making good money. When I gave birth to Tommy in February of 1943, all my girl-friends came and brought expensive gifts. The little room where the crib was was just full of gifts. I don't remember having that many friends, but I guess money was so plentiful that people spent it.

One of the things that surprised me was my lack of knowledge about the facts of life. I really didn't know very much. We didn't really talk about sex or childbirth or things like that. I went through hell the first childbirth. I was in labor for twenty-four hours with my oldest son, Tommy. I was just crying for the doctor to put me to sleep. In those days the only anesthesia was general, where they put gas through your nose.

After I gave birth to Tommy, I can recall thinking, "Gee, I remember a half a dozen of my girlfriends and I were in the sewing circle. We used to meet every night after work, and we'd meet at this Ada Char's Hotel about half a block away from my parents' restaurant. One of them was pregnant and she had a child, but she never talked about childbirth—the labor pain or what you endure for childbirth."

So I mentioned it to them, and asked them why nobody talked about the labor and how much it hurt. . . . And they said, "Oh you forget that." And I say, "Oh NO you DON'T." People don't talk about labor as part of childbirth. It's excruciatingly painful. Girls are screaming and yelling and crying. I remember one girl who was so strong that she tore her pillows apart. Now, you don't hear about those things.

A bunch of my husband's friends also came to visit me after I gave birth. There are still some things about the guys I can't figure out. All of

Tom's friends came up and had a ball in the hospital room. But they never once talked about my being in there because I had a baby. Either these boys didn't know how to talk to women about babies, or they didn't know that I was there giving birth to a baby. And since they didn't know why I was in the hospital, they didn't go to see Tommy, who was kept in a separate nursery. After I got out, one of the guys said, "I didn't know you had a baby!" Can you believe that? It was really strange. Well, to be fair, I lost so much weight every time I was pregnant. And I wore loose clothes so maybe they couldn't tell. But still . . .

And when I went home, my mother wouldn't let me go out for six months.[9] I couldn't even take the baby out for six months. While I was home, a Korean came over and said, *"Buja dweta,"* that I had become rich. I remember thinking, "Gee, I didn't become rich." My mother explained that in Korea, having children is a measure of wealth. I had no idea how wealthy I was going to be back then.

Reflections

When Dora recounts her journey to adulthood, I am again struck by the similarities that I see in our experiences. Cultural journeying has been an integral part of my life since early childhood. Like the Yum children, the cultural milieu in which my siblings and I lived also differed from our educational and familial settings. Like the Yum children, who negotiated their Korean home, the Chinatown environment, and American schools, sojourning was an integral part of our daily lives. We traversed between a Korean home, the Thai environment, and American/Catholic schools. Dora's cultural crossings and their similarities to mine rivet me to her voice, her story. Perhaps in locating and working with Dora's voice, I can come to terms with mine.

The time and place are different, but some of the details are not. Since I attended predominantly Euro-American international schools, I, like Dora, can recall the sting of disappointment when I realized that my mother could not speak English well enough to participate in my schooling. Like Dora, I also retreated into books at a very young age because of the absence of age peers. And despite the appearance of cultural fluency, when I reached high school, I found that I did not easily fit into the monthly dances and socials organized for girls and boys. These similarities, however, do not seem to be a Korean cultural legacy. Rather, these experiences seem to be a phenomenon that emerges for children when their non-

American, non-English-speaking parents send their children to American schools.

There are, however, structural similarities between our families that might be tied to Korean cultural influences. Dora's description of the lines of communication in her family reminds me of the structure in mine. My mother relayed messages from my father, and despite her authority to deal with minor instances of insubordination, my father was the final authority, as was Dora's. Like Dora, I grew up in a Korean Confucian family. I do not know if there are any other kinds of Korean families. People have different religious affiliations, but the common factor is the hierarchical nature of social relations. Confucian ideals are predicated on the notion that human relations are unequal—the ruler and the ruled, man and woman, older and younger.

So despite having had what might be described as a privileged childhood relative to Dora's, both my sister and I thought that we were from an impoverished family. Unlike my brothers, who believed they were entitled, my older sister and I carefully measured how much of the family resources we were expending, trying not to use up "too much." To compensate for the cost of our upkeep, my sister and I started picking up odd jobs when we were twelve or thirteen, tutoring English as a second language to Korean first and second graders, and taking summer jobs in English-speaking youth programs.

And even the other points of difference, such as our respective choices with regard to marriage and children, do not diminish the ways in which Korean cultural constructions have affected our lives. For example, while marriage is one of several markers of coming of age, for women it is still the bearing of children that marks the final crossing into adulthood. So despite credentials and a position that should provide proof of adult responsibility, the fact that I do not have children is a disappointment for my parents, almost a reflection of failure on their part. My mother still occasionally urges me to adopt a child so that I might experience, at least partially, some of the joys of motherhood. I think that for my mother, like Dora and so many others still influenced by Korean cultural norms, having a child in some way, shape, or form is still the final crossing into womanhood.

THREE

A Mother's Devotion

DESPITE *the discrimination that Asians faced, Korean immi-*
grants felt fortunate that they were not living under Japanese rule. Instead of
focusing on the hardships that they faced, immigrants contrasted their lives with
their contemporaries in Korea, and taught their children that America offered
them opportunities that were not available elsewhere. However, given the diffi-
cult financial straits of most Korean immigrant families, and the primacy of sons
in Korean culture, the families that had the resources invested more in their sons
than their daughters. While a surprising number of Korean American women of
Dora's generation and age managed to have careers in mainstream society, the
fact that Dora managed to craft a career for herself is still quite remarkable.

It's my understanding that very few Asian women of your generation worked
outside family enterprises or outside domestic services. In fact, I think it's pretty
safe to say that few women of your generation, Asian or otherwise, chose to have
careers. How did you come to have a career?

I never really thought about having a career or anything until after I
had my first child, when my mother started to say "go to school and get
a job." My mother had retired by then because we had sold the business
in 1942. When I was pregnant with Tommy, I was so sick I couldn't do
anything. The first three months I had morning sickness, and there was
nothing I could do. But after he was born in 1943, my mother repeatedly
said, "I'll take care of your children. I'll bring them up. So go out, go to
school, and get to work." I think she was reflecting on her own life. I
think she figured I was too young to start staying home, especially since
Tom wasn't even home very much. So she insisted that I "go out and take
advantages that exist for women only in America." Like most parents,

our parents wanted us to have the opportunities that they didn't have. But my mother was far ahead of her time in encouraging me to find an occupation, not just a job to supplement family income.

So I started going to City College in 1943. The first course I took was public speaking because I figured I needed to learn how to do that. I got pretty friendly with the teacher, which really helped. In that class we learned how to prepare all sorts of talks, and by the end of the term I was pretty good. It wasn't the speaking that helped me so much as the confidence. That was really helpful. I think I would have gotten better at it anyway because as I got older I had more confidence in myself. But that was the start.

Then later I went to State, and Golden Gate College as well. Any time I saw a course I wanted to take, I went—no matter what the obstacles were.

Did you also work during this time?

When I first went out to look for a job in 1943, I couldn't find a job. In those days it was a girl's dream to get a job on Montgomery Street. That was the Wall Street of the West. And of course, that's where I wanted to work. But I wasn't sure if they would hire me, being Oriental. So I looked at the classified ads and would call the firms. After inquiring about the positions they had advertised, I would ask, "Do you hire Orientals?" They would invariably answer, "I don't know. We've never hired one before." Most of the people were courteous, and some of them would even say, "We'll look into it and call you back."

But no one ever called me back. Not one of them.

I couldn't show my face to apply for work, because I knew I would be rejected right off the bat. You go to an interview and you are supposed to dress a certain way and act a certain way. But it didn't do any good because your color determined that for you even before you walked in for the job. If not for the labor shortage during the war . . . Terrible as it was, the war is what eventually really opened it up.

In spite of the struggle, those early years were really special. In some ways, those were times when the future held the most promise. The entire family was together still: both my parents were alive, my brothers were in San Francisco, and we were living just downstairs from them. Tom was earning enough money, we had started our own family, and I was working on having a career. Those were good times. I remember that my father turned sixty in 1943, after Tommy was born. We had a big *hwan'gap* party for my father at the house. My mother and I arranged for that celebration. I organized the event, and my mother did all the cooking. We sent out invitations and everything. We invited everybody. We moved all the furniture into one room so that we could fit all the Koreans who lived in San Francisco, which was not quite a hundred people, into our place. I believe it was the first *hwan'gap* party that Koreans ever had in Chinatown during that period. Some *horabees* [bachelors] came to that party and cried. They said it was the first time they had *tokkuk* [rice dough soup] in the United States.

Can you tell me how you came to have a career in social work?

It took a long time for me to end up in social work. For about ten years, between 1943 and 1953, I worked at various insurance companies as a clerk/typist when I wasn't pregnant. You have to understand that before the war we couldn't even get jobs as clerk/typists. At that time all Oriental girls could do was be a clerk/typist. My mother wanted me to do better than that. I wanted better than that. But I couldn't, so I worked where I could. In the meantime, I went to school part-time so I could get myself into an occupation. So I was pretty busy. And when Tom came home from sea and I was out working, he would spend time with my mother, watching her cook and enjoying each other's company. I think that's where Tom learned how to cook. That's probably why he's a better cook than I am.

It seems every time I got pregnant I took up another course of study. When I was pregnant with Darlyne in 1945, my husband was in the Philippines, and I went to Golden Gate College to take up all these real estate courses. I took the real estate exam while I was pregnant. The day I gave birth, my mother brought the postcard with the test results to me. She couldn't read it, but she could tell it was from there. I said, "Oh, I passed." I passed the exam and got the license, so I went to the San Francisco Real Estate Board so that I could be a member. Once you're a member, you become designated a realtor as opposed to a real estate broker. In those days that difference was important. Well, the San Francisco Real Estate Board wouldn't admit me as a member because I was Oriental. I remember I didn't want to go to the Real Estate Board alone, so I went with a Chinese girlfriend. And they said very politely, "You really don't have to join." That's just another way of saying, "We don't accept people like you."

That must have been very disappointing. How did you take that?

I got so mad. So did my girlfriend. But there was nothing I could do. I can remember thinking, "Even if you do well, so what?" In those days the opportunity was based on your color alone. I didn't pursue the real estate thing. I continued working as a clerk/typist at some insurance company.

I think running your own businesses, as my father did, was one way to maintain control over your opportunities. In spite of the limitations placed on him as an Oriental, my father was a successful entrepreneur. But even that became more difficult. In 1950 my father bought a hotel business—the Golden Gate Hotel on Kearny. Most of the residents were Oriental bachelors. Both my husband and my brother George, who had also gone into shipping, took time off from shipping to help run the hotel. But my father didn't have the hotel for very long because the union was putting pressure on everyone to hire union workers. He said, "No union is going to tell me who to hire and fire." So he sold the hotel in 1951, and both my husband and my brother went back to shipping.

I also got pregnant for the third time in 1950. My husband was home for Kyle's birth. I remember that because I went into the hotel to work in the office, and Tom came to pick me up at 2:00 P.M. to go to St. Joseph's hospital. My mother really got on my case when I got pregnant a third time. Boy, she was really against it.

All during my pregnancy my mother persisted in telling me, "You're not going to be a good mother, you're not meant to be just a mother. You're meant to go out and work." She was so mad because she felt I wasn't meant to be a mother. I had a son and a daughter and that was enough, right? And she was the one who was primarily raising them so that I could go out and have a career. So she wanted me to stop having children.

She even said, "When you go to the hospital, don't come back home."

But in those days there was no such thing as abortion. There was also no such thing as the pill, you know. So you just took a chance, and if you got pregnant, you had the baby.

I knew my mother didn't want me to give up on a profession just because I was pregnant, and when I was pregnant with Kyle, they started vocational nursing, licensed vocational nursing. So I went to Galileo and took that up. When I was young, I'd always wanted to be a nurse. So I completed the vocational nursing course plan, which was one year. Then they had two-year RN courses at City, so I finished that thing. After we were through with course work, we were supposed to do an internship plan. So they sent me to San Francisco General. When I went out there, do you know where they put me? Not in pediatrics or something like that. They had an all-men's ward, and I had to clean up after their bowel movements and urine.

I came home and told my mother what my job entailed. I didn't like the job, but I don't think I complained. I just told it like it was. She must have known that I didn't like the job when she heard about it. She just said, "Hey, quit that." I think she was trying to make me feel better about quitting because then she told me that they look down upon nurses in Korea. I didn't know that. So instead of feeling like a failure, my mother let me feel that I had quit because she didn't want me to continue.

And despite all my mother said, when I got home with the baby, it seems that she loved him the most.

In 1953 I finally went to the department of employment to see if they could help me find a job. They didn't have a job for me, but the manager told me, "Go down to the office in Embarcadero. I'm sure they're looking for a temporary worker, and I'm sure he'll hire you."

So I went down there, and sure enough, he hired me. He had a Japanese girl that was good, and he figured Orientals were pretty good workers. It really wasn't until after the Japanese girls came back from camp that there were large numbers of Asian women working. I think it was because the Japanese girls worked in the camp and had the experience. Once they got out, they were used to working and continued to work. I started as a clerk/typist. At that time people used to think, "All Asian girls, if they did work, were in the clerical field." I resented that. I think that is one of the reasons I wanted to be a professional.

This was around the time of the Korean War. What impact did the war have on you and your family?

When the Korean war started in 1950, Henry was drafted, and he went off to Korea. This was the first time that anyone in the family left San Francisco for any length of time. In those days the army was discriminatory. He first went to Fort Ord, in California, for basic training. He was selected as a candidate for officers' training so he went to Officers' Training School in Fort Sill, Oklahoma. I have a picture of his graduating class when he was commissioned first lieutenant, and he was the only Asian. No blacks, no other Asians, and hundreds of Caucasians. Then when my brother Henry actually went into the army, he was sent back down to Fort Ord for testing. Apparently they gave him all kinds of tests, and they said, "Gee, he's got such a high IQ. No matter what field he goes into he's going to excel." He was a brain. Then they sent him to Fort Champion, Arkansas, and he came out as an artillery officer. And the life expectancy of an artillery officer in the field was about a minute or something just as ridiculous. They didn't think to use an intelligent Oriental for anything but the field. That's discrimination.

At that time the guys would go up to Travis Air Force Base to get shipped off. When he left, we told my mother not to expect him to return because he was an artillery officer. We really thought he wasn't coming back. But on his way to Korea the plane had a layover in Japan, and they threw him off the plane. They figured it would be easier to teach a Korean than a Caucasian the Korean language. So they sent him to Camp Drake and gave him intensive training for six months, and he ended up being a translator and interpreter at Panmunjom. And he might not have come back if he [hadn't been] taken off the plane to be an interpreter at Panmunjom. Half his company died in combat.

How did your parents react to the war?

By this time, I think Korea had changed so much since they lived in Korea that they were less involved than they once had been.[1] After World War II, Korea was divided into North and South. I don't think they ever got used to the idea. To them Korea had always been one country. They kept up with the war, and we contributed to the war effort, but my parents were more invested in life in America. Maybe the war in Korea changed their minds about going back. Maybe having American grandchildren made a difference. I'm not sure, but in 1952 my father had become really gung ho about getting his citizenship. In 1952 they changed the law.[2]

They [the Japanese and Koreans] couldn't become naturalized citizens until then. He wanted to take the naturalization test as soon as he could, and that was in 1953. I went with him as his witness when he went down to take the test. In those days a witness could go into the room and watch the examination. He answered all those questions. If they had asked me those questions, I could not have answered them because I had forgotten it all by then. A large part of the naturalization test was U.S. history. I realized only then what he had been studying every night in his room. I didn't know that it was because of the citizenship exam that he was always studying. So my father was naturalized just before he died. That was really important to him.

What got me so mad, and I still think about it, is that they misplaced his papers. They didn't know where they had put them. But he went down to the mailbox without telling us what he was going down for. He waited for that letter every single day for nearly a year. He finally got it about a year later, in 1954. That piece of paper really meant something to him.

My mother died in 1954, just after the war. She was only fifty-five years old. I sometimes think that my mother died early because she was worried about Henry, who had been there during the Korean war and was stationed over there. She used to look forward to any mail from Henry. He used to sign his letters, *sarang haneun mangne Henury* [your loving youngest child, Henry].[3] I sometimes think we shouldn't have told her not to expect him back. That might have been too much for her.

My mother died on my birthday. She was making *tok* [rice cakes], one of my favorite foods. In those days they didn't have those grinders for rice flour like they do today. She ground it with a mortar and pestle herself. It was hard work. I think it was too much for her. Tommy and Darlyne, my older children, were going to a grammar school only a block away. The kids would come home for lunch.

I got a phone call from Tommy, who said, "Come home. I can't wake Grandma up."

I hadn't told my children where I worked. I hadn't worked for the Department of Employment that long, and I didn't tell them, but somehow they remembered that I worked for the Department of Employment. So Tommy got the phone number from the operator, and I guessed they tried all over and finally found me. Then he sent Darlyne back to school. He stayed until I came with a doctor. It just happened that I had a doctor that worked with me.

He must have felt funny about the phone call too because he said, "I'd better go home with you."

So he brought me home, and we found her lying on the couch. And sure enough, after examining her, he said she was already gone. She was still warm, but she was already gone. She had had a heart attack. My husband was out at sea at this time.

My mother died in 1954, after I had three children. It was a shock when she died. I had never seen a mausoleum, but I had heard about them. I told my father and my brother George that I didn't want my mother buried. I don't know why, but my father objected.[4]

George also said, "We can't do it. It's too expensive."

I said, "I don't care. It's her money too. Mother died early because she worked so hard for that money. And she's not living to enjoy it. It's her money, so I'm putting her in a mausoleum."

I had no idea how much it cost or anything like that. So we went out to the cemetery to look at plots and mausoleums. And when my father saw the choices, he didn't say anything. He just forked out the money for the mausoleum. I figured he felt bad about my mother dying so early.

My brother Henry tried to come back from Korea for the funeral, but the Red Cross wouldn't let him. . . . I think it was because he was Korean and since it was the Korean War. . . . The lady at the Red Cross said it was like a German trying to come over during World War II. I didn't get it. I lost respect for the Red Cross after that incident.

One Korean woman told the presiding reverend that she felt as if her own mother had died. Another person mentioned that they had never seen so many flowers in her life. There weren't that many Koreans here at the time, but her funeral was really something.

A lot of my American friends came to my mother's funeral. They didn't know my mother, but they called me afterwards and said, "I never went to a funeral where so many people cried for the deceased." She was a well-loved woman.

Then just three months after my mother died, I got pregnant again. It's funny. I didn't expect life so soon after death. Soon after I got pregnant, my boss asked if I wanted to work for the state permanently. And I said, "Yeah, I guess."

He asked me to take the test for employment trainee. I was worried because I was pregnant with my fourth child, but my manager said, "You can even bring the baby down." That's how badly they wanted me. So I took the written test and passed it easily. But you have to pass an oral interview. They flunked me on the oral test because I was an Asian and they didn't want Orientals. So I went back to the office and told my boss. I said, "They flunked me on the oral."

He got so furious. He picked up the phone and said, "Hey, I don't wanna lose this girl. She's the best typist I ever had."

All this was for an entry-level position, the beginning step for the professional ladder. I had to wait six months for them to give the test again. I passed the written, and this time they passed me on the oral because they already knew they were supposed to pass me ahead of time. You needed that sort of connection. I didn't know that I could ever pass the exams so I didn't have the intention of working permanently. But then I passed the exam for employment security trainee.

I wish my mother had been alive to see me move into the professional track.

In 1955 my son Kerry was born. That year, a year after my mother passed away, my father died. I don't think he ever got over my mother's death. He was one of those typical Korean men who never did "women's work." My mother served him three meals a day. He didn't even know how to boil water. Even so, my mother told him, "Even if I die before you, never bother the children."

My mother was that kind of a person. She told him not to be a burden on us, so that's what he tried to do. And all this time we were living in his house. After my mother died, we exchanged apartments. He moved downstairs because it was one room smaller, and we moved upstairs.

But one day he came upstairs as a last resort to tell us, "I have a stomach ache and I can't stand it."

So we called a cab, and I took him to Franklin Hospital. Mr. Chun, a neighbor who lived around the corner, came with us, and he was crying in the cab.

I thought, "Gee, he must have a premonition that something is wrong."

And sure enough, he died on June 15. Apparently his gall bladder or something burst. He should have called the doctor right away when he had stomach pain, but he didn't want to burden us. He didn't even tell us until he couldn't take it anymore. By the time he went to the hospital, it was too late. He died of peritonitis while he was waiting for a doctor to take the poison out of his stomach. June 15 was graduation day at that hospital, and they couldn't find any doctors around.

Three months after my father died, I became pregnant. How, I don't know. Again, it was life in the face of death. Sometime in 1955 I had passed the one-year probationary period as a trainee and become an employment security officer. Soon after that, my daughter Debby was born. It was hard raising two kids when they're only a year apart. The others, Tommy and Darlyne, were about three years apart. And between Darlyne and Kyle there was about five years. You don't feel the pressure when they're spread out because you're really only raising one at a time. And my mother practically raised my first three kids, so it was easier on me. But Kerry and Debby, the two of them only one year apart with no help . . . I took six weeks off after each child, but when I started working again, I remember sometimes I would literally crawl to get milk for Kerry and Debby.

I wanted to stay home with the little ones, but my boss wouldn't let me quit because they needed me. And I just couldn't say no. It was kind of crazy. I told him, "No one's indispensable."

So my boss said, "Bring your kid down with you."

Well, you can't do that. So I found a baby-sitter to live in after Debby was born. Janie [pseudonym] was my first exposure to Indians. She was an American Indian girl, and she was good. Except weekends, she lived in. On weekends Janie would go down to the bars in Chinatown and get drunk. I just accepted that as typical. She was with us for some time—well over five years. I think she was with us until about the time my husband retired.

I hired Janie through the Department of Employment, of course. When she knocked on the door, I thought she was Japanese. I had never seen a Native American, and they look Asian. Well, I found out she was pretty typically American Indian—she was getting a monthly stipend from the government, and it wasn't much. Barely enough for them to survive.

Janie was really talented and resourceful. She could make noodles by hand and things like that. She was a good cook. She also loved my kids like they were her own. That was really good. Once she took Debby on the streetcar somewhere, and Debby apparently left her favorite stuffed black dog Blackie somewhere. Well, Debby couldn't sleep without Blackie. And the baby-sitter went back out to the car barn on Geary to look for Blackie. She found Blackie in a streetcar, which really thrilled Debby. I heard all about it when I got home. Janie did all these little extra things that really amounted to a lot. I was so fortunate to have her. There are so many horror stories about baby-sitters.

Still, there were times when I couldn't keep on top of the household. There were too many times when I would come home late. Once I remember coming home, and Janie said, "We have nothing to eat at home." The kids were starving—but they didn't say anything because they were so young. So I scrounged around and found some macaroni so I cooked that up. I also had a can of tomato soup, so I put the tomato soup in the macaroni and that was our dinner that night. Janie was amazed that I did things like that.

And there were times when I'd come home late and was tired, and couldn't even help the kids with their homework. To me that was neglecting them. I didn't mean to. I don't think that a woman can combine marriage and a career successfully. I say you just can't. Not under the conditions I had my children. It's easier for men because a man doesn't have the primary responsibilities for raising the children.

My husband, Tom, didn't say anything about the way things were run at home. He was still going in and out at the time, when the kids were growing up. He was an officer for the Matson Line. The ship went back and forth from Hawaii to here, so he was home every two weeks or so for about a week. It wasn't too bad. I was used to it. I was used to running the house with the help of the baby-sitter, and when he came home, I pretty much kept the same schedule, working and doing what I had to.

About a year or so after my parents died, we started thinking about moving out of Chinatown. Things just weren't the same without them. And with the two small ones, I felt the kids needed more space. There was just no place for them to play. . . . Actually, we could probably have moved out of Chinatown right after the war, but we didn't even think about it because my parents were settled in Chinatown. It was only after they died [that] we realized there was nothing keeping us there.

Reflections

By the time I was college age, a postsecondary education was equivalent to a high school diploma, and my siblings and I were expected to attend college. But as with Dora, it was my mother who urged my sister and me to study. My mother knew the importance of economic independence for women, and repeatedly told my older sister and me how important it was for us to have an income. I heard the words throughout my childhood, but

I did not understand. Since I did not reach maturity under my parents' protective wing, my mother could not exert the kind of influence that Dora's had. But I can still recall her words when I informed her that I had decided to double-major in comparative religions and sociology. She asked, obviously exasperated, "But what can you do with that degree?" She was equally puzzled when I pursued performance art after college. Despite her disappointment, and her inability to comprehend my choices, my mother, like Dora's, supported whatever decisions I made.

My mother was an embroidery artist, and one of a few women who graduated with a B.A. in Fine Arts from Ewha University in 1949. Ewha became a university after the Japanese Occupation, and it was the only class that was matriculated before the Korean War. I know that she worked to pay her tuition since her older brother, the family patriarch, thought it was sheer extravagance for women to be educated. I do not remember my mother ever working, but I know my mother was a teacher in Korea. I know her wages were essential for our economic independence. When she chose to join my father in Southeast Asia, she gave up her professional life to keep the family together. I think it was difficult for her, and she didn't tolerate my father's role as sole provider very well. She would lie in bed with a migraine for days when my father asserted his economic control over us. And when each bout was over, my mother would ask for jewelry as compensation for her suffering. This happened with such frequency that my father eventually lost track of some of the peace offerings he procured. While I think it was my mother's insurance policy against calamity, my mother often got three of each item, and would slip them to my sister and me as "insurance" toward our futures.

I feel very fortunate that I have not had to cash in my mother's gifts and have been able to make choices about my work. But when I think of my own path to the academy, the professional track, my story is not so different from Dora's. I feel that I arrived at the door of the academy by mistake—that it was a matter of chance events that I have been permitted in. I think about Dora's vision of the academy, and I realize that mine is really not all that different. I have long constructed the academy as an institution that has silenced voices of women and "racial minorities" like mine until very recently. I have always been an outsider in the various contexts in which I have lived, and that I feel somewhat misplaced in the academic setting is not surprising. And while I have settled into the life of an academic, I still struggle with my voice. I suspect that the only place I will feel comfortable is writing of the margins from the margins.

2 *Dewey Boulevard*

WE MOVED out of Chinatown in 1958. At the time we moved out of Chinatown, a lot of Orientals seemed to be moving out. Somehow Chinatown became too small for us, our families. I believe it reminded us of the restrictions that we faced as Orientals. In fact, all of the Koreans of my generation living in Chinatown eventually moved out. We wanted things to be better for our children. We believed that if we moved out, our children would have an easier time than we did. For second-generation Koreans, our parents' involvement with the Korean Independence Movement affected the way they raised us. Our parents taught us first and foremost to feel proud to be Korean, but that wasn't necessarily easy. We were all pretty insecure because we were different; we were Korean. We just took it for granted because we had no choice but to accept it.

At that time [in the 1950s] I think many of us [second-generation Korean Americans living in Chinatown] believed that our children would fit in better, feel less different, if we moved out. We didn't want our children to face that same predicament we had. We didn't want to instill Korean nationalism to the point that it affected their sense of belonging in America. We wanted our children to grow up feeling secure, to feel like they were not that different from anyone else. For us, moving to Dewey Boulevard was the way we were going to do things differently from our parents. We were going to be American in a way our parents were never able to be. And we succeeded in those aspirations. But I'm not sure our children had it any easier than we did. They faced different kinds of issues, but I believe it was as troubling for them as the things that we faced.

I can clearly remember thinking about how different life was going to be when we were about to move to Dewey Boulevard. But when we moved—life just got really busy. It just never let up. If it wasn't one thing, it was another. Between raising the kids and managing their schedules, Tom's work schedule and activities, my job and other activities, there was barely time to think about the changes. So it really wasn't until recently that I've had time to think about how our lives changed when we moved to Dewey Boulevard.

Then my work brought the influx of immigrant Koreans to me when they started coming over after the relaxation of the immigration law in 1965. In the beginning the possibility of having an active and visible Korean community in San Francisco was really exciting. There was so much promise. But in order to establish themselves, the Koreans needed more help than I could provide them at the State Department of Employment. I couldn't do everything I needed to between eight and five. So my work started spilling over into my family life. That wasn't easy. There was so much to do all the time that I barely had time to think or rest.

As I continued to work with the Korean American [immigrant] community that's developed since 1965, I began to realize how different it was from the one we grew up in. The community I grew up in was so small so it was like a family, and we all cooperated when we needed to. I'm not saying there weren't disagreements, but we had common goals—liberation from the Japanese and sheer survival. Now there's a broader range of people coming over, from the wealthy to the destitute, all of whom have their own agendas. So there's much more conflict in the community. It really is two different communities.

In working with the immigrants I also realized how American I am in comparison. While my parents taught me to be Korean, dealing with the immigrants taught me how little I really knew about Korea. I had heard about Korea, but didn't have firsthand experience. And the more I found out about Korea from the immigrants, the more I wanted to learn about Korea. For me it became a personal quest, and I went to Korea several times as an American exploring my heritage.

In Part 2 Dora recounts her life on Dewey Boulevard from 1958 until 1980. Much of the life story information for this section was gathered between 1986 and 1989. However, this section also integrates twelve interviews conducted in the summer of 1992 and notes taken of conversations we had during the many meals we shared after the interviews. The narrative of Dewey Boulevard reflects the changing tenor of race relations in the United States in the postwar era. Since issues of racism were at the forefront of the war against Nazism, notions of white superiority became less acceptable. Legislative reforms systematically struck down laws and covenants that discriminated against Asians, and overt anti-Asian practices and sentiments diminished. Racial concerns shifted from being societal in scope to the matters taken up by specifically anti-Asian groups and individuals. For Orientals in California, especially the second generation, the post–World War II period marked an opening of opportunities in numerous spheres ranging from employment and education to housing. At least half of the veterans of Japanese, Chinese, and Filipino ancestry used their GI bills to buy homes or to acquire college educations.[1]

Dora's move was part of the larger exodus of Orientals out of Chinatown spurred by the lifting of the Restrictive Housing covenants in 1947. The increasing numbers of Asian American college graduates and removal of racial barriers in certain sectors of the labor market allowed many to secure professional jobs. With economic means, Asian Americans started moving into previously restricted, more middle-class neighborhoods. Many older Chinatown residents did not move; however, during the 1950s, the relatively young, emerging Asian American middle class from Chinatown continued to move into what were then considered the outlying areas of San Francisco.[2] For those who were part of the exodus out of Chinatown, the move also signified a major shift in social and cultural life. They went from being centered in immigrant ethnic enclaves to being widely dispersed in satellite communities that retained ties to organizations and activities that were based within the ethnic enclaves. While many middle-class Asian Americans aspired to integrate into the American mainstream, life in satellite communities settled into distinctly Asian American patterns. For Chinese, Japanese, and Filipino Americans in California, "integration" occurred through the creation of segregated ethnic chapters of mainstream civic associations[3] and ethnic divisions of political organizations.[4]

The prewar shift of the California Korean community center to Los Angeles had already affected the level of activity in the San Francisco Korean community. When Koreans dispersed into outlying areas in the postwar era, the Methodist church in Chinatown was the only remnant of what had once been a dynamic community. The numbers that dispersed to the San Francisco suburbs did not constitute a large enough group to form their own chapters of American organizations. Excluded from Chinese and Japanese American organizations, those who wanted to participate in the larger society had little choice but to join nonethnic or multiethnic mainstream groups. Hence, unlike other Asian American groups, the postwar era marked a time of integration into the American mainstream for Korean Americans.

The circumstances specific to the San Francisco Koreans when Dora finally moved out of Chinatown provided Dora with unusual freedoms to reinvent herself when she moved. Unlike San Francisco's Chinatown, which represents minority status and her working-class roots, as well as a period of duty and obligation to her parents, Dewey Boulevard symbolizes a new beginning: her entry into middle-class America. Although initially suspicious about her new social and cultural milieu, Dora discovered that she and her family had choices they did not previously have. The changes to her self-construction are evident in the tone of her narrative of Dewey Boulevard, which starts tentatively with her family's carefully planned move to her new home and becomes increasingly assured as she comes to see herself as an individual in American society.

FOUR

Leaving Chinatown

AS it was for so many people who moved out of the ethnic enclaves, leaving Chinatown was a dramatic break from Dora's parents' immigrant roots to mainstream America. While other second-generation Asians moved their parents with them, Dora did not even consider disrupting her parents' lives. Having resided within the boundaries of Chinatown all their lives, it was only after her parents' death that she and her husband started making plans to leave. And even then, they had great trepidation about the move.

How did you decide to move to Dewey Boulevard?

When we decided to move out of Chinatown, I started looking at probate sales in the paper. I saw one on Dewey Boulevard, which was still a restricted area at the time.[1] Asians weren't allowed to own property out there. I didn't even know where Dewey Boulevard was, so I asked a friend at work about the neighborhood. She said, "That's in West Portal. It's a nice area." My husband was out at sea so one evening I threw the kids in the car and went to look at the house. The house was in really bad shape. The whole side of the structure had terrible termite damage, and it really needed a lot of work—a real "fixer-upper" for sure. But I decided that it was okay.

Since that area, for practical purposes, was still restricted, how did you acquire the house?

The only reason we could buy it was because it was a probate sale. If we had gone through a real estate agent or dealt with owner, they wouldn't have sold it to us. For a probate sale you can do the negotiation over the phone, so that's what I did. And over the phone they couldn't tell what color I was. But you do have to go to court for confirmation. Well, I just couldn't show my face in court. So when the court date came, I made out a cashier's check for the 10 percent deposit and asked a Jewish friend to go to court and make the bid for me. And that's how we got the house.

Moving is always difficult. Can you tell me about your actual move?

When we were finally ready to move, we didn't dare move in the daytime because we didn't want to upset the neighbors. At that point, they didn't know that an Oriental family had bought the house. So we moved in the middle of the night. We packed up all our things and the children and moved in at night. We were afraid that there might be a racial incident. Luckily, we didn't actually have any overt incidents with neighbors. One of our neighbors didn't like it, but they just closed all their curtains when they realized we were next door. Then they moved out shortly after we moved in. Other than that, we didn't have any trouble. The doctor and his family who moved into the house are still there, and we got along since day one. And we get along with all our neighbors now.

So in spite of your fears, I take it that you really didn't encounter any overt racism.

Well, I do recall an incident with some kids that did happen when we first moved to the neighborhood in 1958. I took my two little ones, who were two and three years old, to the West Portal School playground, where there was a Caucasian boy and a couple of girls with Mercy High School uniforms playing. Well, the boy pulled his eyes back with his fingers and started chanting "Ching ching chinaman."

Then the girls all imitated him. I can still hear the children chanting, "Ching ching chinaman" at the top of their lungs and pulling their eyes back with their hands. When they finally left us alone, I was so upset. My heart had started pounding, and I didn't know what to do. What can you do? They're just kids repeating what they've been taught.

I don't know how long I had been standing there, but I knew the playground director from before, from Chinatown, and he came up to talk to me. He must have noticed I was upset because he asked, "What's the matter?"

So I told him about the incident with the kids. And you know, I never went back to that playground after that.

I had been subjected to racial slurs before, but not like that. I grew up in Chinatown, so we were somewhat protected. The kids didn't come into Chinatown to taunt us. It was only if we left, which we rarely did, that we were tormented. But on my first day in my new neighborhood, in a neighborhood park, I ran into that.

So is it accurate to assume that you were, in many ways, more insulated in Chinatown?

We were. In many ways it was a safe haven.

So how did you feel about having moved out of Chinatown?

When we first moved to Dewey Boulevard, I missed Chinatown. Life was really different outside Chinatown. When we were in Chinatown, we knew a lot of people. There was an apartment next door and we knew some of the people who lived there, and we knew the people who owned the stores. There was a corner Chinese grocery store that we always went to. And then there was a Chinese kitchen across the street where we used to buy chow mein and things like that. That part I missed, of course. On Dewey we needed a car to go down to Chinatown for supplies, restaurants, and things like that. The Chinese hadn't expanded out of the Chinatown area yet. So we were always going back to Chinatown if we wanted Chinese food. For a while where I worked was near Chinatown so we would go down there quite often. The kids liked Chinese food. We tried to go down there at least once a week for Chinese food.

But in terms of material realities, our lives were easier in Dewey Boulevard. The house was bigger. We had a yard, which we never had in Chinatown. And with the two little kids, I was able to take them in the backyard instead of looking for a park and going there. I bought them a little children's swimming pool. We set up a swingset in the backyard. That was really nice. We got really caught up in daily life, and I really didn't have time to think about the changes.

So did you feel isolated on Dewey Boulevard?

If we felt isolated on Dewey Boulevard, we didn't feel it for long because we were too busy living—getting ready for school, getting ready to go to work. I had to go to work before the kids went to school so our live-in baby-sitter came with us. The grade school was across the street so my three kids in grammar school just walked across the street and would come home during the noon hour. The younger ones would go to "Tiny Tot" prekindergarten and kindergarten. They were good kids, but it wasn't easy.

Did you stay in touch with the people you knew in Chinatown?

Occasionally. I remember my parents' friends still lived down in China-town at that time. One of them would come up once in a while to visit. I remember the late Reverend Lee's wife once came by with her son, and she said, "We were all wondering how you were going to live without your mother." She said, "Gee you're living better!" with great surprise. The community thought that I couldn't live or do anything without my mother since she used to do everything for me. That struck me as kind of funny.

You mention that you didn't have time to think about the changes after you moved. What do you think about them now?

I suppose in some ways moving to Dewey Boulevard was about being American. While we had been taught of the rights that we had as Ameri-cans, in actuality, our lives had been restricted. But when we moved to Dewey Boulevard, we felt we were finally living as Americans, exercising all our rights. And we took full advantage of that.

A fundamental part of moving to Dewey Boulevard was that we be-lieved the break from the past would be better for us and our children. That extended to all areas of our lives. We started getting involved in new social organizations. I believed that I could and would get a promo-tion at work. And we believed our children would be better off than we had been because they would be raised outside of Chinatown.

During that time, when Tom was home, he was very active—always doing. We [the family] always approved of whatever he did. He joined the Masons and became a Shriner.[2] Although he's no longer an active member, he still pays his dues every year. Looking back, I think a lot of what Tom did was because of racism. I think the only reason he joined some of the activities he did was because it was previously closed to Asians. To join these organizations you have to be endorsed by a former member, and he was able to get that. It's different now; there are plenty of Asians in the Shrine. In fact, the Chinese have their own chapter in Chinatown, where Chinese fellows are Shriners. The female compo-nent is the Eastern Stars, although I don't personally know any Chinese women in the Eastern Stars. And then the blacks have their own. Talk about segregation.

And despite my apprehensions, moving to Dewey Boulevard was rela-tively smooth. I think that gave me a lot of hope. I felt that changes were possible, and in 1959, shortly after we moved to Dewey Boulevard, I took the ESO2 Exam for a promotion to a supervisory position. I passed the exam but didn't get a promotion. There were ten openings for supervisor, and I made number eleven on the list. What I didn't know then was that this would happen over and over. But I didn't know that yet, and I continued doing what I had been doing. I really enjoyed the work.

What exactly did you do at work?

I was in placement. There was a day work desk where the jobs would come in. Workers would come in and wait for jobs. It was for something like $1.50 an hour or so. They would go in and work four hours a day or so. And as the jobs came in by phone, we would call the workers, and they would come in and fill out the applications. We would file the applications. And if they weren't there, we'd call them and send them on the jobs. Sometimes the employers would take a liking to you even if they would never meet you. And they would try to send you gifts like boxes of candy or something. We weren't allowed to accept gratuities so our supervisor would send it right back, but it was gratifying to know that people appreciated the job you were doing.

I'd like to get back to something you mentioned previously. You say you wanted your children to have an easier time than you did. Was it?

Was it better for them? In some ways it was, but in some ways it wasn't. For the older kids, Tom and Darlyne, who were fifteen and twelve when we moved out of Chinatown, I think the transition was difficult because they moved away from their friends and everything they knew. Although Kyle was just seven, since he was in school already, I'm sure it was an adjustment for him. For the younger children, Kerry and Debby, who were toddlers, it was probably easier. But mostly, it was just different from the way we grew up, especially the younger two who didn't grow up in Chinatown or know their grandparents. I really can't say if it was better or worse—just different.

From the beginning, when I started having children, I remember making a conscious effort to raise the children differently than I had been raised. I remember my mother saying, "In Korea . . ." It was always "In Korea they do this or that." What I learned is that in Korea they don't separate a person from his or her family. The person they judge is not that person but the family that you come from. I didn't impose that on my children because I wanted to raise my children differently.

My parents were pretty authoritarian, especially my father. His word was law. Our parents raised us in the strict traditional way. I can still remember my father taking off his belt and chasing my brother George clear around the block when we were living in Oakland. I don't remember what George did wrong or if my father caught him or hit him with the belt, but that incident had a strong influence on me. I didn't ever want to embarrass my children in that way, so I don't think I laid a hand on my children. Whether that's good or bad, I don't know. That incident influenced me.

I don't recall my father doing anything else like that. Well, I think we were all afraid of our father so we just kept out of his way. I do remember that as we got older, if he was mad at us, he never directed his anger towards us or told us. I thought that was more reasonable. Instead, he told my mother, who would gently let us know. Now, I thought my mother had a good way of handling it. And that was the way Tom and I tried to raise the children. We tried not to direct our anger at them. Instead we tried to talk to them about things when they came up.

But when we were in Chinatown, I didn't raise the kids by myself, so I wasn't as directly involved with them as I might have been had I been a full-time mom. As I said, my mother almost pushed me out the door, encouraging me to work and practically raising my older children. I did get help with the children after my parents died, but it wasn't the same as trusting my mother with the kids. In some ways I had to pay more attention to the younger two. It's not like I didn't pay attention to the older kids, but I knew they were okay with my mother. And while the older kids were in grammar school in Chinatown, they went to the same school I did and had all the same teachers I had. The teachers remembered me so it was pretty easy. I had a pretty good sense of what was going on with them.

But when we moved to Dewey Boulevard, I decided I was going to get involved at the children's school. The West Portal schools were new for us, and I thought it was important for me to check on their school. When I was going to elementary school, my mother couldn't come to PTA meetings because of the language barrier. So in 1960, when my second son was in fourth grade, I joined the PTA. I went to the school on parents' night, and I introduced myself to his teacher. His teacher looked at me and said, "My god, your son is so quiet. I just took it for granted that he came from a non-English-speaking family." I think it had to do with his being the only Asian in the class. I'm sure it made him feel diffeerent. . . . So even when you try to do things differently for your children, your children's experience may not be that different from your own.

Could you say a little more about that?

At their schools my children were always the only Asians in their classes—at West Portal Elementary School as well as in Hoover Junior

High School and Lincoln High School. All my children had that experience once we moved to West Portal because there was exactly one Asian family that went to the schools. They had some rough times because of that.

My oldest daughter had the unfortunate experience of being excluded from activities that her friends enjoyed. Many of the girls at Hoover, including Darlyne, had fathers who were Shriners. But she still couldn't be in the Job's Daughters because she was Oriental. I had things like that happen to me too, but it was not that bad because I had alternatives growing up in Chinatown. I hung around all the other Asian kids. My daughter did not have that option. I think when something like that happens, it stays with you and affects the way you act when you become an adult. It also affects the way you raise your children and the way you react to certain things. When you experience discrimination, it makes you feel that something is lost or missing in growing up. It makes you feel like you're not growing up normally.

West Portal was also, more or less, an affluent and white area at that time. Most of the fathers were doctors, lawyers—professionals, and very few of the mothers worked. I'm sure the fact that I worked also affected the children, because it was another point of difference from their friends. And although we weren't poor, like most of the people who had lived in Chinatown, neither Tom nor I were from affluent families. I know the children had some difficulties with that, too.

I don't think my kids were the only ones who had difficulties. I think a lot of the third-generation Korean kids had a hard time. I knew some of the other third-generation Korean children in similar situations, and many of them used to say that they hated being Korean when they were growing up. I'm not sure if it was being Korean they hated or being different because they were Oriental, but once the Korean families moved out of Chinatown, they had very little contact with other Koreans.

How did that affect your children?

Well, since there were so few Koreans in San Francisco, and certainly none in the West Portal area, I wasn't surprised that none of my children married Korean. I didn't think anything of it. My son Tommy got married in 1961, when he graduated from high school. He married his sweetheart, Arlene, an Oriental girl.[3] When they first got married, they lived with us for about a year. We knew that they wanted to go out on their own. At that time they were building the St. Francis Square Co-op on Webster and Geary, where you only had to pay a thousand dollars down. So we paid the down for them, and Tommy is still living there. They called the area multicultural, but I call it a rough area because of the projects all around it. It's a black neighborhood. That's where my two grandsons Thomas and Eric grew up. Thomas was born in 1962, and Eric in 1965.

It's interesting that you didn't think anything of your children not marrying Koreans. It's very different from the way you were raised.

Well, in terms of being Korean, once we moved to Dewey Boulevard, it wasn't something I emphasized. There were few Korean organized community activities to attend even if we wanted to, and there were no Koreans around the area, so there were no occasions to bring it up. If my parents had been alive, it would probably have been different. But since they weren't alive, the whole issue of being Korean didn't come up, especially for the youngest two, who didn't know their grandparents. I didn't even think about that. I didn't feel there was any reason to lay that Korean stuff on my children. And for Kerry, the youngest boy, it didn't even come up until he was eight or nine years old.

How did it "come up"?

It was when we went up to Clear Lake that Kerry wanted to know what he was. Kerry was hanging around with the lifeguard. And the lifeguard asked him, "What are you?" Well, Kerry didn't know what the lifeguard was talking about. We had no occasion to talk about what nationality or ancestry we are. So he came in that night and he asked, "What am I?"

I think I asked him, "How did you answer?"

He thought for a moment and said, "I thought I remembered you were from here and Dad was from Hawaii so I answered, 'half Hawaiian, half American.'"

So I told him, "You're Korean."

Kerry couldn't even pronounce the word *Korean*. And it was only then that I realized that we hadn't emphasized the Korean heritage, and that Kerry had never even heard the word. But until then, it just hadn't come up.

You talk about your life after moving to Dewey Boulevard as fundamentally different from living in Chinatown, as more American, in many ways. Your attitude toward ethnicity and your civic involvement certainly speaks to differences. Were there other lifestyle changes that you made when you moved to Dewey Boulevard?

Chinatown is a world unto itself. Among those living there, there was, and probably still is, a general sense that the world outside Chinatown was off-limits. And at that time, it was. And especially among the immigrants, there was a sense that you'd better work really hard to survive. I think the Asian immigrants of our parents' generation never felt secure about their lives here. Our parents certainly never did, and that influenced us. Our parents encouraged us to keep working so we never thought about taking time off.

But after we moved, things changed. After a while we stopped feeling so insecure, and Tom and I started taking vacations, going away to places like Clear Lake with the kids—something our parents never did. They never even thought of taking time off. . . . To be fair, I think it was also much easier for Asians to move around outside Chinatown after the war, when we started taking short trips here and there.

Then we started planning longer vacations. We went on our first cruise in 1964, right before my husband retired from Matson Company. The officers of Matson Company could go on a cruise for only 25 percent of the cost, so we put in an application. I wasn't too sure about going on a ship for fun. I still remembered what my parents had told me about coming over on a boat, and I had my reservations.

Finally one day I got a call saying, "Your application has been approved for the forty-two-day cruise to the South Seas."

The woman says, "You should see where we put you."

I was thinking, "In steerage?"

But when we got aboard the ship, we were put on the deck right below the penthouse. It was really something. We took only the three younger children. The older two were over the age limit of eighteen. And the kids just had a ball. All I was thinking was that it was forty-two days without cooking. And people wondered what I did for forty-two days. . . . Each of my children found somebody their own age to play with during the entire forty-two days.

This was a luxury cruise where they don't have such common things such as hamburgers and stuff. It was all continental cuisine. The first port we hit was in New Zealand. By the time Tom and I got off the ship to look around, we ran into two kids, Kyle and his friend, and each of them had a hamburger in one hand and a shake in the other. They were hungry for the simple things in life.

After two days back out at sea, Kyle says, "I'm not hungry. I don't want to eat."

We said, "Fine."

It took a while to figure out that he didn't want to get all dressed up in a suit and tie for dinner. So instead of eating with us he made friends with a Chinese cook and went down to the lower deck with the Chinese cooks to eat rice and Chinese food.

What did you and Tom do?

My husband and I also made friends with people on the cruise and just joined in all the activities that they planned for us. One day there was a grandma's tea. They asked who had the most grandchildren, who was the oldest, and all that. I got the prize for being the youngest grandma. I was a little over forty at the time.

My husband made some friends on that cruise, some former army colonels or something. He just carried on with those people like I'd never seen. You would have thought he was a college professor. I found out that Tom was more knowledgeable on a range of topics I never even knew about. Our tablemates seemed surprised at first. I have a feeling that they looked at Tom and saw an Oriental and figured he didn't know much.

But after they talked with him, I'm sure they wondered, "How can an Asian know so much?"

There wasn't a topic Tom couldn't talk about. He could carry on a conversation, argue with them, discuss the pros and cons whether it was sports or history or politics. He knew it all. I was surprised at that, for someone so quiet, Tom could be so knowledgeable when the time comes. It was amazing. I was really proud of my husband.

It sounds like you really had fun on your vacations.

Yes, we really enjoyed ourselves when we went on vacation. But I think it wasn't enough for Tom. It was around then that he started telling me, "You work too hard." Maybe I should have paid attention to what he said, but I didn't. Instead I used to think about how my mother labored. . . . No matter how hard we say we work today, it's nothing compared to our parents. The first generation really endured hardship. That comparison made it difficult for me to take Tom's comments seriously.

You said that you went on the cruise right before your husband retired. When did he retire?

My husband retired from the maritime service in 1965. Up till then he was going in and out all the time. For the last ten years, from 1955 to 1965, it was a lot easier because he was on a regular schedule—just going from San Francisco to Hawaii instead of being gone for weeks and weeks. In the beginning, that was really hard. You have to realize that even after I was married, I was the type that didn't want to go anywhere alone. Even to a show, no matter how bad I wanted to see a show, I wouldn't go alone. But I think my husband's absences slowly taught me to be a little more independent. You also become more independent as you get older anyway, but his being away also helped.

Our life didn't change that much after Tom retired from the maritime service, because he went straight back to work. In 1965 he took the exam to qualify for stationary engineer with the city and county of San Francisco. He worked there for twenty years before he retired as chief engineer for the Water Pollution Department. And we settled into a comfortable routine. Since we both worked, we didn't see each other that much more except for evenings and weekends. But it was really nice that he was always in town.

That was probably one of the best periods of our marriage, when we were in our forties. Even sex became much more enjoyable. It was good before, but it didn't get really good until the children were older. Tom and I had more time alone, and I stopped worrying about getting pregnant again.

It was only in my forties that I began to realize more about life and to be aware of things which I was never aware of before. It was in my forties that I became really confident. I don't know how it happened though. It's interesting even to me. I think it has to do with living longer, and also being more established. That was when he was working for the city, and I pursued my career. And at work I started talking all over the city, and it didn't bother me one bit. I say that because I can't help but remember the first talk I gave in high school when I couldn't stop shaking.

What was happening with your children at that time?

Arlene and Tommy eventually split up in 1965 — the same year that my husband retired. Eric, their second son, was just six weeks old. It really surprised me that any woman could leave an infant son, but she did. Tommy kept the kids and raised them. I really have to give him credit for that. While I didn't doubt Tommy's ability to raise the kids, I worried. I was relieved when my older daughter, Darlyne, moved in with him to help with the children after he and his wife split up. She lived with Tommy for two years, helping out with the kids. In 1969, she married Alan, a friend from college, and moved in with him. They had Marc, our third grandchild, that year.

Other than the help that Darlyne gave him, Tommy raised the kids by himself. He wasn't going to bother us. He did a good job, because his kids turned out okay in spite of the reservations we had about the neighborhood in which they grew up. We were concerned because people say you're a product of your environment. And that environment was rough. So on weekends, we would have them at our house. Every year during summer vacations, my husband would take them camping. He was good with those grandkids. It's funny, because when our kids were growing up, he was at sea so much that he couldn't spend all that much time with them. But by the time Tommy and Arlene split up, Tom had retired from marine engineering, and he was determined to give them all the things that children have under better circumstances. And you know, those kids still remember all the times with us. It's nice to play a part in the grand-children's lives.

We were doing pretty well by then, and by 1968, we had enough money to invest in some real estate. That was before real estate prices skyrocketed in California. I bought a studio condo at the Fontana from my own savings and rented it out to pay off the mortgage. My husband and I also bought a house on Kensington Way for Darlyne, Rick, and Marc to live in, and a condo on Pine Terrace that we rented out.

How was your career going?

In terms of my career, while I did not get a promotion, I was doing interesting work. From 1965 to 1970, I was on loan from the State De-partment to the National Alliance of Businessmen. The federal govern-ment had a contract with large private-sector employers if they would hire our workers. The government would pay for the employees, so the private sector could have free labor if they would train the workers. It was part of the Manpower Development Act. I was writing the contracts for these programs and monitoring them on the job. My work took me to places like Santa Rosa, and as far down south as Palo Alto. I would go to manufacturing plants that would train these workers. I even had a worker training to be a mortician. The workers were mostly white al-though there were a few Chinese, a few Japanese, a few Mexican, and a few blacks. But things really changed over that five-year period. Affir-mative action policies became more common, so the workers became more diverse. So despite the lack of promotion, my job continued to be interesting.

Reflections

There is a dramatic transformation that occurs in the tone of the narrative from San Francisco's Chinatown to Dewey Boulevard: Dora evolves from a working-class-identified Oriental girl to a middle-class American woman. That Dora was not able to become her own person until after the death of her parents is significant in terms of understanding the impact of intergenerational relations on development, particularly for Korean Americans with immigrant parents. Often unable to realize their own dreams and ambitions, immigrant parents will sacrifice themselves in the hope that their children will have more opportunities. If Dora had a different vision of what she might do with her life, it did not bear upon her decisions while her parents were alive. Dora knew that her parents, particularly her mother, had her best interests at heart, and she complied with her mother's wishes, knowing the strength that came from her support.

I am not sure that Dora was fully aware of her mother's responsibilities until she passed away; Hang Shin's death transferred the responsibility of overseeing two households, checking in on her father, and caring for her husband and three children onto Dora. Given the absence of contact with any extended family, her father's death moved Dora into the role of family elder at the age of thirty-three. While the loss of parents is difficult for adult children of immigrant parents, the death of parents can also mark a freedom as they no longer need to mediate the gap between their parents' worldview and the American environment. When her father's estate was finally settled, Dora and her husband had the resources and the freedom to look outside of Chinatown for a larger house that could accommodate two additional children and the baby-sitter she hired to care for her children. While it took two generations to achieve, Dora's life on Dewey Boulevard is a testament to the American dream of upward mobility.

While my narrative, like Dora's, is also one of immigration, in many ways, it is very different. My aunt laid the foundations for family migration by inviting my father over, but I started the migration of my nuclear family to the United States. After three years of trying to make a life in Thailand, where my parents had inadvertently settled, I set performance art aside to returned to the United States for graduate school. This was a practical decision of which my mother approved. My sister and younger brother subsequently followed me to the San Francisco Bay area, and when I finished my training, I decided to stay. The life choices I made separated me from my parents for thirteen years, and I had a freedom that Dora did not know until her parents passed away. I worked hard at my pursuits, not only at developing a professional life, but at trying new things that would structure meaning into my life. I even managed to squeeze in one last foray into performance art. I feel fortunate that I had the freedom to explore my options in my early adulthood, and that my parents have been able to see my progress in life. And while it was not foremost in my mind, I knew that I would have to craft a life that could somehow accommodate my filial duties to my parents in their older age.

In the meantime, my father retired, having accumulated enough capital for my parents to live relatively comfortably almost anywhere in the world. Although there were rumblings about retiring elsewhere, they made no plans to move since they were comfortably settled in Thailand. And so, despite my having immigrated to the United States, home was where my parents lived. I would visit them often there, where they maintained a gracious lifestyle replete with country clubs, maids, and a driver. But because their children had settled here, and because my younger brother had a catastrophic accident in 1994 from which he is still recovering, my parents decided to move to the United States. I am glad that the family is located on one continent for the first time in twenty years (my older brother resides in Vancouver, British Columbia), but their move here has been not been smooth. Their move here was the first instance of downward mobility for them, and the downturn of the Asian economies in 1997 has forced them to downsize yet again. And although they knew language would be a problem, I do not think they were prepared for the culture shock of moving to America. While it has been a tremendous relief that my mother has managed the care and feeding of my brother so far, my parents need considerable help in managing their daily lives and will increasingly need more.

In the instant that my brother had his accident, my narrative shifted: I became an adult in ways that I could not have imagined. Not only did my sister and I take on the responsibility for managing his recovery, in complying with my mother's wishes to be near my brother, we assumed responsibility for my parents' immigration to the United States. And despite my parents' improved financial situation, their continued dependence on my sister and me to mediate their daily lives has placed us squarely into the experience shared by adult children who must care for their older immigrant parents. So in midlife, when Dora had completed her filial obligations, I am just stepping into that challenge. I am grateful for the thirteen-year hiatus from parental obligation I have been afforded, and rather than loosening the bonds of filial duty, it seems to have strengthened my sense of responsibility to them. Like Dora, I am fueled by the dictates of filial duty.

FIVE

The Influx

THE 1965 *immigration law removed "national origins" as the basis for American immigration policy; in its place was a seven-point preference system that included professionals in undersubscribed categories. Designed to facilitate the reunification of families separated during World War II, proponents of the act had predicted that European immigration would continue to predominate. Additionally, it was believed that its implementation would benefit the United Sates by bringing in educated and skilled workers to fill labor needs in sectors of the economy that were enjoying relative prosperity. Few anticipated the rush of immigration that would come from Asia with the passage of the 1965 immigration law. Since 1968, when the law was actually implemented, Koreans have become one of the fastest-growing Asian groups in the United States, surpassed only by Filipino immigration. In 1965, it is estimated that there were fewer than 25,000 Koreans living in the United States.[1] Since the INS started counting Koreans as a separate category of immigrants in 1948, thirty-nine entered each year until 1952. In the 1950s the total number of Korean immigrants for the decade was 7,025. In the 1960s, the number of immigrants increased almost fivefold to 34,526, reflecting the impact of the 1965 Immigration Act. In the 1970s, the immigration figures jumped more than sevenfold to 267,638 in the decade. While the pace of Korean immigration eased in the 1980s, 336,000 immigrated, still indicating a 25 percent increase over the previous decade.[2] The San Francisco Bay Area has not attracted the volume that Los Angeles or New York has, but the increase has been significant. It is estimated that until 1965 there were about 100 Koreans in the San Francisco Bay Area. By 1980 the number had grown to 13,968, and the 1990 figure for the area was 39,459.[3]*

The influx of Koreans in the 1970s coincided with the emerging Asian American movement and the rising popularity of such books as Alex Haley's Roots,[4] which affirmed the necessity of a positive identity for racial minorities who had been historically oppressed in the United States. Many second- and third-generation Koreans, like Dora and her children, started to look toward Korea for their roots and perceived Korean immigrants not just as a link to the homeland, but as people who could assist in the construction of a new, positive identity. The post-1965 Korean immigrants, however, had their own ideas about their situations and their place in America. Very conscious of their cultural and national origins, Korean immigrants were much more concerned with their day-to-day struggles than with racial politics in America. Although they used the services offered by the Korean American activists, they did not have the experience to understand their political agenda. Instead, the immigrants started their own campaign of educating second- and third-generation Korean American activists, espousing their own views as to what constitutes an "authentic" Korean identity. Deeply embedded in 1970s Korean conceptions, immigrants' notions of Koreanness differed dramatically from those of second- and third-generation Korean activists. For American-born Koreans, not only is Koreanness interpreted and modified from their parents' turn-of-the-century constructions of Korea, but much that constitutes Koreanness has been invented in response to the American context.

Instead of seeing the differences as insurmountable, Dora accepted the differences as a challenge to learn about Korea and Koreans. Unafraid of allegations of inauthenticity from immigrants, Dora strove to learn about the multiple meanings of Koreanness.

You worked with the Korean immigrants who came after the change in immigration law in 1965. Yet you make no mention of them until 1970. When did you start working with them?

Well, you know, after the Korean War, in the 1950s, a few Koreans did come to the United States as students or skilled workers. These professionals came to the United States without sponsors. I don't know how many came, but it wasn't many. I didn't meet too many of them in my work because these were professionals, and they settled all over the United States. If they were doctors, they went to New Jersey. Apparently they could pass the state board examinations there. I know they couldn't take the state board examinations here in California. I'm not sure if they were barred because of their education or what, but I know that there are over a hundred who settled in New Jersey during that period.

As you know, the immigration law wasn't relaxed until 1965. When the immigration laws were changed in 1965, that caused the influx, and I mean *influx*. Even though the immigration laws were relaxed in 1965, the Koreans didn't really start coming over until the 1970s. Apparently it took that length of time for the Koreans who were here to take the naturalization test so they could sponsor the rest of their families over to the United States. So many younger Koreans started coming around 1970. They would stay here five years until they could be naturalized, and then send for their parents. And then their parents invited their other children.

If you were married to an American citizen, you only had to wait three years. But most of them waited five years. Apparently sponsoring brothers and sisters is something like the fifth preference, so the waiting period for that would easily be in excess of ten years, so it was easier for parents to sponsor their children. So that's how they got here.

You have a reputation for being devoted to helping Korean immigrants. How did it happen?

First, let me set the record straight: I didn't really set out to do things for the new Koreans. I think I just did what I had to do as it came about. My involvement with the new Koreans just happened because I was working at the state Department of Employment. I didn't realize what was happening until they came in. I was still on loan to the National Alliance of Businessmen in 1970, writing contracts between the government and the private sector, when my boss, Mr. Harlan, called me in.

He looked puzzled and asked me, "Can you speak Korean?"

I replied, "Gee, I don't know. I haven't spoken Korean since my mother died."

That was in 1954 when she died, and after that there was really no one for me to speak Korean with. My father was alive for a year after that, but we didn't really talk. So although I spoke with my father, I didn't feel like I'd really spoken Korean since my mother died. My father was much more distant, as Korean fathers tend to be.

So I replied, "Maybe I can."

He responded, "Well, you've got to go down to the Chinatown office. They're getting an influx of people."

They didn't know where these people were from. A lot of people in those days still didn't know what Koreans were.

So the next day I packed up and went to the Chinatown office. The Chinatown branch of the Human Resources Department was really open to help the Chinese, and here I was, the lone Korean going in there. But I guess word got out, because suddenly there were all these Koreans coming in. They all carried these little dictionaries, and lots of couples would come in together.

What was it like when you first started working with the Koreans?

One of the first Koreans I ran into was this girl and her husband. I gave her a work application and she filled that out beautifully in English. Then I asked her in English, "What did you do in Korea?"

She didn't quite understand me so I repeated, "What did you do in Korea?"

"Pomise" is what it sounded like she said.

"What?"

She repeated, "Pomise."

I still didn't understand what she was talking about. Then she opened up this little dictionary she was carrying with her and pointed to it.

I said, "Oh, pharmacist." That was when I realized that they couldn't pronounce "ph" sounds and "r" sounds.

Her husband was a teacher in Korea, so I asked, "What did you teach?"

He replied, "English."

Well, I thought, there's no problem here, and figured there wouldn't be any problems placing them since he was an English teacher. So I sent them to a job.

Soon after I sent them out, the husband's employer calls and says, "What did you send me? I asked the man, 'How are you?' and he replied, 'I'm thirty-four years old.'"

And then it dawned on me that "how are you" and "how old are you" sounded similar if you couldn't distinguish "r" from "l." The man couldn't hear the difference.

So the Korean man comes back the next day and says, "I didn't understand one word he said." If an English teacher is going to say that, imagine what the other Koreans are going through.

Then one guy who came in was six feet tall. When he was sitting there, I got a telephone call from the garment industry looking for a presser. Now pressers have to be tall. So I looked at this Korean guy and his application, which confirmed his height, and thought he should do.

So I said to the guy on the phone, "I have one for you" and explained who the applicant was.

The employer responds, "No, you don't. Asians don't come that tall."

I sent the Korean out there anyway, and he got the job because he was six feet tall.

The next day, I got a phone call from the employer. I was kind of worried and asked, "What did he do wrong?"

He said, "Gee, he's such a good worker. Do you have any more like him?"

That was when I discovered that Koreans are good workers once they start, even with the language barrier.

Then for the Koreans who couldn't get jobs, they'd come in and say, "We could only bring two hundred dollars over." At that time that was the policy of the Korean government. So by the time they'd rented an apartment in the Tenderloin, all the money was gone. So what could I do? I took them down to the welfare office and applied for welfare. I remember one couple . . . I took him, his wife, and child down to welfare. I was filling out his application at the office when a job came in at Fisherman's Wharf. One of the fishing industries wanted someone to help clean fish.

I asked, "Are you willing to go down and try?"

He said, "Sure," and both he and his wife went down.

A year later they bought the darned place. You've got to give them credit.

My job had put me in direct contact with so many Koreans, many of whom needed help. I don't know how many I dealt with, but I know that I placed one hundred Koreans in jobs one month because the State Department gave me a certificate for doing that.

After a couple of years of dealing with the English problems that the immigrant Koreans had, I wanted to do more. Language is a big issue because communication is essential. I remember when the Koreans used to come, and I said, "You know when you go home with your wife, try and speak English."

They'd come in the next day and say, "We just can't do it, it doesn't work."

But I noticed that when they have young children, in grammar school, they're the ones who parents and grandparents learn from. The kids would come home and use new words that the adults would learn. So I figured that the adults also needed to go somewhere to learn for themselves. So I looked into getting ESL credentials and was told that I had to take certain courses in college. I think I took one course at USF [University of San Francisco], one at UC [University of California extension], one course at State [San Francisco State University], until I finally had all the requirements for the credentials. In 1973 I received an Adult Teaching Credential from San Francisco Community College so I could help the new immigrants with their English.

I started teaching at the Chinatown Resource Center in 1974. I taught every evening, Monday through Thursdays, from six to nine. It was funny that I had a class full of professionals. They knew their ABC's but they just couldn't communicate verbally.

The first thing they would say is "How come they [Americans] speak so fast?"

So the first thing I taught them to say was, "Please speak slowly." If people spoke slowly, they could understand.

Then I said, "The first thing you have to learn is pronunciation." At that time ESL classes didn't teach pronunciation. They would go to school and learn grammar and vocabulary, and that was it. They would never get ahead because even if they knew what to say, no one could understand them. Some of them couldn't even find their way to my office because they couldn't pronounce it. I was at Turk and Fillmore at that time.

One of them said, "I walked to your office."

I asked, "Why did you walk?"

He said, "I got on the bus and I told him I wanted to go to Tuck-ku and Pill-Mo." T-u-r-k is pronounced Tuck-ku in Korean. And since they don't have "F's" or "R's" in Korean, they can't pronounce Fillmore. But I knew no one was going to understand that version, so I told him so. I tried to explain that Turk is one syllable and Fillmore two. But because of the structure of the sounds, Koreans tend to make two syllables out of one-syllable words, and three out of two-syllable words. Even something like Geary Street is pronounced differently. There is no "ear" sound so it's either "Garry" or "Gi-ah-ry." And no one's going to understand that.

And for a while there were half a dozen senior widows living on O'Farrell Street, and they got on the Van Ness bus and wanted to get off at "O-peh-ra, o-peh-ra," and they were dropped off at the Opera House. "O-peh-ra" does sound like Opera. So these were the kinds of daily difficulties that the Koreans faced.

Even numbers are a problem. The class was located on the third floor, and I remember spending half an hour trying to get one girl to say "third floor" and not "tuh-duh-poo-ro." Then the next time I saw her she'd forgotten the pronunciation.

Another thing was getting to where I was. At that time you could take the Number 55 Sacramento to get to my office. But a lot of the Koreans had a hard time reaching me initially. I finally asked them what they were saying to ask after the bus, and they said, "Pi-pu-tee-pie-bu." I tried to teach them how to say "fifty-five," but it was not an easy number. Also, when all the other Koreans understand what you mean by "pi-pu-tee-pie-bu," it's a shock to realize that Americans don't understand you.

I felt the adult language class was a good thing not only because the new Koreans really need to learn English, but also because it was a meeting place for Koreans who are new to the area and the culture. Wednesday was volunteer night, and we had American-born Koreans as well as longtime residents come in and mingle with the new immigrants. It was really fun. When the third-generation volunteers met the new immigrants for the first time, it was really something. Neither was aware of the other, and sometimes it was a rude awakening for both groups.

During that time I also started teaching English to Korean seniors on Saturdays at the International Institute on Van Ness and Broadway. The third-generation volunteers were gung ho, and they wanted to get involved with the Korean immigrant seniors. They were right there, helping me teach the seniors English. It was really something. These were the same kids who hated being Korean when they were growing up. Even if I didn't know them, when I asked them who their parents were, I realized that I knew their parents. There were a group of girls who hung around together. They just finished college, and they were really into community service. At that time, the Asian American movement was just getting strong at State, and there were a lot of young Korean community activists. That was in the early seventies.

The Korean community grew considerably around this time, and because of the tension between North and South Korea at that time, the new immigrants came with strong anticommunist sentiments. At that time no one wanted to look at the U.S. involvement in establishing the thirty-eighth parallel. Anyway, people [non-Koreans] started asking me where I was from, "North or South Korea?" And I said, "Korea is Korea. There's only one Korea." Our parents lived in Korea when it was one country, and when I was growing up, there was only one Korea. And we didn't teach our children to differentiate between the South and the North either. People don't understand that this division of Korea is recent.

The division of the country and the antagonism between North and South Korea have had long-ranging consequences. There are members of the Korean community that still remain strongly anticommunist, but it's not as bad with talk of reunification and all that. The seventies were an interesting time, with the influx of anticommunist Korean immigrants on one hand, and the rise of American-born socialist and communist activists on the other.

I can remember one activist telling me, "You have to tell the Koreans how bad the United States is."

I said, "Are you kidding? The Koreans came to America to escape communism. And you're going to tell them that America is bad? They came because the streets are supposed to be paved with gold, and it's the land of opportunity."

I figure everyone is entitled to their own views, but this is America. To each their own, but don't try to rub it off on me.

After the English classes got started, I started noticing that a lot of Korean registered nurses started coming to me for jobs. I placed them as nurse's aides in convalescent hospitals and rest homes, since they couldn't pass the state licensing exam. I asked about that and started seeing a pattern—most of them failed the psychiatric portion of the test because their training in Korea didn't include psychiatric nursing.

So in 1975 I contacted Steven Shon, a Korean psychiatrist up at U.C.S.F., and Margaret Hanford, who directs the Home Health Aid Program, got them to agree to conduct a series of classes in psychiatric nursing for about twenty of the Korean nurses. I then contacted the Alemany Adult School, where the administrator agreed to issue the appropriate credentials to Dr. Shon and Mrs. Hanford as well as to pay them salaries.

In order to make space for the programs we were starting for the new immigrants, my son, Tommy, and I started a Korean community service center at a storefront on Larkin Street. The nurses' course was already set as a six-month course, so we needed the space for at least that length of time. We relied heavily on donations and volunteers to run the place. My husband, Tom, paid the rent for six months there, my daughter Debby worked at the reception, and that's where I arranged classroom space for the course.

The nurses took the state exam after the course, and although only five of them passed the total exam, all twenty passed the psychiatric portion. I was really proud of them. The rest of them had to take the exam again so that they could pass the other parts of the test. And every one of them passed. It was something else. Now they all are in supervisory positions all over the Bay Area. It's pretty amazing.

You know, in 1992 I went to the wedding of a young woman. She's Mr. Kim's daughter. Now, this Mr. Kim would come in to see me every single day at the department. And one day this Safeway trainee job came up. I believe it was the beginning of affirmative action. Safeway didn't really want to hire Orientals, but they had to, so they put in to train the Chinese. I was in a Chinese office in Chinatown, so I saw this job listing. Mr. Kim was Korean, not Chinese, so I put him down as Oriental. So Mr. Kim got trained as a clerk. He went in as a clerk and he worked his way up from that. He's retired now. He was the first Oriental to be hired at Safeway. I give him credit. He and his wife have brought up their children, and now I'm invited to their children's weddings, even though I don't even know the children. Time flies so fast. That placement seemed like yesterday. I keep wondering, is this the little one I saw? And she's getting married?

I also remember another lady who came to me for employment. She had just come from Korea. She said she would do anything, and that housework was fine. But before I place anybody, I have to find out what their work history is like. And when I started to ask questions, I discovered that she was a relatively well-known pediatrician in Korea. She knew she couldn't get a job as a physician here because of the language barrier and because she wasn't qualified to take the licensing exam.

So I thought about her options pretty carefully. I finally called a laboratory run by a black man I knew and asked him, "Would you hire a technician?"

When he asked about the potential employee's background, I told him, "She's a medical doctor."

Given what the wages were for a technician, the employer knew that he was going to get his money's worth, so he hired her.

But this lady eventually quit because she heard that she was eligible to take the licensing exam in Chicago. So she went to Chicago, leaving her three kids here, and came back with a license. She became a doctor at Kaiser. And her daughter became valedictorian at George Washington High School after one year. That's pretty impressive.

From your experience, how would you characterize the post-1965 Korean immigrants?

There are a lot of success stories, but that's because those who make it tend to come back to thank me. But not all the people who came to the department stuck it out. Some of them never came back if they didn't get a job on the first day. The ones who persevered, came in every day to see me, always got something good. But I don't know about the ones that never came back. . . .

Even the immigrants who came with money had difficulties, so you can imagine what it was like for those who didn't. The saddest cases were the servicemen's wives. They still are the saddest cases. There was one really cute girl who came in. She had two children, and you could tell that she didn't have the best background. The mother-in-law brought her in. Her black husband would not let her out of the house and didn't want her to learn English. She was dying to learn English. She wanted to go out and work. So finally her mother-in-law brought her in. I felt really good when I placed her in a job.

I still have contact with Gina,[5] one of the girls I worked with. When I met her, she had married a guy just to come over. Although Gina never told me, I had the impression she had been a bar girl. She was getting beaten up by her husband and wanted to get divorced so I helped her with that. At that time, Gina couldn't read or write English. She had no money so she had to find work, and she wanted to be a hostess somewhere. I don't really know what to tell her, but I referred her to this Korean Village Night Club. I went to visit Gina to see how she was doing, and she sure looked beautiful at night, with makeup and a long gown. She moved to Hawaii to work in one of the Korean bars owned by Korean girls. I told her she should go to school and learn English. But she didn't.

I remember asking her, "Why don't you find someone good to marry?"
She said, "I'm too busy making a living."
Gina is a nice girl. We still stay in touch.

There are still about a hundred war brides at the Presidio. And the cases are not pretty. I went there for another case about a woman who was getting beat up. She didn't have any children so we told her not to go back. But she kept going back and kept getting beat up.

These girls know they're ostracized by the Korean community so they won't come out. The Korean community looks down on them because many of the GI war brides were prostitutes. They're really isolated, and I feel sorry for them. What amazed me the most about these girls is they can't even read and write Korean. They're illiterate. It came as a surprise when I realized that most of them are girls from poor rural areas who went to the cities to work in bars as prostitutes. They were really poor in Korea, and the girls I worked with said that they married the GI's because they thought all the GI's were rich. There are some really sad stories. Some of the girls ended up in the Ozarks and places like that. There have been cases where Korean girls committed suicide because of their disappointment.

And then because they're married to American citizens, the GI war brides bring their parents over. Dealing with the parents of these girls is another issue altogether. They're really different from most of the immigrant seniors. The seniors we usually deal with at the senior citizens' centers and the Korean community centers can't speak English. Except for the older women for whom education wasn't an option, they're literate in Korean. And while many of them do not have high school or college degrees, their children do. They're the parents of the professionals who came over in the early 1970s—parents of pharmacists, registered nurses, doctors.

The parents of the servicemen's wives are really something else.

They're illiterate, uneducated, and totally ignorant—not just about the way things operate here, but also about how things work in Korea. And they can't or won't even go to the Korean senior citizens' groups because the seniors would look down upon them. So they're isolated and really in need of services. Those are the hardest cases.

Much of the work that you did was for Korean seniors. How did you get involved in that?

After I got my ESL credentials, I started teaching an English class for the seniors, and that really opened my eyes to the situation of the seniors. They really needed help getting adjusted. If you're younger and have to work, you have no choice but to learn about the United States in order to survive. So that forces you to adjust. Since the seniors don't work in the same ways that younger people do, they're more isolated and in need of services. Their situation really stuck with me, so I stayed involved with them even if I was doing other things.

Your involvement with the Korean immigrants extended far beyond your work at the California Department of Employment. Could you talk about that?

It was in response to the needs of the new Koreans that my involvement with them really intensified. I just found myself doing what I had to do. I found myself doing some unusual things. I even accompanied girls to get abortions. This was while I was still working in the department, and I was lucky because my manager always let me go.

I'd say, "Gee I have to take these people to see about an abortion."

And he'd say, "Yes, you should go."

I got involved with this particular issue because I felt that it was the right thing to do, especially for some of these girls who really couldn't afford to have any more children. It must have been in the seventies, because abortion was legal then.

When I had my children, it wasn't legal. I think it was harder then. When you have two or three children, it's enough. So when you get pregnant by accident, again, you are naturally going to think about alternatives. And for me there were none, really.

I think it's really good that women now have a choice. The heck with these pro-lifers. They don't know what it's like when you can't afford to raise a child properly.

Unfortunately, my youngest daughter was too young to understand my position on that issue. I think she took it personally. I once overheard her talking to a friend. She said, "My parents didn't even want me."

That made me feel kind of bad. But whether or not I wanted to have her, I did have her, and I never regretted it, once she was born. And I feel that we were really fortunate because it turned out that we could afford to have her, too.

Even when my involvement in particular issues did lead to misunderstanding, my children supported my involvement with the Korean immigrants.

And during the 1970s I was so busy that I couldn't even see beyond my nose. I think I was just being nationalistic. I was happy to see them and happy to help them. When we were growing up, there weren't more than a hundred of us. That was the total population of Koreans—about half a dozen families and a few bachelors.

But aren't there some fundamental differences between the first wave of Koreans to the United States and the post-1965-ers?

When I first started working with the Koreans, I learned quite a bit about things Korean. I learned very quickly that I wasn't like the new Koreans. They were immigrants starting out in a new country, without the knowledge of the language. I'm American, and there were, and still are, lots of things I don't know about things Korean. But I didn't fully appreciate the differences until sometime in the mid-1980s. I was really blinded by nationalism.

What kinds of things did you learn?

I remember, one lady says to me, "You must be from Pyongyang. You can't be born here. How would you have that accent?"

Apparently I speak Korean with a northern accent. I learned Korean from my mother and she was from that area, so I must have picked it up from her. But I never knew that before. I never even knew Korean had accents.

I really got a sense of how different the Koreans were from Korean Americans. Once I was talking about my daughter in a group of Koreans and I used the word "my"—you know, *neh tal,* and they were horrified and told me not to use the word "my." That's Korean style. You say "our," *uri,* not "my." And they really stick to that. And in a way I came to understand it because it's good family values. I don't think that's bad at all. But that's part of another culture and a different value system. It's a different sense of the family. I suppose my parents were like that. It's different when you grow up here because the individual matters more. So the family is not emphasized in the same way.

The immigrants also talked about Korea a lot. It wasn't surprising since that's all they knew. But after working with them and listening to their stories, I became really curious about Korea.

When I was growing up, I just accepted the things I read and the things my parents told me. But after meeting so many Koreans at work, I wanted to go and see for myself and experience the culture. So I first went to Korea in 1971, when I was fifty.

When I decided to go, I asked my family, "Who wants to go to Korea, who wants to go with me?"

My husband said, "What do you want to go there for? There's nothing there." He spent part of his childhood in Korea, before it started developing, and had his own ideas based on his memories.

My kids weren't too sure about it either.

So I said, "Well, I'm going to go alone."

It was the first time in my life I'd done something like that. I'd never traveled alone before then. So I got this ticket from this Korean guy, who had been one of my clients at Korean American Travel. And for every fifteen tickets the travel agents sell, they get one free. So he sold me this ticket for five hundred dollars.

I was worried about a place to stay, so I asked, "Gee, don't I have to make a hotel reservation?"

He said, "No, there'll be plenty of hotel rooms."

So I just got on the plane and went. But when we landed in Korea, there were no hotel rooms. I went from hotel to hotel looking for a room with no luck. I thought, "What am I going to do?"

So what did you do?

Well, people were always saying, "If you come to Korea, look me up." I hadn't really thought to do that, but I was stuck. I remembered one person who happened to be the secretary of a well-known Korean family so I called him up from the Chosun Hotel. I figured he was a man of influence.

So he said, "Just a minute and I'll be right there." And because of his position, he got me a room for the night at the Chosun.

So I stayed one night at the hotel.

The next morning this woman that I met in the U.S. came to see me. Apparently, this man who had helped me out the previous night had called her, so she came over and told me, "You'll have to come with me."

I figured to myself, "I don't have a hotel room after today anyway."

She said, "I live all alone and I have two maids."

I normally wouldn't have gone, but I didn't have much choice so I went with her and she had this beautiful big home with two maids. Naturally they couldn't speak English, so we got by with my poor Korean. You have to realize that although I can speak Korean, I speak as if I'm speaking to someone of lower position in terms of respect. I've never spoken to anyone in my age group. My parents always spoke down to me, and there weren't enough elders for me to speak up to. I wonder now if they resented it.

But the maids were so happy that I could speak Korean, and I was treated royally by them. I think my host enjoyed going around with me too, because it was my first trip to Korea, and she wanted me to see everything. And we really did do a lot.

Was there anything in particular that you wanted to do?

The one thing I wanted to do was to go to Panmunjom.[6] I really wanted to go because my brother had been an interpreter at Panmunjom on the thirty-eighth parallel, when he was in the U.S. Army. But we found out that Koreans couldn't go up there, and that it was only open to American citizens. My host was actually quite disappointed that she couldn't come with me because she had never been up there. So I went alone.

When I went up there, I met a group of women from an All American Women's Society. The president of the group asked me, "Do you want to join us?" I thought that was nice. She was the wife of an oil executive, and that was how all of the women were living there—their husbands were stationed there. Panmunjom was really interesting, and beautiful besides.

When I got back to Seoul the next day, the president of the All American Woman's Society called me and said, "We're going to a Korean village. Would you like to come?"

I said, "Sure."

We went to this Korean village,[7] about a dozen American women and me. When we got there, we started shopping, and I asked, "How much is this?" in Korean.

The Korean merchant looked at me and said, "Gee, she looks like an American, but she's speaking Korean."

I was there a whole month, and although the people there didn't accept me as a Korean, it was wonderful. I found the little habits, like strangers asking a woman's age, and things like that a little strange, but that didn't stop me from exploring. I spent days going down all these little alleys. I saw all these signs in Korean, and it made me feel good that I could read it, and that I was in Korea. I figure I must look different to the Koreans although to me I'm Korean, even though I'm born in America. But they distinguish between being Korean and being of Korean heritage. Everywhere I went I heard people whispering about me, wondering where I'm from. They thought I couldn't understand Korean.

Still, when I was there, I felt more Korean than American. I was really proud of being Korean when I was there.

But you know, in terms of my experience in Korea, I think it made a big difference that the woman who took me around was from the upper class. People treated her really well. So many people bowed down to her. And as her guest, they treated me the same way. I could tell that my host felt superior—the class difference really oozes out of a person. During that trip I noticed the sharp class difference more than the sex bias. They didn't treat maids and people considered lower-class very well. I didn't like that aspect of what I saw.

So did your trip live up to your expectations?

I expected a very different experience. The fact that there was such an influx of Koreans to the United States, and that my husband had always talked about how people in Korea lived in houses with dirt floors colored my expectations. I was prepared for a lot of poverty when I visited. But I don't remember poverty, people living in houses with dirt floors, or anything like that. I even tried to look for it. When you are in the city [Seoul], you don't see much of it. But when you go out into the country, you do see the thatched huts. But even then, those houses don't have dirt floors.

I suppose you could say that at that time, in some ways, Korea wasn't modern. Even the woman whose house I stayed with, even though her home was modern, and her toilet was supposed to be more modern than other homes in Korea, I still wasn't too happy with it.

I also went to the house of another Korean that I knew there. She had a beautiful house furnished with all this beautiful Korean mother-of-pearl inlaid furniture. Well, I needed to go to the rest room, and I had to go out to an outhouse that was a separate structure outside the house. And they used newspaper for toilet tissues.

And the kitchens in the houses were located down below from the main floor, and the maids were cooking over what looked like a barbecue pit. They spent all day cooking. I don't think I could cook like that. But they brought out the most beautiful meals cooking in that hot room.

But all that has changed since I first visited Korea.

I know your mother's from the North so you couldn't visit her hometown or anything, but your father is from Kangwondo. Did you go up there and try to locate his relatives?

I actually met the Mayor of Kangwon province while I was there, and he invited me up there to see if any of my father's relatives might still be around. But I was advised against it. First of all, the thirty-eighth parallel goes right through Kangwondo and I don't know which part of Kangwondo my father is from. And then the local Koreans told me that if I went up there, and discovered relatives that were not well-to-do up there, they would all want me to sponsor them to the United States. I just didn't think I could handle that responsibility, so I didn't go.

But during that trip I started to wonder why all the Koreans were coming over here. Korea was so beautiful. I suppose I was discovering Korea for the first time, and they had become tired of it, the lack of opportunity there. I think it's the class thing. It's like there is a class system, and it's really hard to get out of the class you were born into. And to top it off, Korea is really competitive, and so it's hard to get ahead unless you're born to a well-to-do family. And while I can appreciate trying to escape the strict class system, I don't know how much better life is here. I think some of the Koreans have unrealistic dreams.

Some people have good lives and throw it all away. Like this one woman—she was a pharmacist. Her family owned a pharmacy that was doing okay and a lot of land, but they heard that they could make a lot more money here. So they sold the pharmacy, and she came over. I think her family still kept some interests in Korea and their land, but she sold everything to come over here. And she can't even earn a decent living here. She came for dreams without knowing what the real possibilities were. Her entire family wanted to come over for this better life, but she told them not to come, that it really wasn't what they thought. But she can't go back. What's she going to go back to? Why come here when things were good there? Is it greed? Can life be that much better anywhere?

And then once the Koreans get here, they still carry on about class and status. It's a real big thing with them. Even if that's what they're escaping, they just create a new version of it here because it's what they're familiar with.

Sometimes I just don't know about those Koreans. . . .

Personally, I don't understand leaving a place when all your ties are there and you are connected to the history. It's hard to live anywhere without having a sense of connection. I see the early immigrants, like my parents, differently, because they came over under very different circumstances. The Japanese occupation really threatened their way of life, which is why they came over. That also prevented them from returning. Since there was really no home to go back to, they had no choice but to stick it out here. But they really had to struggle once they got here.

At this point there are five generations of Yums or four generations of Kims from the San Francisco Bay Area. So it's home for us.

Were you satisfied with your trip to Korea?

I really loved Korea. I started going back as much as I could. I think I went back four times in the 1970s. And each time I had a different experience. I went again in 1974, and that trip I knew more people, and looked more people up. Then after I retired from the California State Department of Employment in 1977, I got involved in the travel business and went to Korea again that year, and again in 1979 for these travel agents' conferences.

And in 1979, I had an entirely different experience from my other visits. Previously I had gone as an ordinary citizen trying to find her roots. And when you go like that, you end up doing tourist things, and you don't see how the Koreans live. And while I understood that the class system was rigid, I still had this idea that Korea was a perfect society because I was fortunate enough to meet people who treated me very well, and took me around.

What made it so different from the previous three trips?

Just before my 1979 trip, I met Mary Pajalich, a retired female judge in San Francisco. She had just been in Australia for a conference on women and law, and mentioned that a Korean attorney had won the award for service to women. This Korean attorney, Tai-Young Lee, was the first woman attorney, and the only one working for the rights of women, because in Korea, to this day, women are considered nothing.

Well, I was staying in the Chosun Hotel for the conference, and when I was in the elevator, I asked the elevator man, "Do you know Tai-Young Lee and how I might get in touch with her?"

He looked at me and said, "If you don't know Tai-Young Lee, you aren't Korean."

So I realized that she was a very famous person fighting for the rights of women, and I knew I wanted to meet her.

I know you met her because you told me to look her up when I was in Korea.
How did you meet her?

During that trip I looked up a woman I met in San Francisco. She was a teacher who had been visiting from Korea. She had said, "Be sure to come and see me."

So I did. What I hadn't known was that she was the principal of In Duk Park Vocational, which she owned, her own huge school. She had her own car and driver in which she took me to her private residence. And while having a car and driver is more common in Korea, you still have to be plenty wealthy to afford it.

Her residence was spectacular. Her apartment was comparable to a really nice apartment here. This is in comparison to what you see on the streets, where you peek into the store and the family is actually living in the store. Some of them are so dark they look like caves, and there are entire families living in there.

And as soon as you entered her house, there were servants right at your feet, removing your shoes, taking off your coat, and making you comfortable.

Anyway, I asked her about Tai-Young Lee, and she said, "Oh, I know her."

And she took me to the Korean Center for Legal Aid to meet her.

When I met Tai-Young Lee, I found out that at that time women couldn't even become attorneys. Without the support of her husband, who was a high government official, Tai-Young Lee couldn't have become one.

I also learned that Tai-Young Lee was disbarred for helping women. So this was the first time that I connected the things that my mother had said about women in Korea to the current status of women in Korea.

We talked to her about Korean history, and the position of women in Korean society. That really opened my eyes to life in Korea. I didn't experience any incidents against me, but then I'm also treated as if I'm not Korean when I'm there so I wouldn't know.

Anyway, I started looking at Korea through different eyes after that. I realized that the things my mother had told me still affected women in Korea even today. I started realizing the problems that existed in Korean society are problems that are just as difficult as the problems in American society.

But there was something else I discovered through Tai-Young Lee. When Dr. Lee realized that my father had been involved with the Korean Independence Movement in San Francisco, she had her chauffeur take me to Independence Hall. That was something. The *Hungsadan* has the history of Korea from the beginning to the end. And the seventh building has the history of the Korean emigrants that came to America, and pictures of Korean life in America as early as the late 1900s. They also have the Korean history of fighting the Japanese. I was looking around, and I saw these two pictures that I recognized from our family albums. My father's picture was hanging on the wall. It was a picture of the delegates that Ahn Ch'ang Ho had assembled here in the United States. And there was my father. There was another picture of the Red Cross volunteers assembled in San Francisco taken in 1920. That was one of the first pictures of my mother that we have, of when she first arrived in the United States.

It was something, to see our connection to Korean history. It made me feel really proud to be Korean, and I could see the connection between my parents and Korea in front of me. Then Tai-Young Lee took me to an exclusive club in Namsan to eat. That was really a perfect day.

Your experience with Tai-Young Lee sounds wonderful.

When I returned home, I told my husband again that Korea was beautiful—the subways, the hotels, the restaurants, and told him about my experiences. When I related my experiences to him, he responded, "That's not Korean. That's the upper class."

Well, it just happened that these are the people I met. It's not that I'm a wealthy person. I didn't know that the teacher was, in fact, the principal of a famous school. And I didn't know that Tai-Young Lee was such a famous person in Korea.

Given the experiences that I did have, I've since dreamed of going to Korea for a year and work. Even now, I occasionally think of it, although I don't know what I could do there. I think it would be fun, just to see. I know that sexism is really bad there, but Koreans don't think I'm Korean, and I'm older, so . . . you know, older women are exempt from a lot of the sexist practices.

What is interesting is that just in the time since I started going to Korea, I've noticed a lot of changes. Now there are a lot of modern apartment buildings, just like here, and I think I could be comfortable there. I've also learned a lot about the culture and the traditions there over all these years that I've been working with immigrants, and I know those have changed as well. The fact that I can speak the language, read and write Korean, also helps me to understand how that society is changing. But it may be that nationalistic thing I have that fuels to my desire to live there.

Reflections

The influx of the Korean immigrants occurred during an interesting moment in American history—during the flowering of the Asian American movement. This movement called for people of Asian descent to reassess the viability of assimilating into the dominant culture and stressed the importance of cultural heritage. Fueled by the idealism of the times, her recollections of the difficulties that the immigrant generation faced in the 1920s and 1930s, and her memory of the powerful solidarity that Japanese occupation created among Koreans, Dora did not question her responsibility to her new compatriots; she responded passionately to the needs of the new Korean immigrants.

I was born to a Korea very different from the one Dora learned about. The Korea I knew had already been "liberated," and although there were shortages of luxury items that I now take for granted, the country was undergoing dramatic changes. The national goal was economic development: modernization, industrialization and furthering global trade relations. Although my father eventually started his own business in Thailand, he actually left Korea as part of Korea's economic development program. An employee of Korea Shipping, a government-owned corporation, my father worked in the economic sector of Korea's foreign service and was sent to Taiwan and Japan before my mother and the children joined him in Singapore. Eager to forge productive relations abroad, the brightest were selected to go abroad to represent Korea's interests, lured into service with the promise of compensation packages that allowed for vast improvements in standard of living. After my family left Korea, the few Koreans to whom I was exposed were educated and of middle- or upper-middle-class backgrounds. So while Koreans came together for social support, the notion that Koreans needed to band together for survival never even crossed my mind. I grew up with the middle-class belief that affiliation was a choice grounded in shared sensibilities and interests, and did not feel any special affinity with Koreans.

Nonetheless, both Dora and I carried around Korean cultural constructions that had their origins in early childhood, Dora from the 1920s and I from the early 1960s. Given the inevitable changes to culture over time, both Dora and I felt compelled to explore Korea for ourselves. We were at different points in our lives when the opportunity presented itself to us: Dora at age fifty and I at nineteen. But our experiences were remarkably similar. Koreans are quick to locate each other, and with the increasing numbers of Korean Americans visiting the homeland, there is a Korean American sensibility that is quickly recognized. But it seems that neither

Dora nor I fit easily into this category, and it arouses the curiosity of the Koreans we meet, even here in California.

I wonder if the impression we make is related to the kind of shuffling we did between various cultural milieus. I realize that cultural journeying has been an integral part of my life since early childhood. Like a well-trained pigeon, I find myself making the return "home," the pilgrimage between Korea, Thailand, and the United States. I am now a naturalized U.S. citizen and have come to feel more American than anything else. Since my sister and I consolidated the family by moving my parents to the United States, I have gone through all the motions of taking my stand in one place. But I still have the need to make the rounds. I like to imagine that the trips will allow me to rest, to come to terms with the decisions I have made. But like Dora, whose cultural journeying I document, it is the voyage and not the destination that feels most like home to me.

SIX

Centering Service

TWO *kinds of political activists emerged from the movement:* *radicals who articulated the "correct" leftist political ideology and reformers* *who put their energy into setting up services for both immigrant and non-* *immigrant Asian Americans.*[1] *For reformers like Dora Yum Kim, who focused* *on the immigrant community, the need for services specific to particular Asian* *ethnicities was a priority. So while the focus of the Asian American movement* *was the pan-Asian liberation from oppression, activists were torn between issues* *that were pan-Asian and issues specific to particular Asian ethnic groups.*[2] *De-* *spite differences in their agendas, Asian American activists were united in their* *search for a positive Asian identity that articulated the ethnic dimension of their* *experience.*

In 1975, after six years of working with Korean immigrants, Dora and her *children participated in cofounding the Korean Community Service Center, the* *first Korean community organization in the United States. The center started* *losing support in the mid-1980s, after ten years of activity. In 1990, when Dora* *was still recuperating from a stroke she sustained in 1989, the center lost its* *funding. While Dora is no longer involved with the community center, there* *have been efforts to reestablish the center, although the viability of a Korean* *American–run organization is questionable.*

I know you cofounded the Korean Community Center. Can you tell me about it *and how it started?*

It was really my son's influence. My son Tommy was really active in the Asian American movement at San Francisco State. He was fired up about the need to help the new immigrant Koreans. Koreans certainly became more visible at this time, and I think Tommy believed that the new immigrants would enhance the claims of the Asian American movement. By that time I was already pretty deeply involved with helping them. So we put our heads together and started talking with other people about the possibility of opening a center.

In 1975, Tommy and I opened a storefront on Larkin so that we could have some space to run the programs we had started. Well, that very next year, my son Kyle bought a three-story building on Fulton Street. He was planning to occupy the top floor and rent out the second-floor flat. So a group of us went over there to look it over. We realized that if we did a little work on the bottom floor, we could probably put in a kitchen, a bathroom, and a lunchroom. So we decided to use the bottom two floors for the Korean Community Service Center. We moved out of the Larkin storefront after six months, which is all the rent we had secured anyway.

We got our first funding—start-up money—from the Vanguard Foundation and the mayor's office Community Development Fund. At that time Tommy was in a master's program in social welfare at San Francisco State University. He was into the Asian American movement, and he and a half dozen Koreans got three-hundred-dollar stipends from State to work at the center. I was still working at the state Department of Employment, but in response to the need in the community, I got really involved with the center.

What was your role in the Korean Community Center?

I primarily focused on Korean seniors. I think their situation reminded me of my parents'. They didn't understand the culture or have the language skills to adapt. I can recall that we—me and my brothers—tried to explain what we could to our parents, but we were just kids and didn't really have the know-how. As an adult, I had the ability to really help the seniors in ways I could never help my parents. Times had changed too, which made it easier for us to set up services for the seniors. I think my involvement with the seniors had something to do with the fact that my parents, especially my mother, didn't live long enough to fully enjoy any fruits of their labor—they never got the kind of attention that adult children can give their parents. I guess you could call it filial piety in old age. I wanted to help the seniors in honor of my own parents.

I was the coordinator for the Senior Meals Program. In 1976 I wrote up a proposal for a senior meal program saying that the Korean seniors couldn't participate in other senior centers in the city because of the language barrier and because of dietary habits and preferences. The Korean seniors aren't going to change their dietary habits, so we worked to provide a well-balanced, nutritional menu for the funding agencies. I wrote sample menus for the state nutritionist.

The nutritionist came back and asked what *kimchi* [spiced pickled cabbage] was, and said, "You can't serve this *kimchi* dish every day."

And then I realized what I had to do to explain the Korean diet, and how important it was to find nutritional justification for food. People didn't know anything about Korean food at that time. So I found out about the nutritional value of all the foods, and I remember writing about the vitamin C content in *kimchi* as justification for including it. We hired a full-time Korean cook, and had an in-house lunch program there for ten years. I think I started putting my energy there because I was frustrated with my job. At lunch time I would dash over there to supervise the cook and the volunteers who served lunch. After about a year of running back and forth, I quit my job at the state Department of Employment.

When did you quit ?

I didn't actually quit. It was officially an early retirement. I retired early from the state Department of Employment on 7/7/77. I picked that date on purpose, for luck. My retirement was long in coming. While my job was interesting, I seemed to go nowhere in the organization. I was passed by every time I came up for promotion. They kept doing that. So even if I was on a professional track, I was in a dead-end job.

I finally protested because I realized that they weren't promoting me just because I was Asian.

After I protested, the head of the California State Employees Association, who happened to be a black guy, came over to me and said, "Do you know that they have your name down as the one protesting nonpromotions?"

I replied, "No."

Then he said, "Since your name is down as being the one who protested it, you will never get promoted."

So finally, that's one of the reasons I took the early retirement. You know I retired at age fifty-five instead of sixty-five. They started promoting Asians only after I retired in 1977. I guess they were under pressure from somewhere.

How long did you work at the Korean Community Center?

I started working at the Korean Community Center in 1976, so there was a year in there when I was working two jobs. In total, I spent ten years as a full-time worker at the Korean Center. Actually, I took a year off somewhere in there. First I was a meal site manager, and then I was called a senior coordinator. I was there from 1976 to 1981 as the coordinator of the Senior Meal Program. I took a year off from 1981 to 1982 for personal reasons. When I went back to work, I returned as the coordinator of the Senior Center from 1982 to 1986. I certainly didn't work there for the money. I got two hundred dollars a month from the Korean Center when I worked there as coordinator of the Senior Meal Program and then coordinator of the senior center. Good thing I got that small pension from the Department of Employment after I retired. When they couldn't pay me anymore, I retired from the center. However, I did continue to go in as the volunteer coordinator until I suffered a stroke in 1989.

You mention two local funding sources as the start-up for the center. What other kind of support did you get?

We had both state and federal funding at different points. And I've done my share of lobbying for our proposals, but I never got used to the politics. It's really dirty.

From my perspective, the Korean Community Service Center was set up to serve the Korean immigrants. There was a great need. At that time there were few services available, and after all I'd seen at my job, I thought it was a good idea.

When we went for our funding, we wrote our own proposals. The first time we turned in a proposal it was turned down. I heard afterwards that someone from another agency told them not to give it to us.

When it was turned down the first time, someone told us, "Get your politics together."

It was a very political issue, getting funding for the Korean Center, and apparently someone in a high political position said, "Don't give it to them," because we didn't do the right things.

It was funny—the second time we submitted to the state for funding was in 1977, when I was a trainee in the CORO Foundation Public Affairs for Women. Well, we drove to Sacramento to do our internship for a couple of days at the government agencies. So while I was up there, I thought I would go to the main office in Sacramento to see how our second proposal was doing.

So I went into the granting office and talked with them. I mentioned, "I'm here on the CORO Foundation Public Affairs Training for Woman," and talked with all the people at the office.

Apparently talking with them and being part of the CORO Foundation Public Affairs Training for Women was the right match for them, because they gave it to us right after the visit. I don't like playing politics. It's dirty. But it helped us.

With no professionals to help you run the center, how did you manage?

When we first started, we didn't really know how to run the center, but we focused on service. It was hard. To have a service center you need volunteers and commitment. There were periods when we had more, and then periods when we had less, but the focus was service.

What kinds of programs or services did you provide at the senior center?

I remember the rush for taking the citizenship exam. After the seniors had been here for five years they wanted to become naturalized. There were a lot of seniors I tutored through that. One of the older men I helped was a Mr. Kim [pseudonym]. He came to the Korean center for two weeks, and I put the citizen test on the tape. He took it home and must have really studied that exam because he passed. So he became naturalized. But to this day he still can't speak English. They all memorized the whole thing and passed the test. As soon as he passed, he sent for his whole family. I also helped Mr. Kim and the other Korean seniors fill out all the paperwork to bring families over. I never realized what a large family he had. And that was a pattern that I started noticing with the rest of the seniors who passed the exam. As soon as they passed the exam, they would send for their adult children.

There were many Koreans who studied with me for the intensive two weeks for the citizenship test. They always wanted me to put it on tape, because I told them hearing the language was the most important part of taking the test. If you can't understand what he's asking you, forget it. Then you have to learn to speak so that the examiner can understand what you're saying. And everyone that I taught eventually became citizens.

I never got one penny for it. The reason I mention that is because by this time other Koreans started getting involved with the new immigrants. Businesses that catered to the immigrants started to open all over the place. One guy was telling me that he asked one of them to help him study for the exams, and the going rate was twenty dollars an hour for tutoring. This guy thought that was too much and didn't go for it. He came to me, instead, because it was free.

Another important thing was taking the seniors down to apply for MediCal. If you're sixty-five, you're eligible for MediCal. Of course, you're also eligible for Medicare. But Medicare doesn't pay for it all. The federal government pays for 80 percent, and you have to pay the rest yourself, whereas if you get MediCal funded partly by the state and partly by the city, everything is paid for. You're not supposed to have any assets when you apply for MediCal, but the people at the office have it all figured out. One of our clients was actually told to put his twenty thousand dollars of savings into his son's name so that it wouldn't cause problems. The people down at MediCal will tell you exactly what to do with your assets.

I personally think that's terrible. I don't like that. I never had twenty thousand dollars in cash at once myself. But that seems to be the system. And the people at the office even tell you how to get around it.

Didn't you also plan activities for the seniors?

In addition to doing all the administrative work for the Senior Center, keeping the Senior Meal Program going, and setting up all sorts of activities like calligraphy classes and that sort of thing in the afternoons, I also arranged trips for them.

After I retired from the state Department of Employment, I also started working in outside sales at a travel agency. Through the agency connections, I used to take the seniors on trips to Reno about once a month. It was a really good deal. I would rent a bus, arrange for room and board for free so that the seniors could gamble up there. And did they ever gamble. It was pretty amazing. The bus rides were also a lot of fun. We would bring food and drinks, and the seniors would sing all the way up there.

But the trips were also hard. The Korean seniors don't have any manners, not in the American sense. I guess it's just different in Korea. Or maybe they don't care because people aren't Korean. I can't tell. In Reno they pushed right up to the front of whatever they wanted to play. With the seniors there's no such thing as standing in line. They just push right to the front. They would also plop right down on the floor and squat, Korean style. At first I was embarrassed.

I would say, "Don't do that!"

But after a while I stopped caring because it's no use saying anything to them. They won't listen.

The first time I took them to a restaurant in Reno I didn't realize that they'd never been to a non-Korean restaurant in the United States. I'd never thought about that. So I had to go to each one and order separately. So after that when I took them to Reno I made sure I took them to a buffet. But even that had drawbacks. When you order individually, you can take out leftovers. But in a buffet you're not supposed to do that. The seniors didn't care. They stuffed whatever they could into their bags. One man just went up to the table and started putting things into his bag.

I thought, "Oh my god, I hope no one is looking." You can tell them to stop, but they won't listen to you.

I also used to take Korean seniors to Calistoga. The Korean seniors really like hot springs, so I thought it was a good idea. So we went up there and we all got into a big Jacuzzi, to relax, I thought. But then the seniors started taking a bath in there. They brought out soap and bathing towels and started scrubbing each other and washing their hair. It was pretty empty, and I hoped that none of the Caucasians would come in. I was embarrassed and afraid of being talked about. You know, people might say, "Those damned Chinamen" and stuff.

I asked them to stop, telling them that this wasn't a public bath. I told them the Jacuzzis were used like swimming pools, but they didn't care. They acted like they didn't hear me and just went right on. They just went on having a good time, laughing and bathing.

They wanted to go again, but this time I made sure I told them about the way things are done in the United States. I told them I wouldn't take them unless they behaved, so they agreed not to use the hot springs like a public bath. But then when we got there, it was the same thing. You just can't stop them from doing what they want to. So after a while I simply stopped taking them. I felt bad because these trips were really important to the seniors because it gave them something to look forward to, something to do.

They still talk about it and ask me to take them. But I know what will happen. They'll promise to behave, and then go and do what they always do. So now I just use one excuse after another.

It's called acculturation, which they refuse to do. That's bad. I know they're older, but I feel that the seniors should learn American ways. If they want to live in America, they should learn the laws, the language, and the way things are done here.

Did you ever take the seniors on longer trips?

Once I took a whole bunch of the seniors to Las Vegas and the Grand Canyon. That was fun. We just had a great time. But after I came back, some people started saying that I made a lot of money off the seniors from that trip. You know, I paid my own way, like everybody else. I just organized the trip for the seniors because there were no agencies that organized tours for Korean seniors at that time. We got a really good deal on the trip. And for that, people started talking about me behind my back. The trip was a lot of fun, but I didn't enjoy the backstabbing after the trip. So I didn't plan any long trips after that trip.

It seems that there's a downside to dealing with the seniors.

The Korean seniors are fun, but they aren't easy. And for me, it's also hard because I have to negotiate things for them. I have a couple of girlfriends who volunteer for the senior meal program at Kimochi, at the Japanese center. And they told me about the trouble they have with Korean seniors. First of all, Kimochi serves a lot of people, about three hundred meals a day. So people start lining up at ten o'clock for the noon meal. But what do the Koreans do? They come late and cut in line, push and shove, and act like they deserve everything. So, for a while, the people at Kimochi would try to arrange to serve the tables of Korean seniors last. It's obvious that the Koreans just aren't welcome because of the way they behave. If I was served last anywhere I wouldn't go back. But the Koreans don't care; they continue to go. The food is good there, but it's not *that* good. No meal is worth the humiliation.

The Japanese Americans just hate the way the Korean immigrant seniors behave. I can certainly understand that. And what I don't understand is why the immigrant Koreans seniors even go to Kimochi. The immigrant seniors always go on and on about the animosity they feel towards the Japanese, even American-born Japanese, but they continue to go there for meals.

You mentioned earlier that it was in the mid-1980s that you started realizing differences between old-timers and post-1965-ers. Can you talk about that?

You know, when the Koreans started immigrating in the 1970s, American-born Koreans jumped in to help because of this attitude of solidarity towards all Koreans. But from the beginning there were signs that the Koreans from Korea didn't feel that way. I went to one meeting trying to get the third generation to work with the first and vice versa, and this one guy who was the president of the organization at that time says, "We [the immigrants] are not like Koreans who were born here. We have to try to remain Korean and not be like those who were born here. But they have knowledge so let's work with them." I thought it was pretty awful to talk like that, but we still managed to work together.

There was always a gap between the new immigrants and us old-timers, the American-born Koreans. That just never diminished. But I didn't really catch on to that until sometime in the mid-1980s. By then I got to know the new people pretty well and realized that the new Koreans came from upper-middle-class families. The post-1965 Korean immigrants were pretty well off because you had to be relatively rich to be able to afford to pay the cost of application and relocation.

That certainly wasn't true when my parents came over. When my parents came over, they were not rich. I think my father said he had five dollars. And he sent for my mother in 1920, who came over as a picture bride. After a while I couldn't help but compare the two groups and the difference in our experiences. When I was growing up, we were so busy working that we never thought about our lifestyle or what our lives should be like. At that time it was just a matter of surviving and overcoming obstacles, mainly discrimination. I remember hearing stories about Chinese men in the early 1900s, how they wore their hair in pigtails. And some Americans used to come down Grant Avenue and pull on the pigtails and beat the Chinese to death. And nothing ever happened to the Americans. They were never sent to jail. Hearing about things like that bothered me. The stories taught me that we just couldn't do the things Americans could, and we accepted that as fact. Still our parents did their best to give us a sheltered life. And we were well sheltered in Chinatown.

The people who came over after 1965 are different; they had goals and ideals. They're upper-middle-class people, and they're really status-conscious. They try to one-up each other. They still use Korea as their frame of reference, and measure themselves against Korean standards. The new immigrants come primarily because they want to improve their quality of life, and that's primarily what they struggle for. The immigrants at the turn of the century didn't have time to do that; they were struggling just to survive. Except for the war brides and servicemen's wives, Koreans who come over have to have money just to come over. There's plane fare to begin with. Then some of them say they bribed officials to get over here.

So there must be some tension between the old timers and the post-1965-ers.

My husband likes to say, "If your parents were alive here today, the immigrants would look down upon them."

And it's true. Many of the early immigrants lacked education and didn't necessarily come from good families. And in terms of wealth, although my father was known as the richest Korean in San Francisco when he died, we weren't that rich. He was just the first and only Korean to acquire that much property in San Francisco.

I suppose we lived in the ghetto, in poverty. But it didn't seem bad at all. Poverty is relative and money isn't really everything, although it helps. I feel sorrier for the children of rich parents who get shunted off to boarding schools because many of them never know a parent's love.

In the mid-1980s the post-1965 Korean immigrants started organizing themselves. At first we tried to work together, but it was hard to get past that attitude many of them had. It became pretty apparent that the differences were irreconcilable. So I eventually said to them, "Gee, we just can't work together. You're just trying to use us." They had certainly talked about us in that way all along, and after trying to work with them for ten years I figured they didn't really want to work with us. They really couldn't, anyway, without translation services. The third generation can't speak Korean, and the first generation can't speak English. So there was no way they were going to get along in the long term.

Maybe it would have been different if the immigrants had been easier to work with. But they weren't, and by the mid-1980s the young third-generation activists had moved on; some went back to school, others got better-paying jobs or started families, and drifted away. They're not into the community at all anymore. It's too bad. We really need the volunteers.

You mention that the post-1965-ers started their own organizations. What sorts of organizations are you talking about?

For the first ten years it was really up to us old-timers to provide services for the post-1965 immigrants. And they really appreciated it. But towards the mid-1980s, the post-1965-ers started their own service centers. And around that time there was a change in the immigrants as well. Or was it a change in me?

In any case, I started noticing that the Korean immigrants who arrived since the mid-1980s were really different from the old-timers or even the first people who came after 1965. Part of it was that by that time, the immigrant community was large enough so that new immigrants could just integrate into the Korean community. In many ways the Koreans who came over in the mid-1980s were much harder to deal with. The main difference was the issue of commitment.

Commitment to what?

I had the sense that many of the newer immigrants were less committed to making it here. When the Korean immigrants first started coming over after 1965, it was considered "losing face" if you couldn't make it here and returned to Korea. During that time, there were really more opportunities in the United States, and the standard of living was still much higher here. But that changed in the mid-1980s, and when the immigrants got here, they realized that things weren't so easy here, even for those who had been here for over ten years. Koreans started going back because it was just easier to make a living there than here.

And the standard of living—I sometimes took people from Korea on tours, and sometime in the eighties, I started hearing from them that the standard of living of the general population had improved dramatically. One man told me that he had two Western bathrooms in his apartment. So large apartment complexes have all the conveniences that we have over here. And middle-class people could also afford to hire help, have maids and chauffeurs for their cars. Not a bad way to live.

But these "improvements" in life seem to have been accompanied by other changes that are not necessarily better. One change they talked about is the commitment to taking care of your parents. In Korea it used to be that the eldest son took care of the parents. I was told that was breaking down in even in Korea. I could also see this change in the more recent immigrants—as soon as they get here, forget it. When they bring their parents over, they have to sign an affidavit saying that when they sponsor their parents, they are not going to make public charges out of them. But the minute they come over, the first place they take the parents to is the social security office to apply for supplemental security income. which is nothing but welfare. And I don't think that's right.

What about attitudes toward their children?

The more recent immigrants are even more focused on Korea than the first post-1965-ers. They even send their sons to Korea for a *chungmae*, and the sons go and bring their brides back. Some Korean parents arrange the matches, and go back to Korea to have a big wedding. For some reason, Korean parents think that American-born girls or the Korean girls who grew up here are not good enough or spoiled because they're Americanized. I don't know what Korean girls are supposed to do. I suppose it encourages them to date boys from other backgrounds.

But when the boys bring their Korean wives here to live, a lot of couples get divorced because the wives get Americanized too fast. They bring them over so they can have subservient Korean wives, but even Korean women from Korea don't want to be subservient in this day and age. A lot of the women agree to marry Korean men from the United States because they figure that if they come to America they won't have to be subservient.

To what do you attribute the change in Korean immigrants?

I think it really has to do with changes in Korean culture. That's what is affecting the changes in the immigrant population. There's such a difference between those who came in the early 1970s and those coming over now. For instance, in the seventies, the immigrants said that middle class women never worked in Korea. From what the newer immigrants say, that's not true anymore.

And even in the seventies, no matter how young you were widowed, it wasn't proper to remarry. Nobody would have you, for one thing. According to the newer immigrants, that is no longer the case. I understand that now there are divorces, just as there are here.

Underlying all the changes is the simple fact that Korean values have changed. When I first started dealing with Koreans, the focus was on family, you protected the family no matter what. But even that has changed. People still talk about protecting family over everything else, but that's not what you see.

There was recently a case of a Korean immigrant family in which the father apparently beat the mother and the daughters. Well, that's not unusual in Korea, and you're supposed to put up with it. And the early immigrants adhered to that because it's a family thing. But not anymore. In this family, the daughter, who was sixteen at the time, called the police on her father. A restraining order was put on the father by the courts. Now that's a change from the Koreans who came over in the 1970s, and also not in keeping with what the Koreans say about family.

Things in Korea have changed considerably, and the behavior of the newer immigrants reflects the changes in Korea. So even in dealing with the Koreans who are supposed to be from one culture, you have to pay close attention.

Did the Korean Center continue to serve the newer Korean immigrants?

We did service some of the newer immigrants in the mid- and late eighties, but they started going to the other Korean Service Centers that were cropping up. By then, the Korean population in the San Francisco area had shifted, so that there were a lot more immigrant Koreans than American-born people like me, and that made a difference. In some ways, I can see that the earlier post-1965-ers are in a better position to help the newer immigrants—the immigration experience is much closer to them. But I'm still not too keen on the way they run their centers.

I understand that the new Korean community centers, which were subsidized by the Korean government, hired professional proposal writers just to write for them. It's an area of expertise in and of itself. We just couldn't afford to hire professionals to write our proposals for us, and our funding suffered because of that.

Many of the other centers are different from ours in other ways. The "Service Center" part is good for getting nonprofit organization status, but many of them are run like businesses. Within that structure of the center, they open day-care centers so they can get additional funding. I suppose that's money-smart, but I'm not too sure about it. If they really wanted to help the kids have a place where they can go, that's one thing. But I'm not sure that's the rationale. It's more of a business choice.

It seems that the new immigrant Korean community just isn't that big on volunteerism or service. All they want is money. I don't know if that's because they're immigrants struggling, or if it's because they just don't know how important it is to support social causes here in America.

There's also a lot more dirty politics in the "Service Center" business now, and that seems to be what it is—a business. It seems the only way you can get ahead is by playing dirty politics. And it gets plenty dirty in the Korean community.

On the other hand, I can see that immigrant Koreans need representation, and that's, in part, what the new organizations do. There seems to be no justice in the world today. I continue to fight against injustice. It's everywhere. There are a lot of articles about the racial bias against minorities that exists today. But I figure everyone knows that.

I've been to court a couple of times down in South San Francisco to interpret for Koreans. The language barrier is really difficult. Both cases were auto accidents, and the Koreans had good cases. Well, in one case the American guy driving the other car knew the judge and the clerk, so he went to talk to them. And before we got there, he was allowed to put a drawing on their board, and the man I was interpreting for got the short end of the stick. I say that's not right, no matter what. It made me so mad. And there was nothing I could do.

There are lots of cases like this, and the injustice really burns me up. I won't interpret for courts anymore because it's depressing. I get emotionally involved, and I can't sleep for nights when I see injustice done.

The Korean immigrants really need to get services because there is injustice and discrimination against Asians, especially if you didn't grow up here and you don't know anyone. But it doesn't make the way the new organizations are going about it right either.

The program you started was Hot Meals. What exactly happened to it?

The Hot Meals Program at the Korean Center lost its funding in 1986. Part of it had to do with funding sources, and part of it had to do with what was happening with the seniors in the community. As the community grew, people started fighting with each other. Some of the seniors wanted to have their own organizations, and started their own senior citizens' groups that met on Saturdays. I thought that was great, but then they started recruiting from the Senior Center, and people started fighting with each other and factions formed. And then rumors started flying. Some of the seniors had started saying that I was making a lot of money on the Senior Center. Yeah, two hundred dollars a month. Instead of people just coming in for the services, some people wouldn't come in because a member of the other faction was there, and so on and so on. So the center usage became inconsistent, and even though we still serviced quite a few seniors, we lost the funding.

Although we lost funding for our own cook and kitchen in 1986, we still continued to serve lunch. We worked pretty closely with Kimochi, and they sent food out to us as one of the satellite locations for food service. I still worked there without the funding, and that's when I started calling myself the "Volunteer Coordinator" because that's what I was do-ing—volunteering. And that continued for about four years.

During that time one of the new organizations spread rumors that our Senior Hot Meals Program was completely closed. We heard that because one of our regular clients said when he was on a bus, and another Korean senior asked, "Where are you going?"

He said he responded, "To *Han Il Bong Sa* [Korean Service Center] for lunch."

And the reply he got was, "Oh, they're closed. That's what the people at the other center told us. That's why we're going over to the new place."[3]

Another time a couple of the older seniors I knew came down to the Center, and out-and-out told me that they had come down to check on us. There was nothing to check because we were going along as usual, but I guess the other center was working on an angle and wanted infor-mation about our center to use against us or something.

You see, funding for service centers is limited, and the agencies don't want to fund two organizations that serve the same population. So you need an angle. And after you get some sort of angle that you're going to take and evidence to support it, you have to talk to people, know the right people, say the right things, and be connected to the right organi-zations. I don't like that. I never have. And sure enough, since I don't play those dirty politics anymore, we don't have any grants for the seniors.

In 1990, after I had my stroke, the granting agency gave funding for a Hot Meals Program to another Korean center. After that we couldn't even justify being a satellite lunch service site for Kimochi, so we shut down the lunch program completely. Quite a few of the seniors asked me why they did that saying things like, "I wonder why they did that? You seemed to be doing okay." It's true that even at the end we still served a constituency, but we just didn't have the funding. So we've shut down the services. So I stopped volunteering there after I had my stroke in 1989.

In terms of the funding issue, is funding limited to just one ethnic organization in an area?

They say it's a matter of how many people you serve. Supposedly, if you can show that there's a need for two organizations, it's not an issue. But it's not viable to have two Korean centers in such a small area as San Francisco. The funding then goes to the center that seems better posi-tioned to serve more people, and apparently the other center did do that.

But I think that's because the new Korean organizations have a lot more funding than they show. If they're connected, and many are, then they have strong ties to rich and powerful people in Korea who will give financial support for endeavors here. And the post-1965-ers do fund-raising Korean style. They believe in giving all sorts of banquets and fund-raisers where they invite all the people they are trying to "butter up," and give them huge plaques and stuff like that. That kind of stuff flatters the agency workers and they like that. Those Koreans really know how to play the game. It's a different system.

We never had that kind of money to spend on public relations. Even if we did, we American-born Koreans don't know how to do that sort of thing.

What do you think of the new Korean service organizations?

I don't know. The other centers say that they're doing all this stuff for the seniors. You know, the workers take the seniors down to the Senior Referral Office, and got them gold cards and discount cards. But that isn't a big deal. Anyone can do that.

The seniors then come back to us and say, "We can't even speak English. How are we supposed to use the card?"

They still come to me and ask me about it. Apparently they aren't taught how to use the cards. But that's the kind of action that you can build a reputation on, by doing these little things that you can count. You can certainly count how many people you've taken to get gold cards or discount cards. Never mind that the seniors can't use the cards. And they arrange really high-profile activities, like organizing the seniors to go on Senior Walks. But most of the seniors don't ever figure out what the event is about even if they show up; the seniors show up because it gives them some place to go. Then the Korean center people invite the agency people in for a site visit, and bring them around while the staff try to explain the walk to the seniors. The agency people don't even know what is being said, and the seniors don't understand what the agency people are saying. But it sure looks good from the outside, particularly if you can't understand what's being discussed in Korean.

Those are the games you have to play. And that sort of thing gets a lot of media coverage and hoopla. The seniors also like the attention. But it still doesn't help them to learn how to manage from day to day.

You sound concerned, but you also sound a bit jealous.

I used to be jealous that others could be so smooth and get so much support without really having to do the work. But I'm not anymore. I just don't have the energy or the inclination for that. I just hope that the people who actually do the work know what they're doing. I believe that what goes around comes around. Do unto others as you want others to do unto you. I sure wouldn't want to be in those shoes when it comes back around.

What is your involvement in the community today?

These days I try not to get too caught up in what's going on in the community. I sometimes go to community organization meetings. Because of the high proportion of Korean immigrants here, whenever there's a meeting of Koreans it's all in Korean. So the meetings tend to exclude second- and third-generation Korean Americans. I used to try to mediate, but it became too messy. I've come to the view that this is America, and if you're going to have a meeting that pertains to life in America, you should conduct it in English. But that's not how the Korean immigrants see it.

And sometimes, when you listen to the Koreans, or even read the Korean papers, they have it all wrong. There's no one to interpret it correctly for them. And even if they did, they probably wouldn't listen. That's too bad. I guess it's one way of saying, "I'm proud to be Korean." But I'm not proud about that. I'm not proud of the Koreans when I see how close minded some of the new immigrants are.

And it's not even as clear-cut as the Koreans against the non-Koreans. There's also a lot of conflict within the Korean community. It's a mess. If you look at just the seniors you can get an idea of what's going on. There used to be just one Korean Senior Citizens' Group. And then the officials of the group had a disagreement. It was bad. They had to call the police because it was so out of control. So after that, one of the guys left the group to start his own. That started a precedent. Once one person started his own group, other people who have slight disagreements figure, "Hey, if I don't like it I can start my own group."

It would be a lot better if there was one large group that could ask for funding for services. But now there are so many splinter groups that compete with each other for limited resources. And they just hate each other more and more because of the funding situation. It's pretty bad.

As I've said before, this pattern is not just with the Korean seniors. You know, there used to be only one Korean church when I was growing up—the Korean Methodist Church. I can understand the need to have different denominations represented, like the Korean Buddhist Church and the Korean Catholic Church, but the growth of Korean churches is ridiculous. A new church forms anytime anyone has a disagreement. This has been happening more and more in the past ten years with the influx of more Koreans. There are now over a hundred Korean churches in the Bay Area.[4] Can you believe that? It's the men, of course. They fight and then start a new church. They just can't stay supportive of each other. Everyone needs to be the boss. It's like they're all on ego trips.

You don't paint a very pretty picture of the Korean American community.

Well, some of the things that are going on aren't particularly pretty. For instance, there are also many new Korean American "heritage" groups that have been established. And you know, almost all of the members are Korean-born. I have been to some of the meetings, but I'm not part of the group. One of the groups is trying to document the history of the Korean Methodist Episcopalian Church—you know, the first Methodist Church. The disturbing thing is that history is blatantly being rewritten.

One of the things they are saying is that Ahn Ch'ang Ho cofounded the church. I don't remember him as a cofounder. Reverend Lee Dae Wi was one of the founders in 1903. He was the one who invented the Korean typewriter. But there's not even a mention of him. And I supposed there's no one alive to dispute that point but me. Dae Wi Lee died working for the Korean community in 1928. Reverend Lee died young of TB because he worked so hard. He used to stay up working all night to help the Koreans. When he died, the entire community came out to honor him because it was common knowledge that he had dedicated his life to the community and the nation of Korea. That's what the community put on his tombstone. But people don't even acknowledge him. All of that is being forgotten in the revision of history.

I ran into this Korean social worker from Chicago when I was a delegate to the White House Conference on Aging in 1981. You could tell he was an old and learned man. He told me that he was one of a bunch of students that came from Korea. I don't recall the reason for it, but they were all going to be deported right back to Korea. Dae Wi Lee heard about it somehow and came down and spoke for them. According to this social worker, it was only because Reverend Lee had come down and spoken for them that they were able to stay. And I know this was not an isolated incident. Reverend Lee was like that.

Can you tell me what your concern is?

As I've said before, many people are rewriting Korean American history. I think that, in and of itself, is good. But I am concerned about the way it's being rewritten. Many people think they have the authority to write the history without consulting those who lived through the time period. It would be one thing if we were all dead and couldn't be consulted, but that isn't the case. I can't believe the arrogance. And it's one thing if things are forgotten from ignorance, but I think they purposely "forget." At one of the meetings I asked if they knew about this and the other that they were leaving out of the history. And one man responded, "Yes, we heard about it." But they're not writing it down. It's being excluded.

I don't know. I remember once I went to church and there was a group of people talking and the reverend's daughter-in-law proudly says, "I've been coming here since 1965, from the beginning." It's that notion that if you came in 1965, you're in the first group of Koreans who came over here. The people who were here before don't count. I sometimes wonder if it's because our parents came over as laborers. Can people really be that shallow?

The Korean immigrants are very status-conscious. That's why members of the *Han In Hwe* [Korean Residents' Association] fight every year. Everybody wants to be president. So I've been asking, "What's so great about being president?" One answer I got from a fellow was, "Then I can make cards saying that I'm the president of the Korean Residents' Association in San Francisco and go meet the President of Korea." I want to know what's so great about that? Is it really worth fighting and screaming over?

They're still living in Korea. Immigrants have their hearts and souls in Korea.

They always say, "In Korea this" or "In Korea that."

After years of that I sometimes want to say, "Hey, don't tell me about it. You're in America now."

I know the heritage is important, and that nationalism was the unifying issue for the early Koreans, but I don't know how long you can continue to cling to that. At some point you have to decide to be in America and to build a community that really lives in America.

So are you saying that the post-1965 Koreans are the ones distorting history?

I don't think it's fair to say that it's just the post-1965 Koreans that are rewriting Korean American history. I think the movement of Koreans rewriting history started long before the emergence of Korean American "heritage" foundations. There was one reverend who tried to change everything, including the past. This man wrote the first history of the Korean Methodist Church. Well, a third-generation activist happened to see it, and this minister had left out her grandfather, who had been the minister of the Korean Methodist Church for the longest time. This third-generation woman is a real thrill in terms of action, and she raised hell. So the minister had to put her grandfather's name into it after that. But all the original history and the papers are gone. Apparently he threw it all out before he started his version of the history of the Korean Methodist Church. Members of one of the "heritage" groups came right out and said it. This reverend destroyed all the records. Isn't that something?[5]

When I think about it, I suppose that for a lot of Koreans, the community is all they have. Many Koreans, especially the immigrants, only participate within the narrow limits of the Korean community. So when all is said and done, the Korean community is the only place where they can satisfy their needs for recognition. So that's where they go to make claims of self-importance.

Since the Korean community has gotten pretty large, the audience for your claims of self-importance has also grown. I think that affects everyone, both the post-1965-ers and those descended from the first Koreans who came here. There are people making claims about their parents' and grandparents' role in the early Korean community, the independence movement. Well, they're mostly dead, and almost all the people who knew them are dead, so I suppose the descendants can say what they want to.

There's one woman who's still alive. And the *Sun* ran an article about Korean independence and how the Korean community read the Korean Independence document every March first. That's true. Then the article went on to say that this woman was the one who read the whole thing. That's absolutely false. When I was growing up, Korean women didn't read in public. It was Kim Dong Woo who read it.

I suppose people are making claims to the past to make themselves look more important. Maybe they think the immigrant community will think better of them. I don't know. But I don't think it's really going to change who you are now. Why pretend to be something you aren't?

Do you think the Korean community was more cohesive before the post-1965 influx?

I'm not saying the community was perfect when I was growing up. Even when the community was smaller, there were tensions. But they seem minor by comparison to what we have now. First of all, the community was really unified around liberation. And the community was so much smaller that the tensions couldn't be acted out the way they can be today. There were fewer factions to which you could go for support. And we really needed to stick together for survival. But there were still plenty of petty politics.

We used to have a church picnic once a year at Golden Gate Park. There's a little piece of land on the right side of the Conservatory, and that's where the Koreans met every year for years. They used to have a cooking contest. Well, we owned a restaurant, and my mother was known to be a good cook in the community. I remember that she once won the contest making *mook* [a gelatinous dish made from mung bean paste]. Anyway, the Korean women used to bring out gallons of *kimchi*. My mother had a reputation for making good *kimchi,* and once, at the end of the picnic, another woman slipped her glass jar where my mother's was and took it home. These small jealousies are silly, but it damages good will among community members. And this sort of thing happened often enough to make an impression on me: I remember the small Korean community as full of petty jealousies and ill will.

There were even rumors that my dad paid to have an article on my grades put into the *New Korea,* the Korean newspaper. But I know he didn't. The daughter of the editor was a good student at Girls' High School, and I'm sure she showed the newsletter about all the honor roll students to her father because she was on the list. Stupid rumors that came out of petty jealousies and just plain ill will created problems in the community. I realize now that my father fought against that all these years, never saying a word against fellow Koreans. He was silent when rumors went around, and didn't dignify gossip with a response.

I know there has been plenty said about me over the years, and there are many things I've let slide. But I'm not as generous as my father. There are some allegations that I just can't stomach. I have spoken out against some of the ill will against me, and I will continue to do so. I've spent my life doing what has to be done. And I've struggled against racism and sexism all my life, and now ageism. I know I can't change the world, but I do what I can to help people who need assistance. But the Koreans can't believe that.

Once someone asked me, "Do you do those things because you want to be liked?"

That comment really hurt. I never thought of doing things so that I would be liked.

But the comment did make me think about motivations, and how that works. And the conclusion that I came to was that you can't do things solely to be liked. It's certainly rewarding to be appreciated for the things you've done, but I don't think that alone can carry you through. You have to do it because you believe in it. I do things because they need to be done. Whether I can do it, whether I want to do it, or whether I should or shouldn't do it—those questions are irrelevant. If you think too much about doing something, it won't get done. And if you have to think that much about doing something, maybe you shouldn't be doing it. You just have to do what needs to be done, if *you* know that it's the right thing.

But since the Koreans do not know community volunteerism, they think I'm crazy to do the things I do. I don't really care what people think of me if I don't know them, but it's hurtful when people you know question your motives. But what can you do? You can't control what others think of you. But it still hurts.

Those Koreans . . . They just don't know how to help each other. There's just no support. The Koreans have good heads on their shoulders, old and new immigrants alike, but they have no cohesiveness, no support system. It seems that if they think you're doing well, they'll pull you down. It doesn't matter what you're doing, no matter how big or small the project. They won't help you in any way if they think you're getting ahead of them.

That's a pretty strong indictment of the Korean community.

I say the things I do about the Korean community because that's the one I'm most familiar with. I don't think the Korean community is any worse than other communities. As with other communities, there are those who are honorable while others are not. But no one is honorable all the time. All you can do is try. And that's the real issue.

I think all communities, ethnic or otherwise, suffer from pettiness such as jealousy and ill will. It's just managed differently, and looks different from the outside.

The Koreans are just not very good at managing conflict. Not only is there a lot of conflict within the community, there's also conflict with other communities. Recently there's been a lot of press about the Korean-black conflict. But that's not the only problem. The Koreans have had conflict with other Asian groups as well. We [Asian American community groups] try to support each other, but it's hard when there are new Korean organizations popping up all the time. It's hard to know who to support when the players are always changing. So, other Asian organizations have a hard time coordinating with all the various Korean groups.

You brought up the Korean-black conflict as an issue that needs to be addressed. Can you elaborate on that?

As I said, the Korean-black conflict is just one of many issues the Korean community needs to address. And they have gotten better at dealing with it. But with the media the way it is today, just magnifying tensions to sell papers, it just doesn't help.

The aftermath of the Rodney King decision really brought those tension to the media. That was terrible. Instead of shooting all those people afterwards and having all that senseless violence, they should have dealt directly with the justice system that permitted that decision. It really was a matter of dealing with the four policemen and the jury who came to that decision, not destroying innocent people's lives and property.

But if you want to understand the roots of that Korean-black conflict, it's in the attitudes that Koreans had towards blacks even when I was growing up. Actually, around here, there weren't that many blacks until World War II so it wasn't a big deal.

But even before the war, the older Koreans tended to be afraid of blacks because of their skin color. You know, it's not unusual to be afraid of people who are unfamiliar. And you know the Korean standards—the darker you are, the less respect you get. People just see you as being inferior in terms of class and education if you're dark.

I suppose Koreans and other Asians believe the stereotypes about blacks. Even in those days because they used to say, "If you want to make money, you have to go into a black community. The blacks will spend the money they have. They don't have much, but when they have it, it goes out."

Well, at that time, there weren't many stores in the black areas because blacks didn't have access to capital to start businesses. And while we were restricted from American neighborhoods, Asians weren't restricted from black neighborhoods, so some started businesses there. So the money went into the Asian pockets. And once they made enough money, the Asians left. Strange as it sounds, we accepted segregation as the way things should be.

During the war, blacks came in droves because jobs were plentiful, and discrimination against blacks was less because of the war effort. I suppose at that time no one really thought about it because everyone was so up in arms about the Japanese, the "enemy at home." With the influx of blacks who came to work on the war effort, neighborhoods were set aside for them to live in. And they were encouraged to move into the neighborhoods that the Japanese had evacuated. So they settled into well-demarcated neighborhoods. At that time I didn't think anything of it. You know, we were all segregated into certain areas of town until after the war, so that seemed natural.

So, are you saying that there is historical precedent to the conflict?

Definitely. I don't think tensions like that develop overnight. It takes years of misunderstanding to work up to open conflict. And in recent years there has been more conflict between the Koreans and the blacks. I suppose that's because there's more contact without the benefit of further understanding.

More recently, in New York, Chicago, and Los Angeles, all the businesses in Harlem and neighborhoods like that were already closed. The Koreans went in and built it up. I think the blacks were jealous of that. But the Koreans didn't make it any easier. Koreans are kind of paranoid. And there's reason to be when you don't understand what's going on. They believe that blacks will go in and try to steal everything. And given the stereotypes that Koreans come in with, they don't consider all those who don't steal. Instead, they pay attention to the negative incidents, which only makes the sentiments against blacks stronger. The Koreans get their views of blacks from the media, and that has always been unfavorable.

Also, when you go to the back of these "mom and pop" stores, you see a master's diploma. The Koreans were engineers or writers or some type of professional in Korea, and they're now working sixteen hours a day in a store. The Koreans feel a keen sense of injustice about their situations in the United States. So many of the Koreans want to go in, make money quick, and leave. And that's a problem.

Can you elaborate on why you think it's a problem?

The problem with the Koreans, like other immigrants, is that they don't understand what it means to be American and what America stands for. It's not just about getting rich, although opportunity is important. In this day and age, being American is also about getting along with people who aren't like you, and accepting differences. I keep telling the Koreans when something comes up, "Look, you chose to live in America. You wanted to come to America. You're here, so familiarize yourself with the laws of the country. They're different from Korean law. And if you want to live here you should learn the language and learn about the community you're in, whatever it is. You need to understand and follow rules of the community you're in."

But it's not that easy. Koreans fall back on what is familiar, and what they know is family. And while the focus on family can be positive, it can also be divisive. Even within the Korean community, when push comes to shove, they forget all the other Koreans and think only of their families. So much for community.

What about you? How do you feel about blacks?

We had a few blacks when I was in school, and other than their color, they didn't seem that different from anyone else. But while I didn't agree with Korean ideas about blacks, I personally didn't think much more than that because we had so little contact with them. I knew that the majority of blacks were not well off, and like us, did not have social advantages.

I have to admit that I've become more cautious around black kids. I've had my purse snatched three times in the past few years, and unfortunately, all three times the snatchers were black kids. So I've had a few bad experiences. But to be fair, I think I've generally gotten more cautious around young people. This kind of crime is new, something we've never had in these proportions. And kids do have physical strength over me. I'm just not as strong as I once was. I don't recall being afraid of people when I was younger. Maybe the fear has developed because I've become older, and it's easier to take advantage of an older person.

Did your work at the Korean Center affect your family life?

The years at the center were really busy. I was always writing proposals for the seniors while others were focusing on other aspects of service for the Korean immigrants. But, for the first five years things at home were pretty stable. The kids were grown up and had lives of their own, so I didn't worry too much about them. Even the little ones moved out. But in 1980 my youngest son, Kerry, got married to Nancy, an Asian girl, and they moved into the Dewey Boulevard house for about a year so they could save some money before getting a place of their own in 1981. In the same year Debby, our youngest, moved into the studio condo at the Fontana. So Tom and I were on our own for the first time. But our lives weren't meant to be as simple as that. 1981 was a year of personal tragedies. I had to take an entire year off just to recover. I know I haven't been the same since.

But within a year I was back, working as ever. But I cut back on some of my activities like teaching English. We were still always writing proposals for this or that so it was pretty hectic.

What have you been doing since you've retired from the Korean Center?

Now I don't work directly with any of the Korean community centers. However, I still work with Korean immigrants. These days, I spend a lot of time up at U.C. Medical Center interpreting for patients and doctors. I work through the language bank, and I get a lot of calls. I enjoy the work, and the language bank pays me for going up there. Of course, with this kind of work, I tend to get really involved in the cases, and end up following the cases well beyond the paid interpretation. That's just the way I am. I think that's the social work background coming out. But people can be pretty suspicious about the work I do.

Recently, when I went to interpret after hours, I think the nurse was surprised to see an interpreter at that time of night. So the nurse asked, "Where does your salary come from?"

I said, "What salary? I don't get a salary."

She was surprised and asked, "Well, why are you doing all this?"

I replied, "Well, it has to be done, and there's no one else to speak up for them [the immigrant Koreans]. The only place I get a salary is from the language bank, when they send me for an appointment. U.C. Medical Center pays the language bank and the language bank pays me. That's the only way I get paid."

I had helped these Koreans before, and they were in another situation where they needed help. Since they didn't speak any English, they called me. What could I do? I had to go and interpret for them.

I run into this kind of thing every now and then. You don't do things because it's structured as part of the job, or because it's your duty to do it; you do it because it has to be done. I never thought about what it was going to get me. I never expected anything in return. . . .

I'm up there at U.C. Med. almost every day that I'm in town, doing one or two medical interpretations a day. It keeps me centered on service and in touch with those who really need the services without having to deal with the messy community politics. And you know, I'm finally making use of the things I learned in vocational nursing school. I'm able to interpret clearly because I have the background. Some of the doctors have begun to specifically request me, because the other interpreters don't seem to understand the doctors. The doctors complain that they say ten things and the interpreters sum it up in one sentence. When I interpret, I try and explain everything. That's what we're supposed to do. I've even gone up to Novato to interpret. They pay for mileage since it's far away.

While new immigrants continue to face cultural problems, there seem to be more services for them now than when your parents came over.

Things have certainly changed since we were growing up. With the emphasis on multiculturalism and all that, there are so many more services for immigrant families. But the thing that surprises me is that, given the influx of so many different types of people from all over the world, you'd think I'd be less conspicuous here. But you know, I still have these incidents where my identity is called into question.

It happened again, another mini–identity crisis. When I was growing up, it was always, "Are you Chinese?"

"No."

"Then you must be Japanese."

"No."

"Then what are you?"

"Korean." And then a long explanation of what that was. Today it was more of the same. Only now I get it from Koreans as well as Caucasians. It was a new Korean person who didn't know me from Adam. I said, "I'm here to translate for you."

And she says, "Are you Korean? You don't look Korean."

I responded, "Well, what do I look like?"

"You look American. Can you speak Korean?"

So I asked, "What language do you think we're speaking?"

When I was growing up, it was the Caucasians who asked me about my background. And they still do, but I guess I'm much more used to that. Now the Korean immigrants ask the same types of questions. It's funny but when you're Korean American in an immigrant community, you don't really fit with the majority of the Koreans, and you don't fit with the Caucasians. So there's a lot of explaining, a lot of mediation. I feel like I have to explain things to both sides. The Koreans can tell that you're not from the old country by the way you move or something.

Reflections

Dora's involvement with the immigrant community coincided with her realization that she had reached the glass ceiling at work, and it was important for her to redirect her energies. I am still in awe of Dora's persistence and conviction in "doing what has to be done" for Korean American immigrants, her ability to rise above the conflicts and tensions in which she became embroiled, and her continued commitment to service even after the rupture between the American-born and immigrant Korean communities. Her untiring desire to serve and care for those less fortunate than herself reveals a strong commitment to moral action, as well as a remarkable compassion and kindness.

I cannot make claims to the kind of virtue that Dora has exemplified or the altruism that blossomed in her midlife. I had other motives when I started volunteering at the Senior Meal Program and at the Korean senior citizens' associations in 1986. It was the one way that I could gain access to the elderly population that I wished to study for my dissertation. When I started this project, I knew it would be difficult because I had very little contact with people of Korean heritage, and I found the experiences of both Koreans and Korean Americans very foreign to me. And when I left for fieldwork in Korea in 1989, I used the opportunity to retreat from all my activities in the Korean American community.

Although I reconnected with Dora to work on her life story, it wasn't until 1995 that I became involved with the Korean American community again. I was recruited by a colleague to the board of the Korean American Museum (KAM) when I moved to Los Angeles in 1995. While the contexts of our immersion into Korean America differ, like Dora's experience in the community, my involvement on the KAM board has pulled me into the highly factionalized and contentious orbit of Korean America. The KAM is a noble project that attempts to map the social and cultural issues salient to Korean Americans, but it is a complex undertaking fraught with difficulties. I do not know about the long-term viability of such a project, given the state of Korean America, but I do what I can there, as it combines my academic concerns with my interest in cultural production—a passion that I set aside in 1986, when I had to study for my doctoral exams. And although my involvement was not a conscious response to Dora's concerns, I can see her influence. The KAM project is one that attempts to address the concerns that she voiced: it has the potential to unify the diverse social body as well as build bridges between Koreans and non-Koreans in America—a legacy for the current generation of community workers.

A
FAMILY
GALLERY

Man Suk Yum's female relatives in Korea.

Wedding Photograph of Man Suk Yum and Hang Shin Kim, 1920.

Hang Shin Kim (on right) with Ahn Ch'ang Ho, seated, 1920.

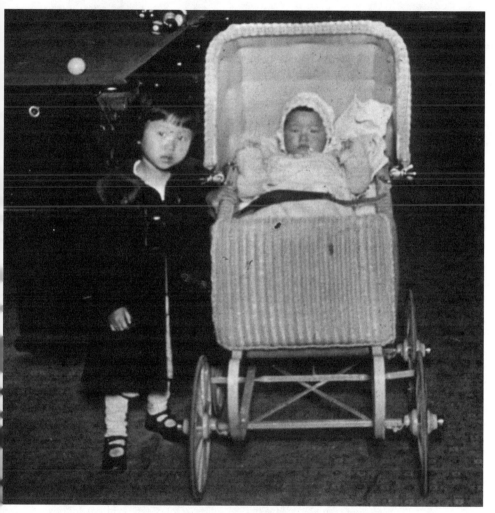

Dora with brother George in pool hall that Man Suk Yum managed, circa 1923.

Family portrait, circa 1925.

Hang Shin Kim and her children, circa 1931.

Dora, at the cigar stand, circa 1935.

Dora and friend Arlene, at Sawyer, CA in the summer of 1937.

Family portrait, circa 1937.

Man Suk Yum, outside
Lee's Lunch, circa 1937.

Dora's high school graduation
portrait, 1938.

Wedding portrait, Dora Yum and Tom Kim, 1942.

Dora leads Korean constituents in American Day parade, the first time Koreans were
publicly recognized as separate from the Japanese, 1942.

Dora and Tom (left) socializing at Forbidden City, the first Asian American
nightclub, 1943.

Dora, second from left, sings with Korean women at the half shell in Golden Gate Park on The First Korean Day with the first Consul General of the Republic of Korea, 1953.

Last family photo before the death of Hang Shin Kim, circa 1953.

Dora speaking before the United Nationalities, 1981.

Dora receiving the Korean President's medal, 1989.

In honor of........

KOREAN COMMUNITY SERVICE CENTER
상항한인 봉사회

Line drawing of Dora Yum Kim by Min Paek for the cover of the pamphlet for her hwan'gap/retirement party.

PART

3

A Room
of Her Own

SIXTY was the worst year of my life. I can barely remember anything about it except the losses. I lost my two brothers and my youngest daughter that year. I stopped doing everything after that, and I don't think I came out of it for about a year. I think I just stayed home. It was a terrible year.

Part 3, a narrative of Dora's later life, covers the time span from 1981 to the present. In 1981 Dora turned sixty. Age sixty, the hwan'gap *year, signifies rebirth, the completion of the zodiacal calendar, and a return to the year of birth. The increasing numbers of people reaching age sixty has diminished its significance as a rite of passage into old age, celebrating longevity and retirement from active life. However, Koreans continue to mark the* hwan'gap, *especially of those whose lives are considered exemplary in some way.[1] Although her service to the Korean American community warranted celebration, for Dora the sixtieth year was not marked with one. Not only was Dora unprepared to retire from active life, she was busy with funeral preparations for the three family members she lost in 1981. The timing of the losses also precluded celebratory preparations, as they would have been inappropriate. Although Dora's* hwan'gap *year did not include celebration, in that year she was honored by the city and county of San Francisco. Dora was recognized as president and one of the founding members of the first multicultural organization in San Francisco, the United Nationalities, estab-*

lished in 1942. She was also an elected delegate to the White House Conference on Aging. Public acclaim, however, was eclipsed by ethnic Korean community discord and the losses she sustained.

When Dora entered "young" old age in 1981, the ethnic Korean milieu in San Francisco had changed dramatically. By then post-1965 Korean immigrants, predominantly comprised of an educated middle class, outnumbered the descendants of the first wave by approximately 200 to 1.[2] With business savvy and access to resources, they began to emerge as the dominant force in the ethnic Korean community. While prohibitive land costs deterred Koreans from physically demarcating their own enclave as they had in other urban areas,[3] it did not deter the growth of Korean businesses. Pockets of Korean establishments opened in the Japantown area, and along Geary in the inner Richmond District. Small businesses proliferated: the entire range of Korean-owned establishments, from laundries, video stores, flower shops, bookstores, green grocers, liquor stores, garages, retail clothing stores, delis, to medical offices, opened.[4] Korean churches, the center of ethnic Korean communities multiplied accordingly.[5] Additionally, Korea-based operations such as banks, department stores, car dealerships, and computer outlets opened branches to serve both Korean and non-Korean clientele in San Francisco.

While the success of Koreans in carving out an economic niche for themselves was widely publicized, there was also a fast-growing need for social services. Not only did businesses falter and fail, economic downturns and downsizing made for limited employment opportunities. Additionally, many adult immigrants sent for their parents after they settled in America. While children sign promissory documents to fully support their parents after they immigrate, they are unable to keep up with the exorbitant cost of elder maintenance without the support of the extended family system.[6] Hence many are forced to seek government assistance. Given the multiple strains on immigrant Korean families, in addition to the growth of for-profit enterprises, there has been a growth of nonprofit community service organizations.

Despite growing need, second- and third-generation-run community service centers experienced a decrease in activity. On the service front, the passing of the era of civil unrest and radical Asian American coalitions had consequences. *Disillusioned and burnt-out, many student leaders, community organizers, and volunteers who once believed they could change the world had moved on. This left a gap for post-1965 immigrants to organize community services for themselves. Concurrently, the rapidly expanding population of post-1965 immigrants had become dissatisfied with the cultural and communication gap between themselves and their second- and third-generation mediators. Post-1965 immigrants broke away from the grassroots community centers and organizations established by American-born Koreans to found their own. Underutilized and unable to claim a broad enough constituency, many second- and third-generation-run nonprofit organizations felt the sting of underfunding. Competition for state and federal funding from immigrant-run institutions further fueled the decline of these nonprofit service organizations. Savvy to funding sources in Korea as well as the United States, their middle-class and educated immigrant counterparts set up nonprofit and profit service organizations with capabilities that surpassed those operated by American-born Koreans.*

Feeling betrayed and used, many of the remaining second- or third-generation Korean American community workers and volunteers continued to seek alternative venues of service. Dora, a strong advocate for continued service to needy Koreans, watched powerlessly as factions and divisions formed within the ethnic Korean community service sector. Not only did the factions within the immigrant community begin to battle for resources, at that juncture it was difficult, if not impossible, to bridge the growing gulf between the "Korean American and Korean Korean."[7] *Amidst community turmoil and chaos, family tragedy struck. In 1981 the death of her two brothers and her youngest daughter derailed her. Grappling with personal losses, she was unable to work or socialize. This period was one of the few times in Dora's life narrative where she did not focus on race, ethnicity, and community concerns.*

I have called on a variety of sources for the chapters in Part 3. Chapter 7, "Hidden Costs," was constructed from one interview conducted in the summer of 1992. While Dora often talks of 1981 as "that terrible year," the only time she directly addressed the circumstances of that year was in one very short meeting, which I have reproduced almost verbatim. In that particular interview, she uncharacteristically remained extremely focused on the topic and left little room for questions or comments. In this chapter Dora speaks of her two brothers' and daughter's deaths with a precision and flow that can only come from practice. While she may not have told the story before, this was not the first time she had thought it through. It is told in a detached, rehearsed manner common to people who speak of incidents that still are emotionally difficult to discuss.

Chapter 8 is constructed from two interviews in which Dora finally talked about the circumstances that led to establishing a room of her own, separate from her family. Initially, Dora was reticent to talk about the tensions in her family life from which she needed time out. She was particularly concerned with the possibility of portraying her husband negatively. However, as we started discussing the issues off-tape, she became more comfortable about revealing the situation that led to the establishment of a room of her own. She understands that Tom had his own difficulties with the loss of their daughter, difficulties that she could not help him with. While Dora initially found a room of her own in response to an altercation she had with her husband, she sees the incident as just the catalyst that allowed her to express her need for solitude and self-examination as she was entering her latter years. Dora constructs her need for solitude as essential to managing her own pain and anguish, as well as confronting her own issues around mortality.

The final chapter of Dora's life narrative, "Hwan'gap" is Dora's account of her celebration. It is a composite from two interviews conducted five years apart. The first of the two interviews was conducted in 1987 and the follow-up in 1992. Dora's version of the day lends insight into the issues to which she pays attention—not necessarily the points I find relevant—and the way they influence her reconstruction of the event.

SEVEN

Hidden Costs

IN 1981 Dora lost her two brothers and her daughter. The way that Dora talks about these deaths highlights her experience of grief and mourning.[1] For Dora, the pain of loss does not diminish; what has occurred over time is the ability to manage her feelings of loss and anguish in order to resume her responsibilities: work, social obligations, and caring for surviving family members. Her narrative of loss and mourning does not easily fit into the popular American conception of loss, which views mourning as a finite process that leads to enhanced functioning and the diminishing of pain and anguish.[2]

You often refer to 1981 and even refer to the losses, but you have never really talked about it at any length. Would you be comfortable talking about that year?

Like I keep saying, 1981 was a terrible year. So many losses. Three deaths in one year. It was devastating. It's still hard to talk about.

Are you sure you want to talk about it?

I'll be okay talking about it. Like you say, I keep referring to it. That's because that year really changed things. Things have never been quite the same since. I used to believe that all could be well in my life. Now I'm just thankful for the things I have, and take it one day at a time.

So who did you lose first?

My brother George was the first to pass away. I didn't expect it at all. I went to see him in sometime in mid-May of 1981, just to visit. At that time he was living alone in the apartment on Bush Street. He had moved back to San Francisco after spending thirty years in Los Angeles. George worked as a stationary engineer for the city and county of Los

143

Angeles for about twenty years, then worked as a real estate broker down there for about ten years. When he moved back to San Francisco, he worked for the St. Francis Hotel on Powell Street for a couple a years in there, but in mid-May he was not employed.

So I was just stopping in to visit, and I found him really out of it. I was so alarmed I called an ambulance and had him hospitalized. I think he had a heart problem. Once he was in the hospital, he just got weaker and weaker. He died a week later of heart failure. He passed away on May 23, 1981. He had some money when he died, which I used for the funeral and the burial.

George was married several times, but at the time of his death he was single. His first wife was a Korean girl from Honolulu. He had a daughter with her, but after three years he divorced her and sent them back to Honolulu.

Then he married again to a Korean girl, Lillian, who was a public nurse in L.A. Lillian was the first Korean public health nurse. George lived in L.A. with her. They were only married a couple of years when Lillian died of aplastic anemia at the age of twenty-nine. It was tragic.

Then he married a Chinese girl from L.A. who was a schoolteacher. He was married to her for at least five years and had two boys with her, but that marriage ended in divorce too. George had moved back up to San Francisco after that and was living alone. I used to just stop in to visit.

I guess what was really hard was that he had no family of his own at the funeral. My brother Henry and I were the closest surviving relatives.

That must have been very difficult. What happened next?

Then my brother Henry passed away suddenly. Again, it was totally unexpected. I guess he was staying over with some friends because I got a call from them saying that they couldn't wake him up. The autopsy revealed that he had walking pneumonia. He never knew it. He died June 14. He just went to bed one night and never got up. And I was the closest surviving relative. He never had any children and was not married at the time.

After the Korean war, he became a cryptologist and worked for the national intelligence agency in Washington, D.C. I can't remember why, but he went down to L.A. and met a Korean girl and married her. He was in the military so she traveled with him on his military sojourns.

They finally settled down in L.A., and Henry worked for the department of employment down there. He started the affirmative action program down there. They never had any children, and I guess they weren't getting along because he eventually divorced the Korean girl.

Henry remarried a Chinese girl. They didn't have children, but his second wife had three children whom he adopted. That marriage ended in divorce too. So he eventually moved back to San Francisco, and he was single again when he died.

Both my brothers were in their fifties.

When you get older, your siblings become really important. They share a kind of history with you and know you in a way that can't be reproduced. There isn't enough time to build that kind of knowledge with new people. And sharing that family experience—it's special. Many people don't like their families, but it builds a kind of closeness that's really important.

I still regret not spending more time with my brothers, because having brothers or relations doesn't mean much until you lose them. I could have helped them more, but I felt more allegiance to my husband and children. But it's not like that with everyone. My brother Henry didn't have children, and George's children were raised by their mothers so his kids weren't close to our family. That's sad.

I remember thinking during that time that I'm the only surviving member on my side of the family. My mother died in her fifties, my two brothers died in their fifties. . . . And I'm in my seventies. It still makes me feel funny. But I guess my father died in his seventies. I don't know what it is. I try not to think about it. But at my age—like today, I was running around and it was really hot, and I wondered, "Am I going to drop dead?" The old lady [one of the many Koreans she helps who is also a well-regarded fortune teller] says, "You have to live until you see your grandson, Kerry's son, become something." He's so sharp. But that's a long time. . . .

When did you lose your daughter?

My daughter died in October—October 23. She was twenty-five years old. And here she was the one who had a couple of certificates for fitness. People used to say she was so beautiful. And she was. My youngest daughter was beautiful. She turned heads wherever she went. Everyone thought she was so pretty. In some ways, she was too pretty for her own good. I remember one time, I think she said she was coming down the stairs one day at the state building, or the federal building. Anyway, some guy stopped her and said, "Gee you're the most beautiful girl I've ever seen. Would you have dinner with me?" But she was never one to fall for anything. Anyway, he gave her a card. So she showed me this card, and it turned out that he was some big executive, CEO of a pretty well-known company. She really turned those heads.

She was the one who worked the reception at the Korean Center when we were over on Larkin Street. She was also the one who worked for the summer youth program run by the city at city hall when she graduated from high school. I suppose she was following in my footsteps in many ways. I knew some of the people there at city hall when she worked there in the summer program. Anyway, Debby came home one night says, "Jeez, everybody introduces me as Dora Kim's daughter. Don't I have a name of my own?" She was really independent—so much energy, so much drive . . . When she died, many people said, "Well, you have other children."

But it's different. Whether you have one or five or ten, losing a child is the greatest pain that a mother can endure. I don't think people understand it in this day and age. It's been over ten years, and there isn't one day that goes by that I don't think about her.

How did it happen?

I remember Debby called the night she died, and we had made some plans for the next day. Her last words to me were, "Oh, I'll see you tomorrow."

You just never know. Her girlfriend was the one who contacted us and told us that something had happened to her. She said she was talking to her on the phone, and all of a sudden Debby stopped talking.

So she called us and said, "You'd better go over and look."

We tried to call but couldn't get through. We found out later that she never put the receiver back on the hook. Since I had just talked with her, I wasn't too worried—but we called, just in case. . . . She was living at the Fontana then, in the condo I owned, so we called the doorman, and asked him to go in and check.

But he said, "We're not allowed to."

I'm still mad about that. If they'd caught her in time, taken her to the hospital and pumped her stomach, she could have lived. I guess it wasn't meant to be.

So when did you find out about her death?

The next day I was at the center helping this girl fill out a form when I got the phone call. I don't remember the conversation very clearly, but they said she had been dead just seven hours when they found her. It was just too late. I remember going into shock. She died of pulmonary edema—her lungs just gave up. I didn't know that until I got the autopsy report.

I had just experienced the death of my two brothers, and that was bad.

I was having enough trouble with that. But when a child dies, it *really* shakes up your life. You know, children aren't supposed to die before the parents. Most people live with the sense that even if terrible things can happen, somehow you're safe, that things will go according to some kind of schedule. But that sense of safety gets shattered when you lose a child.

We buried Debby on my brother George's birthday, which happened to fall on October thirtieth. And that's when we buried her. I put her in a mausoleum. And after that, I just cut off from everything. I was teaching ESL, and I just quit that and let others do it. There were a couple of organizations that I was active in, and I resigned from that. Three major losses in a year is devastating. My life unraveled on me. That was the hardest year of my life. It took me about a year to gradually start coming back. I didn't go to the center for about a year. . . . They say time heals, but it doesn't heal. You just get used to the pain, and you learn to live with it. If that's what they mean by healing, I guess time does seem to help somewhat. I started to gradually get back into activities.

How did Debby's death affect other family members?

If I took Debby's death really hard, Tom did no better. Debby's death really shook him up. But he's always dealt with things differently than I have. Tom places the responsibility on things outside himself while I tend to question myself and the way I contributed to things. So Tom dealt with Debby's death differently than I did. He blamed me for my daughter's death. He said I wasn't around enough, that I didn't spend enough time with her. I don't know what he would have been like if she hadn't died, but it really changed him. And when he blamed me . . . As I said, I tend to look inward anyway. Then to top it off, I had my own doubts because I never thought I was a great mother, so . . .

I just went around and around on this.

Now I say, "Hey, you don't have control of your children after they're twenty-one.'

But I sometimes think if you're a successful woman, you pay for it with one of your children. Around that time, Clare Boothe Luce's daughter died in an auto crash. Her daughter was going to Stanford at the time. There are other women with public lives who lose their daughters. It seems like you're paying for your sins. I can't help but wonder if success is a sin for women.

You're so hard on yourself.

You can't run away from it. The pain is always there to remind you.

How did you recover from that year?

I don't think you ever recover from something like that. I don't remember what I did for that year. I must have kept busy, but I really can't remember. That year is a blank. I do remember gradually coming out of my shell again. I eventually got back into the flow of life. I suppose I realized that regardless of how I was doing, life just goes on. You can either be part or it or not. I don't understand it, but there seem to be cycles of things. I wonder if life events happen in threes. In 1981 I had three deaths. It's funny, ten years later in 1991, I had three weddings. And weddings tend to lead to births. Life runs in cycles—deaths and births, death followed by birth, followed by death, and on and on.

Reflections

Dora does not falter as she speaks of "that terrible year." But I hear the sadness in her voice as she recounts the events of that year. I do not want to cry. I feel the lump in my throat, and I am doing all that I can to keep the tears at bay. I do not know if Dora is aware that a large tear is trickling slowly down her face. I feel the tears roll slowly roll down mine.

As the tragic narrative unfolds, I know that I agree with Dora in her belief that many do not recover from the trauma of loss. This is not to say that there is nothing to be gained from loss. On the contrary, there is much to be gained. But these are life's hardest lessons—to learn that life goes on, that our lives go on, and that, even without us, life will go on. The experience of loss can, indeed, nurture resilience.

EIGHT

On Her Own

THE losses sustained in 1981, particularly the loss of their youngest child, had long-term effects on Dora and her husband. Not only did they have trouble coming to grips with Debby's death, it intensified the differences between them. Unable to contain the anguish of losing a daughter in adult life or find comfort at home, Dora sought solitude so that she could come to terms with her own pain, as well as with issues surrounding her own aging and eventual death.

When did you start going back to work?

I guess I started going back to work at the center sometime in 1982. I kept busy, but things weren't going smoothly at home. The deaths of my brothers and our daughter Debby were really hard. For about ten years I had been going in one direction. The children were all grown up, and I had become really involved with the Koreans and different organizations. So our marriage had gone through some changes. But I didn't think too much about that because the changes had occurred gradually. It's part of life to discover little things as you go along, but you don't necessarily put things together until you have time. And I had the time after Debby's death.

What did you put together?

It wasn't until after that horrible year that I realized how different Tom and I were, how differently we felt about family. I think that's because I grew up with parents, and he was sent to Korea for school. That makes a difference in the way you treat your own children. When our kids and grandchildren got married, I was really involved. My husband acted very differently than I did—he was more detached.

I also realized how much he really resented my working. I had known that Tom didn't like me working when I started, but he was in and out of town, and my work hadn't really interfered with home life. When Tom retired from Matson Company and started working for the city, he stayed home and took care of the kids—like he did when he was home from sea. He had never said anything about my working when he was working for Matson, so I just assumed it was okay.

Then in the 1970s, when we still had five children at home, I started getting more and more involved with the immigrant Koreans as they started coming to the office. So I was working a lot, and just couldn't be at home as much as I would have liked. He did occasionally say I shouldn't work so hard, but I didn't pay any attention to that. And then, when immigrants called me at home after hours, he said that he preferred if they didn't call me at home. However, since they generally called in the early evening, for emergency situations, he didn't press the point. But then the calls started coming in more often, and Tom started asking me not to bring my work home. Like I said, he had never pressed that issue then, and by that point, I think it was already too late. What was I going to do? Take back our phone number from all those immigrants? I think if he had it to do over, he would have spoken up a lot sooner.

So when it happened, it really took me by surprise.

What happened? What was "it"?

One day he just blew up and started yelling at me. "It" was the yelling and hollering. It was as if it had been building up for some time, and he couldn't hold it in anymore.

I was still working for the state Department [of Employment], and unfortunately, I got a phone call in the middle of the night, at three o'clock in the morning. Naturally it woke up the whole house. This Korean woman was at General Hospital, and they couldn't get out of her why she was there. The only thing they found on her was my name and my phone number. So they called me. I wasn't exactly thrilled myself, but Tom didn't like it one bit.

He started hollering, "I told you not to bring your work home with you." It was not the first time he had told me not to bring my work home, but the hollering . . .

And what could I do at that point anyway?

Since they asked me to come out, I went out there and asked the girl, "What's wrong? Why did you come here?"

She said, "My stomach hurts."

I went on asking the where, how, for how long and all that, and then came home when I was done.

What happened when you got home?

When I got home, Tom just went on and on about my work interrupting our home life. But at that point I couldn't stop them from calling. And I couldn't stop working. You can't just stop doing something like social work. There's a need, and you just have to continue. So I just kept quiet until he finished hollering.

And I suppose I should have tried to reason with him, but I didn't. I couldn't. He was really upset, and I just let it pass. But maybe I shouldn't have, because it just got worse. After that incident he became much more open about expressing his displeasure that I was so focused on work. And me, I just sat there and took it.

You know, my father was like that when he was younger. He used to yell and scream about this, that, or the other. But he's really mellowed with age.

What did your mother do?

When she was younger, she used to just take it.

I know. That's Korean style. I sometimes think it's a thing with Korean men. That's all I hear about. So many of them just yell and holler when they don't like something. It's not easy to live with, but that's Korean men for you.

But it wasn't until after Debby's death that it got really tough. It was after Debby's death that Tom started blaming me for everything. That was not fun.

In other words, he's really Korean, like your dad. He's so Korean-ish. He sees the world from his point of view and his needs. He doesn't want anything to interfere with the smooth running of his life. And after fifty years he's become more and more Korean. Some parts of the old Korean traditions are good, but this is 1992, and things change. Things should change.

He wasn't like that when we were younger, but then maybe I tried to please him more. I'm not sure. The older we got, the more he seemed to just go on and on when he got upset. And then after Debby's death it got really bad. He still goes on and on when he gets upset, but he doesn't get upset as often. He wants things his way. Thinking back to the early years, I guess he's always wanted everything his way. I suppose some women wouldn't have put up with it, but I was the type that was patient enough to accommodate him. I shut up and put up with things, even if I didn't approve of it. I felt I had to *chama*—you know, keep things in and live with it. I tried to continue to do that, but one day I knew I couldn't do it anymore. All of our differences just came to a head.

It was a long time in coming.

What did you disagree about?

We had a lot of differences in terms of what family meant. I first began to appreciate how different our family values were when our children and grandchildren got married. I don't really care who our children or grandchildren marry—as long as they love each other and can work things out between them. But Tom isn't like that. Even back in 1965 when my daughter Darlyne got married to a Caucasian fellow, she knew her father wouldn't approve. So she waited until she turned twenty-one and got married in Carson City, Nevada, on her birthday. In some ways, it was very romantic because her fellow wanted to marry her more than anything else, no matter what anyone said.

I didn't think that much of it then, but looking back I think that was the first event that stands out regarding our differences. I didn't know how traditional my husband was, but apparently the children knew. What are you going to do? He is a real old-style Korean who's always objected to Koreans marrying Caucasians. Given the lack of Koreans in San Francisco, he figured that other Asians were okay, but Caucasians were out. That's just the way he is.

On the other hand, I'm not at all against interracial marriage. This is America. Besides, family is family. Your children choose who they think they can spend their lives with, and you just have to stand by your children. I think Tom has always been different about that. He's disappointed by the children when they do things he disapproves of. And he just didn't approve of interracial marriage.

I think it makes a difference whether a Korean from Korea or a Korean American marries a Caucasian. It's two different things. My daughter was born in San Francisco, she met her husband at college; he was Tom Jr.'s friend. My daughter is all-American, even though she is Korean in looks. There are a few differences between a Korean American and a Caucasian, but I think they're minor. Even though I was born here, growing up with a Korean heritage, we had *pop* and *kimchi, rice* and *kimchi.* So my daughter is used to eating Korean food. Since she married a Caucasian, even though she is an American, she misses that rice. Her husband really is a steak-and-potato man, and my daughter is a rice and *kimchi* person. But they both compromise, and they go out to eat quite a bit.

I'm impressed with my children in the choices they've made and the ways they've chosen to live. But my husband thinks differently. Like I said, he's easily disappointed by the children.

I don't know what he expected from them. He didn't even pay for his son's MBA. That made me mad because he was in a position where he could have helped, and he didn't. I don't even know if Kyle wanted his help, but I didn't like that. If you don't have the resources, there's nothing you can do. But if you can help your children out, you should. That's the way I feel.

Then there was the situation with Darlyne. When she went back to get her master's degree, she and her husband didn't have that much money. And my husband didn't offer to pay for it. My brother George had just moved back up here from L.A. after his marriage broke up and had some extra money, and he just gave Darlyne some towards her education because he knew her situation. He shouldn't have had to do that. We should have done that. My parents sacrificed everything for us, for our education. There's no reason why we couldn't have done it because our sacrifice today is nothing compared to our parents' sacrifice.

To be fair, I think I sometimes forget that our parents were different. I had shelter, love, and support of both my parents and Tom didn't. And that makes a difference.

So you were saying that things came to a head?

Yes, they did. And when they did, it turned out to be a good thing that I bought that studio condo at the Fontana back in 1968 as an investment. You know, I rented that condo out until my daughter Debby wanted to move in there in 1981. That's where she died in 1981. Then we rented it out again for a couple of years.

So what happened?

I was still working with the Koreans at that time. Well, one afternoon my husband was home when I was about to go to General Hospital for an appointment. And he said, "I want you to be home at six o'clock and get dinner ready. If you can't be home by six to get dinner ready, don't come home at all."

There was just no way I was going to be home by six o'clock. Besides, he's a good cook, and when I wasn't around he usually did the cooking. But Korean style is: you'd better be home by six or not come home at all, if that's what your man wants. While Tom had never come out so strong before on this issue before, he did that time.

It was seven o'clock before I got out of the hospital, so I didn't go home. Instead, I went over to the apartment of a couple I know. They know my husband because the man is Tom's childhood friend.

He said, "Go ahead and stay here."

They had an extra apartment they were fixing up, so I stayed there a while. Well, while I was there, the tenant at the Fontana moved out. And I thought, "Here's my chance." So I moved in there. But I knew that, eventually, I had to go back home. And I did.

When I did go home several months later, my husband couldn't say anything, because he was wrong. But he's got that Korean pride. You know, the male chauvinist thing.

So what was it like to live alone?

As you know, I had never lived alone in my life. I'd always lived with my parents. Even during the war, when my husband was away, my parents were there. And then after the war, when my husband was at home, I had both him and my parents there. And then the children came, and it was hard to be alone, even if I tried. Living alone for that time was good for me.

When I first started living alone, it was hard. There were so many things I had never done by myself. For instance, I had never even been to a movie alone. And you know, when I was younger I had been the type who never did things alone, never went places alone. Even when Tom was out at sea, I carted the children around with me. It was only in my job that I had to do things by myself. But even there, I was always interacting with people—there was always some new client to deal with. For the first time, I was completely alone.

How did it feel to be completely alone?

At first I was a little scared to be on my own. But it didn't take long for me to learn that I didn't have to cook for anyone, or take other people's needs into consideration. I also realized that I had lived all my life in places that were overheated for me, and that I sleep much better in cooler rooms. At the place on Dewey Boulevard, the radio and the TV are on all the time. But at the Fontana I had the choice of turning off the radio or the TV when I wanted. And I found that I work a lot better when it's quiet. At the Fontana I learned what I liked. I ate when I wanted to, what I wanted to, and just managed myself. It felt good. I went to a movie by myself, for the first time, when I moved to the Fontana.

And you know, to this day I don't know what I was afraid of. I guess growing up, I was taught that girls didn't do things alone, just for themselves. Girls were supposed to go along with what everyone else wanted to do. Now I like to do things alone. When you do things like go to a museum, you don't have to worry about looking for the person you went with.

There are still some things I just can't or don't like to do alone. I don't like to eat alone. That I still can't do. I've done it a couple of times, but I don't like to. I still feel funny about that.

But in general, I really believe that the older you get, the braver you get. It's been true with me. I don't think I had the courage to live by myself when I was younger. I relied on other people's reactions and interactions with me for my sense of who I am, so I don't think I would have done so well on my own. But for the first time, when I got older, I started wanting to get away from the ties. I want and need the time alone to think about my life, as well as my death. It's hard to think about those things when you're in the thick of things. . . .

After living alone for several months, you went back home to Dewey Boulevard. How was that?

I think living alone was particularly good for my relationship with Tom. Even when I was living alone, I was really busy working at the center. But living alone gave me some time out. It's hard to get perspective on a person when you live with them. I don't know why, but after a while, you just assume that you share all the same experiences. Given the direction that our relationship had taken, I needed the time and space to think about the different ways in which we had changed. And for the first time I realized how Korean Tom was, and how much more Korean he had become as he aged. And getting that perspective really helped me in terms of dealing with him. There are still times when I wonder, "Why is he like that?" Then it dawns on me again and again that he was sent to Korea to go to school, and it was his upbringing in Korea that influenced him. Then I'm reminded that the way he grew up and the way I grew up were totally different.

Was this a helpful insight for you?

Given the point that we were at, it was extremely helpful. I've come to think that a person's early experiences have a strong influence on who they become later on. And even if it isn't apparent for a time, it can emerge later. If you haven't had a loving childhood, it affects you later. Tom's mother died when he was thirteen, when he was in Korea. I don't know how long he was in Korea total, and being a Korean man, he won't say. He returned to Hawaii after his mother's death. But after his mother died I don't think the family did too well in Hawaii. I think it's hard when the woman of the house passes away early.

Tom doesn't talk about what it was like in Korea. I guess it was that bad. I hear more about what happened in Korea from his older sister than from him. His sister once told me about an uncle that they lived with. The fellow had a son, apparently the same age as my husband. And in the winter she said it was deathly cold. She said the uncle would send my husband out in gloves, with holes in it, to bring the wood in for the fire. And the son wouldn't do a thing. His older sister didn't want anything to do with that uncle after she came back to Hawaii because of the way he treated Tom. And Tom didn't want to have anything to do with them either. The uncle and his wife are both dead, but the wife lived for some time after she was widowed.

Tom's younger sister is still in Honolulu, and she grew up ignorant of the way the uncle treated Tom. She believed that they're family and that she had to help them if they needed it. Well, apparently that family was not doing well. Tom's younger sister insisted that he send money to them. And while Tom may not have wanted to, he thought it was the right thing to do. So until the uncle's wife died, he sent fifteen dollars a month to his sister to send to Korea. But in spite of the fact that Tom gave financial support, I've never met his family in Korea. Tom never gave me their address or anything. And I think meeting with family is as important as sending money.

Why do you bring that up?

There is conflict in that, the difference in our values. But I don't want to change him. I know I can't, so I just let him be. But sometimes Tom won't let me be. I used to put up with it, just shut up and let Tom say what he wanted. But after being on my own, I won't put up with it like I used to. I used to think it was part of marriage to put up with whatever your husband and children dished out. I don't think so anymore. I think a good marriage or family life is one in which there's room for everyone to be who they are. And now, I can just leave if things get bad. And I do. It's not an issue because everyone knows where I'm going, and that I'll be back.

But you know, I don't want to give the impression that I think badly of Tom. That's not it at all. I think marriage is just hard work. And being married and having a family is one of the most important things in my life. But having a place of my own has allowed me to have a much better marriage than ever before. I think a little time away is good for us because it allows us to appreciate each other more.

What kind of arrangement do you have now?

Since I moved into the Fontana in 1983, I've been going back and forth between the house on Dewey Boulevard and the Fontana. I figure there's no use in renting it. Since everything is paid for, I would just have to pay taxes on it if I rented it out. It's now my retreat. I sometimes have to go there so I can be alone, be by myself. It helps me get perspective on things to be alone. Also, anytime Tom goes on at me, I just walk out of the house.

Sometimes, when his father goes on like he does, our son will say, "Go on home."

And I just smile and say, "Yeah."

The other night he was really going on, so I left. And as I was going to the Fontana, I noticed that it was a full moon. So I called Kerry to let him know.

He laughed and said, "We should have known."

He seems to get out of hand when the moon is full.

So is it safe to assume that things have been pretty smooth since you got your own room?

Well, I had two strokes, one in 1989 and another one in April of 1995. Health problems are difficult for everyone. But besides the health-related problems, we did have a difficult period back in 1986, when Tom also retired from the city and county of San Francisco, where he was the chief engineer. I think retirement is really hard on men. Since men see them-selves so much more in terms of their work, they can really be at loose ends when they retire. I was really worried about him. You always won-der about the man. With women, there's no problem—a woman can always keep busy. Women are more involved with people—social activi-ties and daily living. I retired, but it didn't slow me down at all. I got involved with starting the Korean Community Service Center, helping people, and have never been busier. It's different with a man. So I was really concerned.

At first I tried to include Tom in more areas of my life, and tried to get him to come down to the Korean Center and stuff. But he wasn't having any of that. I even tried to bring Tom with me to the apartment just to keep him occupied, but he wouldn't come with me.

After Tom retired, a couple of things happened. Because I was moving back and forth from the Fontana to Dewey Boulevard, Tom started getting into cooking. He gradually took over the cooking and the grocery shopping. As it turns out, he's a much better cook than I am. I'm not really surprised because early in our marriage, when I was working and Tom was in town, he would spend time with my mother. The activity that they shared was cooking, and my mother taught him to cook in a way that she didn't teach me.

Then in 1987, my son Kerry and our grandson Kerry Junior moved in with us. That has turned out to be one of the best things for Tom. Kerry Junior is the center of Tom's life. He's really tied to his grandson. In some ways, he's more involved with Kerry Junior than he was in his own sons. He's doing things with his grandson that he never did with his own children. Tom really loves to cook for the kid. I think it's worked out well for both Tom and Kerry Junior. Children need as much love as they can get. My mother lived to see three grandchildren before she died, Tommy, Darlyne, and Kyle. My younger son and daughter always say they regret not having grown up with a grandparent. I think about what Kerry and Debby said, and I try to do as much for my grandsons as for my own sons. So it's nice to see Tom doting on Kerry Junior. His involvement with his grandson is the focus in his life.

What happened to the mainstream organizations he joined?

Tom used to be involved with social organizations like the Shriners, but not anymore. I know that one of the reasons that he isn't involved with those organizations anymore is the segregation of those groups into ethnic chapters. He doesn't want to be relegated to a Korean chapter of the Shriners. I think that's been really disappointing to him—it perpetuates ethnic divisions within larger social organizations. But Tom doesn't talk about it. He just keeps everything to himself.

Maybe it would be helpful for him to talk about it more. I don't know. But he reads a lot and he's knowledgeable. Whenever we go someplace, like on cruises and on vacation, he opens up and talks about things. So, it's really important for us to go on vacation together. That's how I find out what he thinks about a lot of things. I wish he would open up and be more sociable when he's at home, but he's not.

Do you and Tom socialize with the Korean American community?

Tom will accompany me to the parties that the Korean consul general gives, but that's pretty much it. I don't think he likes to be known as Dora Kim's husband. And I can certainly understand that from his perspective.

But because Tom is so unsociable, especially with the Koreans, people still aren't sure that I have a husband. I don't know what they think, but it always comes as a surprise that I do. It happens all the time.

For three years in a row, members of our family got invitations to go to visit Korea on Korean Airlines. We didn't go the first year—the invitation was extended to me, and Tom didn't want to go. The second year, my son Tommy was invited to go to Korea, but he didn't want to go because he was too busy. So I went in his place. The following year I got an invitation, so I figured I would give my husband a chance to go. It was a free trip.

So we were at the party at the consul general and I was talking to Mr. Yang, a man I know, and I said, "I hear you're going to Korea."

He replied, "Yes. You are too, aren't you?"

"No," I said, "I'm going to let my husband go."

"Husband! You have a husband?"

After all those years of working with the Koreans, most of them don't even know I'm married. That's how active my husband is in the immigrant community. But to be fair, when you're in the social work field, you don't have time to talk about your own family or children. So the people don't know.

That's pretty surprising, given how small San Francisco is.

It's just not my husband. Just the other day, a prominent member of the Korean American community called me about the Korean Methodist Church. They are still fighting. Sunday they are having a final vote and there is one group that wants to keep it as a historical site, because that is where the *Hungsadan* started, the independence movement. And then the other group, including the minister, wants to sell it and buy a larger church on 3030 Judah street at 36th Avenue. And they are still fighting over that. So they were having a meeting with the superintendent of the Methodist Church.

He said, "You should to tell Tom Kim [Junior] to come, because Tom is a pretty good speaker and he can talk from the third-generation perspective."

Then he asked, "Is he related to you?"

After all these years of sitting in meetings with Tom Jr. and me, he didn't realize Tom was my son. I don't even think he knew I was married.

But that's typical of the Korean community. Totally self-absorbed. So it was easy for Tom, my husband, to just stay in the background. He didn't want to get involved. And he didn't have to.

How would you describe your relationship with Tom today?

When I was younger I probably wouldn't have come here today if Tom didn't want me to. Mind you, Tom has always done what he's wanted to. But things have changed. This morning I had him drop me off at U.C., and I just told him then, "I'm going to be here all day, and afterwards I'm going over to Soo's for an interview." If he didn't want me to come over, he didn't say anything. He knew I would come over even if he didn't want me to. He's finally learning to just let me do my thing. I really like that change in our relationship. We're much better companions now than ever before. You could say we have equal rights in the relationship.

Would you say you're a feminist?

I believe in equal rights, but I'm not a feminist. I think believing in equal rights is different from being a feminist. To me feminists are women who have lives in which they're the head of everything. They want to make all the decisions independently. In other words, they don't need a man. That would be really hard for me. I still need a man to make my life complete. I like being loved by a man. I still like it when a man opens a door for me, or helps me. There's also real comfort in having a man to share the joy and pain with. My understanding is that feminists don't want any of that. And if that's feminism, it's not for me.

I'm still with Tom, and I'm happy about that. Overall, I think Tom and I get along better now than we ever have. We've had a lot of fun, especially during the war, but when we were first married, we had five kids. Abortion was not legal at that time, and there were no birth control pills; so when it happened, it happened. There wasn't much time for just the two of us, as we have now. After they're grown, it's wonderful. It was fun when I first met Tom, but it's better now. We drove up to Reno the other weekend, just the two of us. It was nice. I drove halfway up and he drove the last half. And without the financial worries, it's so much better. We didn't even have that much time to think about it, but somehow it worked out okay.

Through it all, our children, our ups and downs, Tom and I have stuck together. And there have been down sides, but Tom's just part of my life. Now, Tom may not agree with everything I do, and is pretty unhappy with some of the things I've done. But then, I don't agree with everything he's done either. Still, one way or another, we've managed to work things out.

I think it takes a lot of courage to stay with it and work things out as you have.

I don't know about courage. I just did what I had to do. And these days I sometimes wonder if it isn't time to let go of that studio apartment. So the other day, I was telling my son, "Maybe I should rent that place out again. Dad says I'd be here more if I didn't have another place to maintain. I'm here most of the time, certainly more than I am there, and most times I go just to pick up my mail. The place is in a mess too. . . ."

And he said, "Don't you do that. Don't you dare do that."

The children say the best thing I ever did was to move into that apartment, because when things get rough at home, for whatever reason, I can just go back there. They think it keeps things more balanced. And it does. And I really do like the way things have worked out. But I sometimes wish I didn't have to maintain two places.

The option of having a room of your own is a wonderfully refreshing alternative. Many people think about it, but few have the resources or the courage to do it. I think it's really great. Have you read Virginia Woolf's A Room of One's Own?

You and Virginia Woolf may think it's wonderful, but I don't know about most other people. I'm especially uncertain about what the Koreans will think. Korean standards of acceptable behavior are more narrow. Maybe you shouldn't include this stuff about living in my own place, because people will think I'm crazy.

For me, it wouldn't be your life story if we omitted such an integral portion of your life. I don't think I could write your life story without including that. What do you think?

It makes me feel odd that other people will know. But I'm okay with it. After all, it is an integral part of my life. And you know, that's where I go to clear my head. I do all my thinking and planning there—I do my best work there, alone. And that's just the way it is.

Reflections

Debby's death became a focal point for existing tensions in Dora's marriage and accentuated the differences between her and Tom. But even when their relationship faltered, Dora did not give up. Although I am aware that people in Dora's generation had different expectations of marriage, Dora is so independent and forthcoming that I attribute to her the sensibilities of women of my generation. So I am surprised that she didn't walk away when she had the resources to. Instead, she used her resources to craft a viable alternative. I have great respect for people like Dora who are committed to working through differences in relationships. I admire the courage it takes to acknowledge differences, and the creativity it takes to negotiate a way around them.

While I have been aware of Dora's living arrangements throughout her life, she is so comfortable with herself that it surprises me to think that Dora had not experienced living alone until she was sixty-two. I can only imagine what it might be like to live one's life entirely within the family fold. Not only must family hold different meaning, it must also heighten the awareness of others—what other people need, what other people want. As such, the very idea of establishing a room of her own was foreign to her. Nonetheless, Dora has discovered that having a place where she can be alone is very important to her in later life.

Since I left home at sixteen and started living alone when I was twenty-two, I am so used to living alone that, for me, the idea of living with others is more alarming. But even so, I am just learning how to take time for myself. I am more oriented toward others and find that I am generally healthier and happier when I am socially enmeshed. While the pull of duty is sometimes exhausting, it is the tangle of obligations that makes me feel alive, and I find great satisfaction in caring for others, satisfying their needs. I realize that I am more like Dora than I had thought. Like her, I am most comfortable when I am in a role of giving to others.

NINE

Hwan'gap

April 1987

         DORA'S version of her hwan'gap *celebration focuses on her experience of the event as its honored guest. When I met her at the Korean Community Center to interview her about her celebration, Dora set up the videotape machine so that we could view the tape together while she narrated:*

Can you tell me the circumstances surrounding your hwan'gap *celebration?*

In 1986, when the funding for the Senior Meal Program ended, I decided to retire officially. I wasn't going to get paid anymore, and I didn't see myself fighting for funding. I was sixty-five, and I thought it would be a good time for me to call it quits. I didn't really think too much about it. I figured I would have time to pursue my other interests like the travel business when I retired.

When I retired, the seniors gave me a retirement party on my birthday. I knew the seniors were going to give me a retirement party at the community center, but I really didn't expect the celebration I received.

How was it different from your expectations?

Although the *hwan'gap* is the sixtieth birthday celebration, not the sixty-fifth, the immigrant Koreans called it a *hwan'gap*. I believe that's because the *hwan'gap* is supposed to indicate a retirement from active life, and although it was my sixty-fifth birthday, that's what I was doing. I also think that because I'm second-generation, American-born, the community decided it was appropriate to make my sixty-fifth birthday the *hwan'gap*. I guess it was a concession to my being American.

Were you involved in the preparations for the event?

Well, I knew a woman from one of the senior citizens' groups was organizing the food and going to do all the cooking. When I found out this woman was going grocery shopping for the party, I insisted on going with her. And when I realized how much food they were getting and how much money they would have to spend, I insisted on paying for the groceries. I just couldn't let them pay out of their pockets.

The seniors initiated the event. They knew that my part of the program at the center was ending, and I was turning sixty-five, so this was, in fact, my second retirement. My sixtieth year was really rough, and I wasn't in the frame of mind for any celebration. I was in mourning then. And since I didn't have a *hwan'gap* party when I was sixty, the seniors thought it was a good time to have it then.

But in terms of other preparation, I guess the Community Center coordinated the entire event. Just the decorations for the party alone must have been a lot of work because it was pretty elaborate. Min, the Korean artist, made all the signs in beautiful calligraphy to hang on the walls. She also arranged the ritual table with all the oranges and persimmons, and all piled up the way it's supposed to be. I don't know the rules, but apparently she did. The senior groups sent floral pieces, and so did the consul general's office. I was really overwhelmed at all the attention that I was getting.

Geez, so much work. It really was something. I know the seniors were spreading the word. But then, announcements of the party got into all the Korean papers. Reporters from all the Korean newspapers showed up that day. The Korean TV crews showed up, too. I remember a newscaster asking me to come outside to the sidewalk so he could interview me. The place was too crowded for them to do it inside. I think there were over three hundred people at that place. I was just overwhelmed. I think my son, Tommy, also arranged for someone to videotape the entire event so that I could have a copy for myself. I don't know when I'm going to ever look at it again, unless it's something like this, where someone else wants me to look at it with them.

Were there any special concessions that you made for the event?

When it came near time for the retirement party, I decided to wear my *hanbok* [traditional Korean dress]. It seemed right because I was retiring from service to the Korean community. I didn't buy the *hanbok*. I got it from one of the Korean clients. I guess she wanted to thank me for what I had done.

One day she asked me, "Do you own a *ch'ima chogori* [Korean skirt and blouse]?"

I said, "No, but they are beautiful."

"I'll give you one."

"No, that's too much trouble."

"Please don't say no. I want to give you one."

I finally accepted. How can you refuse a gift from a person who feels indebted to you? There wasn't much I could say to that, so I agreed to it. Then she asked about my favorite color and size and all that. And in a couple of months, she brought me this beautiful white *ch'ima chogori*. I was speechless when she brought it to me. So I wore that because it was part of my life with the Korean community.

I later found out that it was the right thing to wear by Korean standards. You're supposed to wear white to the *hwan'gap* if your parents have passed away, and since my parents aren't with us anymore, it was the appropriate clothing. I chose white because I've always like the look of a white *ch'ima chogori,* not because I knew that was what the customs were. Anyway, it was nice that my idea matched those of the Korean custom.

Can you tell me about the people who came to the celebration?

When the celebration got under way, I was really surprised. I had thought that the guests would be primarily family members and Korean seniors. And indeed, the Korean network showed all the children that did show up on the TV news. But I think my children were surprised because they didn't even know the people who came. Apparently my niece Lorna came with her boyfriend. Afterwards she called me and said, "There were so many people that we couldn't get in. So we left." And then people that did show up wanted to meet my family and take pictures, so I introduced them to the family members that did show up.

My husband didn't come. It was supposed to be a birthday party that the seniors were giving to me, and since he didn't know the seniors, he didn't come. When you're doing social work, you don't talk about your own family; so even if I'd been working with these people all that time, some of them didn't even know I had a family. I know Tommy was involved in the planning of the party, but my other children weren't really involved in the planning. They heard that I was going to have a birthday party, so they were invited and they happened to come. So they were as surprised as I was when the event got under way.

And all the seniors were there. At that time there were two Korean citizens' groups. There used to be just one, but one of the officers of the group wanted to become president. When his bid for the presidency failed, they had this huge fight at the center, which required police intervention. This officer left the senior citizens' group in a huff and formed his own senior citizens' organization. Seniors from both of the groups were resentful of me because they thought that I should only help members from their senior citizens' group. But I told them, "No I can't do that. I'm a social worker who helps everybody no matter what group or what church they go to." People from the two groups didn't even talk to each other after that split, so I was surprised to see members of *both* senior citizens' groups there having a good time.

It wasn't just my family and the Korean Seniors who came. The Korean consul general—I don't think he came, but he sent a representative with a gift and a plaque for me.

There were just so many people I didn't expect. There were people I'd helped years ago at when I was at the Department of Employment who came—you know, Koreans who had since established themselves in their professions. And so many people made speeches. I remember one couple that I had helped over ten years before the event, and he made a little speech.

He said, "I have never forgotten Dora Kim for all the help that she has given me and my wife and my family when we came from Korea. Dora referred me to job training, and the job I still have now at the Bank of America. I've been too busy with my own life to contact her, but when I heard that she was having a *hwan'gap* party I knew I had to come as a show of my appreciation." He came with his wife and brought me a beautiful gift. Some of the seniors that I worked with didn't know that I had worked in the Department of Employment and had helped all these professionals. They were surprised to hear that.

There were so many people from all areas of my life who showed up, from the Korean Center years as well as much earlier. I don't know how it happened. Colleagues from the department somehow heard about it and they came. People from various churches came. People from Kimochi came. My Chinese girlfriend Tillie and Japanese girlfriend Kemi from childhood came. I guess Tommy must have contacted them. At that time I was active in the Business and Professional Women's Club, and some people from BPW came. They were interested in seeing the Korean customs.

There was another surprise. I didn't even know about it until Tillie, one of my Chinese girlfriends from childhood, called me over and said, "Gee, this is wonderful." I said, "What?" And she showed me a pamphlet that they had made in honor of me. Min had made a pencil drawing of me in the front. I looked through it for the first time when Tillie showed me. I was shocked. I didn't know what to say. I didn't even know they had made the pamphlet. I thought it was really nice. They did a good job.

Tommy, who was, and still is, the director of the Korean Community Service Center must have gone through a lot of trouble to put it together. I think he must have asked Min to see what she could do in terms of artwork. I didn't know anything about it, but they put a short biography of me and my family in it, and included pictures from my childhood as well as recent photos. I remember Min, the artist, coming over to Fontana and taking pictures of me. And a couple of the pictures that she took then ended up in the pamphlet. A couple of the other pictures were ones that she had taken before. I thought whoever did the layout did a beautiful job. That must have been Tommy who organized that. I know I'm his mother, but I didn't expect it. I was really honored that everyone went through so much trouble.

Then after the party, people told me that there were so many people at the center that the party spilled over into the street. The entire place was open, even the garden, but there still wasn't enough room. People came and went for the entire afternoon. I don't know how many people came, but I think it was in the hundreds, over three hundred, maybe more. All day the center was full, and people continued to come all day.

The seniors, Tommy, the people at the center, and the community members really coordinated it well. They call it a *hwan'gap*, I call it a retirement party. It doesn't matter what you call it. It was a real honor.

Reflections

Dora was surprised at the magnitude of the *hwan'gap* / retirement party and at the number of people who came out to acknowledge her assistance. Although she is aware of the number of lives she has touched in her life, for Dora helping others is just an integral part of doing what is right, not something remarkable for which she deserves recognition.

I do not think that Dora can comprehend the enormity of her life's work. Dora grew up knowing that being a Korean female placed severe limitations on her. Practical and productive, she learned to focus on the possibilities in the present. Dora is extremely gifted at problem solving— crafting possibilities where others might not see any options. Without social or political aspirations, Dora simply acted on her desire to help others less fortunate than herself. Consequently, Dora sees herself as an ordinary person trying to live in compliance with her moral imperative. She understands the myriad of things she has done for others as fulfilling duty and obligation, or, as she puts it, doing what had to be done.

And while each of Dora's actions falls within the range of common acts of kindness or ordinary acts of duty, when one person's actions affect so many people, it is a remarkable feat, worthy of recognition.

CONCLUSION

Doing What Had to Be Done

Summer 1992

IN many ways I've had an ordinary life. Like most of the girls from Chinatown that I grew up with, I got married and had children. Growing up, most of us worked in our parents' businesses. But we didn't really think of that as real work. For us, real work meant working in an office in the financial district. We thought that was glamorous. However, for us girls from Chinatown, working in the financial district was just a dream. I don't even think we really thought about what working outside our family businesses entailed. It didn't take long to realize that those dreams were not available to us. So when we were young, we focused on getting married and having children.

My life has been different from my Chinatown girlfriends', because I ended up working.[1] I ended up having a career outside Chinatown after I had my first child. I don't think it was really that unusual to want both a family and a career. But wanting something is different from going out and doing it. I think most of my friends were content to raise children without having to work as hard as their mothers had. It was a luxury to be able to stay home and raise the kids.

Finding work outside Chinatown wasn't easy, and I was rejected many times. My life work as a social worker certainly wasn't a career I intentionally embarked upon. I started out as a typist at the California Department of Employment, and eventually managed to become a social worker. It's funny—initially I was barred from working because I was an Oriental female. As it turned out, sometime in the early 1970s, my career actually became dependent on my Korean heritage. I was one of the few people who could work with the influx of Korean immigrants who came after 1965. And for me, the experience with the Koreans really shook up the way I thought about my heritage.

169

When I think about my life, it's as if I've lived in many different worlds. The world has really changed in my lifetime. Not only have there been advances in our standard of living, my life has been marked by the opening up of possibilities for Orientals in America. This isn't to say that racism is gone. My entire life has been a struggle against racial and sexual discrimination. In my lifetime I've washed dishes at my parents' restaurant in Chinatown and ridden in presidential motorcades. I've been prevented from leaving Chinatown and have traveled all around the world. I've known garment workers as well as international lawyers and businessmen. Looking back, I've had a very full life. But I think my early years really stuck with me. In those days we had to struggle for survival—not just in terms of making a living as Orientals in America, but also in terms of maintaining a positive sense of who we were as Koreans, one of the minority Asian groups clumped in with the Chinese in Chinatown. When you have to struggle for survival, you learn that there are things you just have to do. And that's how I've lived my life. Through it all, I just did what had to be done.

The conclusion of this book analyzes the meaning of "doing what has to be done" over Dora's life, and how this survival strategy evolved throughout her life. It explores the mother-daughter dynamic that laid the foundations for "subversive obedience," a form of resistance based on notions of filial piety—familial devotion that transcends duty to serve purposes that extend beyond traditional definitions of family. It also discusses the strength it takes to engage in subversive obedience, an everyday form of resistance, and questions the characterization of everyday forms of resistance as weapons of the weak. The conclusion analyzes Dora's hwan'gap which finally brought her into the mainstream of the Korean American community, and elevated her life of subversive obedience into a version of cultural heroism.

In framing her life in terms of "doing what had to be done," Dora instills her life narrative with moral imperative. Dora was seventy-one when we started recording her life story, and she had maintained a room of her own for eight years at that time. I do not know how Dora might have constructed her personal narrative at earlier times in her life. The personal life story is constructed in early childhood, sometime after the third year of life[2] and successively revised throughout life. As life unfolds, the life narrative is modified to bridge the gap between expectations and actual experience. Cohler, who examines the meaning of significant others across the life span, notes that this may be particularly true in later life. In old age, the essential other may not necessarily be a person, but a narrative of one's historical self.[3] Butler claims that there is a universal process called life review that older people go through in later life to settle their accounts, the way they lived their lives.[4] While claims to a universal process of life review cannot be empirically substantiated, there are people across cultures who review their lives in old age.[5] In Korea, as well as in India and other parts of Asia, there is precedent for people to go into the monastery in their later years to contemplate their lives. In later life, reminiscence and the ordering of one's life may, indeed, be a source of solace and morale building.

The hwan'gap celebration, the Korean version of the rite of passage into old age common to many Asian societies, is not directly related to the psychological process of life review or creating a coherent personal narrative. However, the collective process of rendering virtue and coherence to a life creates a focal point from which to think about a life narrative. The convergence of personal, cultural, and psychological elements may influence people to utilize life narrative as a vehicle to reanalyze their experiences. Like other hwan'gap celebrants I interviewed in Seoul and San Francisco, Dora freely discussed the tension between elements of the public life narratives and personal life renditions.[6] These tensions are the very materials that an elder has license to revise in old age.

While it was not our purpose at the outset to sort through unresolved issues, the recounting of her life forced Dora to confront some problematic disjunctures in her life. In an attempt to relay a coherent narrative to me, she often worked through various moral dilemmas that resulted from conflicting moral codes: Oriental versus American in her early life, Korean versus Oriental in her young adulthood, and American versus Korean in the latter half of her life. In mediating incompatible social systems and their differing values, Dora was exposed to feelings of entitlement and injustice on the part of people from various strata of society. As such, the larger issue with which she grappled in her adult life was the juxtaposition of privilege and privation—the issue that shaped the moral ordering of her life.

Having been awarded a hwan'gap by the Korean American community, her life was recognized, in part, as that of a virtuous woman who had fulfilled her duties as a gendered entity. The qualities most venerated in women are obedience and self-sacrifice, and that which marks a Korean woman as virtuous is to have acted as a dutiful daughter, wife, and mother. Since fulfillment of these roles is limited to the private, familial realm, there is little reason for her to be awarded a public celebration; that is, unless a woman has a large extended family network or happens to be born to a distinguished father, marry a prominent husband, or raise an ambitious son. Since Korean families in the United States do not have the vertical nor horizontal depth of their Korean counterparts, women are not regularly awarded public celebrations.[7] Nonetheless, the hwan'gap is an important life stage marker, for it formally designates the end of gendered social duties. There are, of course, examples of unusual women whose obedience and self-sacrifice have been directed toward community, whose efforts have made a significant difference to communities. Dora fits into this latter category.

*As mentioned in the Introduction, the post-*hwan'gap *period is a time when both men and women become elders or living ancestors free to pursue interests previously restricted along gender lines. The* hwan'gap *celebration not only marked the community's acceptance of Dora as elder, but as news of this event spread, she started being recognized by San Francisco city and California state organizations, Asian American groups, and Korean government offices. With her accomplishments, Dora brought attention to the margins between spheres of cultural authority, transforming the margins to a central site. Dora has moved beyond the liminal spaces she has occupied as a second-generation Korean woman born of first-wave Korean immigrant parents. As a Korean American elder, she now feels that she has license to speak out in a way with which she was previously uncomfortable. Dora casts herself against the youth, and worries about the state of her community. Dora confided, "If you live long enough, you become history." This is in sharp contrast to the way she sees the majority of young people today: "If you talk about something that happened last year, it's ancient history." From the perspective of this Korean American elder, if you live long enough, you can become a forgotten living ancestor.*

Dora's concern about young people today is grounded in her experiences growing up. She found the ability to understand the past and use it to create a vision of the future to be essential for creating meaning in life. Dora believes this is particularly true for issues of ethnic identity, and she has struggled to weave different cultural threads into her life. Dora grew up during a time when non-Asians believed Orientals were either Chinese or Japanese. As a Korean, she found herself not only contradicting others' inquiries of "Are you Japanese?" or "Are you Chinese?" but having to explain where Korea was and why Koreans constitute a separate people. Since the influx of large numbers of Koreans to the United States, being Korean no longer elicits curiosity; the questions Dora now faces are "How long have you been here?" or "How come you speak such good English?" from both Koreans and non-Koreans. Because her parents immigrated to the United States when relatively few Koreans did,[8] Dora has always felt like an ethnic anomaly, not easily placed. This forced her to confront the notion of a usable past as an essential component of ethnic identity. Dora feels that it is important to leave younger Koreans Americans with as much historical information as possible so that they can build usable pasts for themselves.

However, it is not just the ahistorical youth that concerns Dora. The telling of Dora's story coincides with a revisionist trend within Korean America, and multiple versions of the Korean American past have emerged. While versions of the past vary, the multiplicity draws attention to the Korean American commu-

nity's desire for coherence despite its diversity. According to Myerhoff, "When cultures are fragmented and in serious disarray, . . . individuals . . . seek opportunities to appear before others in light of their own internally provided interpretation."[9] *In the last thirty years the composition of the Korean American community has changed dramatically. Currently about 90 percent of its members are Korean-born. Among this majority of Koreans in America, there are many in the community who are unaware of the first wave of Koreans to the United States. In fact, there are numerous versions of Korean American history that focus only on post-1965 immigrants. Dora fears that if she does not get her story out, the stories of the first wave of Korean immigrants may be lost. Dora is contributing to a larger Korean American project that gives voice to both the ancestors of early Korean migration as well as the more recent Korean pioneers.*

SUBVERSIVE OBEDIENCE: MOTHERING CHOICES FOR THE DAUGHTER

Reflecting the legacy of the Korean Confucian family system, Dora's refrain, "doing what has to be done" captures the obligation and duty of an obedient woman. Obedience, the first lesson in filial piety that Korean children learn, governs Confucian social relations between ruler and ruled, old and young, male and female. Implicit in obedience is the naturalization of unequal personal and social relations. Matters of gratitude, obligation, and indebtedness are determined by one's position in the hierarchy. For females, this translates into lifelong deference to the wishes of men—first to fathers and/or brothers, then to husbands, and finally, to sons.

While Dora's parents abided by these principles and socialized their children to these "facts" of life, migration to the United States also opened counterpossibilities. When Man Suk Yum brought his picture bride over to San Francisco in 1921, the Korean Methodist church was the center of the small immigrant community. The church served as a social and educational center for culturally and socially disenfranchised Koreans and their American-born children, as well as the headquarters for the Korean Independence Movement.[10] *In its formative stages, the church was still a fluid structure in which women were able to assume active roles. Ilse [first- or immigrant-generation] women who migrated to Hawaii and the mainland United States between 1910 and 1924 have been characterized as "assertive and decisive in domestic and public (church) matters."*[11] *For women, participation in church affairs also led to involvement in the independence movement. This not only allowed them to develop a strong political awareness, but taught them the importance of social activism. Nonetheless, women's contributions in the public arena were still structured as acts of obedience and self-sacrifice, qualities consistent with traditional ideals for womanhood.*[12]

In keeping with new possibilities of virtuous Korean womanhood in America,

Hang Shin dedicated herself to the church and the independence movement. But she was also a devoted wife and mother whose household was structured along more conventional Korean lines. As the pakat orun [outside adult], Man Suk mediated all legal transactions such as lease agreements, mortgages, and land purchases, which generally involved large sums of money. Hang Shin Kim, the chip saram [house person], was allotted a monthly budget with which she managed all household finances such as groceries, clothes, and daily expenses for the family. Her labor contributions were critical to the household income but did not alter the conventional Korean economic arrangement. The only money that Hang Shin Kim had for her own purposes was what she could save from the household budget.

Dora characterizes her father "like other Korean men"—as "distant, authoritative fathers of whom children are afraid." Hang Shin was responsible for all household affairs, including raising the children, and Man Suk did not communicate directly with his children. Since all messages were relayed through his wife, through reinterpretation and misinterpretation, Hang Shin had considerable power to influence and subvert the patriarchal order. And there are clues that while she told her children what was absolutely forbidden, she also negotiated freedoms for her children, particularly her daughter. For example, instead of keeping Dora at the restaurant all day, as her husband wanted, Hang Shin encouraged Dora to read by giving her breaks to visit the library. And while the monthly savings were not a large sum, in ten years she had saved enough to buy a piano for Dora. Although there were practical advantages to investing in her eldest child, as Dora would be able to assist her sooner than her sons, she also made special efforts to ensure that her daughter would have opportunities that she, as a girl in Korea, had not had.

While language and cultural differences limited the scope of her own public participation to the immigrant community, Hang Shin did not lose sight of the possibilities for Dora. She conferred on Dora the hope for fuller participation in American society and directed her to take advantage of opportunities available "only in America." While the ideas that Hang Shin imparted to her daughter were modern, the vehicle for their inculcation was not. Under the guise that most parental directives were from her husband, the first and most important lesson in virtue Dora learned from her mother was that obedience to the parental authority, particularly her father's, should not be questioned. This lesson is deeply instilled in Dora, and she defers to her father, beginning her own narrative with her father's entry into the United States. But it is her mother's voyage to America that captures Dora's imagination.

Dora accords her mother agency in her marriage choice, envisioning Hang Shin as a twenty-one-year-old girl in Korea deliberating over and selecting the man who would be her husband.[13] This is despite the fact that she characterizes her mother as "just a subservient woman," and understands women to be "virtual slaves" in Korea from the stories she has heard. The specifics of her mother's marriage arrangements are not known, but the more common tale she heard in childhood from her mother and her Korean picture bride friends is one of lack of choices and compliance to parental wishes. Dora's contradictory rendering of her mother's marriage to her father reflects her understanding of Korean gender relations. Dora tacitly recognizes women's abilities to maneuver within the cultural norms to gain control over their lives despite directives that compel virtuous Korean women to be obedient and compliant.

Consequently, despite Dora's presentation of her mother as passive, there are hints that Hang Shin stood apart from her contemporaries and was not "just a subservient woman." Unlike other Korean women, who typically bore more than five children, Dora's mother controlled her fertility.[14] Using space and Korean childrearing practices as her rationale, she insisted that she and her husband sleep in different rooms after the birth of her third child. She allotted one of the two bedrooms in their apartment to Dora, the only daughter and oldest child. The second bedroom was reserved for her and her nursing infant. Her husband and second child George were relegated to the living room. It is not clear if Hang Shin and her husband ever shared a bed again. What she did tell her daughter was that she had decided to stop having children after the third child. While Hang Shin constructed motherhood as a requisite for womanhood, she did not embrace the enterprise uncritically and took the necessary steps to control her fertility. Later, when Dora was pregnant with her third, her mother criticized her harshly, saying, "Two is plenty." As if trying to excuse her inability to live up to her mother's standards, Dora commented that in her childbearing years, barring abstinence, there was no adequate means of birth control.

When Dora describes her parents' educational aspirations for her, she assumed that both her parents, "like most Korean parents," wanted their children to go to college. It is not true that most Koreans of that era wanted their daughters to go to college.[15] While some families may have wanted to send their daughters to college, very few could afford to send even their sons to college. In fact, in many immigrant Korean families, daughters were obliged to work so they could help pay for their brothers' educations.[16] More likely than not, it was Hang Shin Kim who negotiated that privilege for Dora before encouraging her to continue her education.

When Tom asked Dora to marry him, she "jumped at the chance," fearing that she might not meet another single Korean man to her liking. At that time, Tom Kim worked as a merchant marine on the line between Honolulu and San Francisco and could have settled in Honolulu or San Francisco. Dora simply states that they settled in one of the units below her parents in the Mason Street building. When questioned about that decision, Dora responded, "My mother *thought I would be lonely when Tom was at sea so she thought we should settle in the apartment upstairs from her." Once again compliance with parental wishes serves as the rationale. However simply Dora presents it, Hang Shin must have negotiated with her father. Man Suk was a man raised in a culture in which responsibility to daughters ends upon their marriage.*

Hang Shin Kim, on the other hand, appears to have wholeheartedly supported the arrangement as intimated by Dora when she explains that it surprised her mother's women friends that Hang Shin embraced her son-in-law as part of her family. While Dora attributes this behavior to her mother's compassion, I believe that Hang Shin had a larger vision. If she could persuade Tom to stay in San Francisco, Hang Shin Kim could spare Dora the hardship of being separated from her natal family. While little is known about Hang Shin Kim before she arrived in San Francisco, what is known is that in Korea daughters did leave their parents' homes and separate from their family of birth. And for most picture brides, the separation was traumatic since most never saw their families again.[17] It is likely that Hang Shin worked to ensure that Dora was not subjected to the difficulties of a new bride entering a new kin group, knowing that continuity of kin affiliation could afford Dora a social and personal strength not available to her, or many other Korean women.

Since Tom spent so much time away from San Francisco, Dora had license to structure her life for herself and had considerably more freedom than the women of her age who grew up in Chinatown. After the birth of her first child Tom, her mother began to tell Dora that she would raise the children so that Dora could go to school and get a job. Not only did she tell Dora "two is enough," in order to counteract the social pressure that privileged motherhood over work, she also told Dora that she would not make a good mother. While her mother's insistence started her on her career path, Dora's ability to maintain a career was also contingent on her husband's work as a merchant marine. With an absent husband who could not dictate terms, Dora could take her mother's advice and explore professional options for herself in various fields, which in her case meant passing the test for a real estate license and completing the coursework for nursing.

Unlike other married Korean women who might have been criticized by their mothers-in-law for seeking work outside the home, Dora "did what had to be done"—she obeyed her mother. While it was highly unusual, her mother's open encouragement allowed other Koreans to interpret Dora's actions as eminently filial. Community members attributed Dora's eventual success in securing employment to Hang Shin Kim. However, there were also repercussions from Hang Shin's actions. After her mother's death, one of her mother's Korean friends expressed surprise that Dora could keep her family fed and clothed without her mother's support. This seemingly innocuous comment reflects the talk there had been about Dora and her mother, that Hang Shin Kim had encouraged Dora to pursue a career without regard to her training in domestic matters.

HONORING CHOICES FOR THE MOTHER

While her mother's death devastated her, it was the death of Dora's father in 1955 that precipitated her family's move out of Chinatown. No longer able to evoke filial duty, Dora adjusts the logic of "doing what has to be done" to her mother's reasoning—from filial responsibilities to motherly obligations to her children. Since Dora had two more children and relied on a live-in baby-sitter to help with her young children, there were three new members in the household. Dora cites space considerations as the primary reason for moving out of Chinatown. Dora's understanding of space needs for the family, like her mother's, is grounded in the view of families as corporate entities, and privacy is not a construct she employs for herself in considering living space. On the contrary, the new four-bedroom house did not provide any more privacy for Dora and her husband as they shared the master bedroom with the two younger children. Space needs referred specifically to the children: particularly her adolescent daughter's need for her own bedroom and the lack of accessible playgrounds for her two young children in Chinatown.

Despite practical reasons for moving, the move marked an ideological transition for both Dora and Tom. Instead of feeling isolated in the "American" neighborhood as they feared before the move, family members settled easily into a new pattern of having increased choices and personal liberties. For the first time family members started making decisions based on personal preference without legal or social constraints. Dora and her family began to structure their lives according to the standards of American society—the ethics of autonomy. Tom Sr. joined the Masons; in 1965 Dora reapplied and was admitted to the San Francisco Real Estate Board, an organization that had rejected her application in 1946 because "Orientals weren't allowed to join"; the children began befriending "Americans"[18] and started participating in previously restricted activities such going to summer camp; the family started going on nonorganized vacations such as cruises and trips to Tahoe—then unheard-of for Orientals. Given the lack of ethnic organizations, the Kim family was not regulated, as were the Chinese or Japanese satellite communities, to continue ethnic associations.

Despite the ease with which the family adopted the ethics of autonomy as their modus operandi, and the apparent success with which both generations of Kims integrated into the nonethnic organizations and activities, issues of race and ethnicity continued to shadow them. Recalling her own self-consciousness about her Korean heritage in Chinatown, Dora stated, "I didn't impose Korean traditions on my children. I didn't want my children to feel that they were torn between two or three cultures." In keeping with their new surroundings, Dora raised her younger children to think of themselves as American and did not instruct them about their race or ethnic heritage. This, however, did not make things any easier for her children. They were still prohibited from joining activities based on their race, and continued to be questioned about their ethnic heritage—questions they were unprepared to handle.

While her family was on Dewey Boulevard, the Johnson Immigration Act of 1965 changed the demographic makeup of people immigrating to the United States. People from Asia who had previously been excluded started to trickle into the United States. The trickle gradually grew into a major flow, with one in three immigrants to the United States being Asian.[19] Strategically situated as an employment officer in the California State Employment Service, Dora was asked to help with the influx of non-English-speaking Koreans who were coming in for social services. Dora frames her initial involvement with Korean immigrants as part of "doing what had to be done," a response to a directive from her manager, her duty to a superior. However, Dora also understands her charge as an opportunity to mediate a fair chance for the new immigrants, immigrants who reminded her of her parents. The combination of a sense of duty to superiors and the chance to fulfill filial obligations offered a powerful incentive.

The influence of the social milieu during this period was significant in shaping her relationship with the incoming Korean immigrants. The civil rights movement foregrounded issues of inequality, and social unrest forced this issue into the consciousness of Americans, whether or not they wanted to be aware of it. For Dora, these issues were brought home by her eldest son, who was heavily involved with the emergent Asian American movement. With the growing awareness of racial inequities in American society, Dora took on the problems that faced new Korean immigrants as an assault to her sense of justice and equality. Dissatisfied with the services provided by the State, Dora began to spend her free time championing the rights of individuals of Korean descent. It did not take long for her to become aware of the differences between the new immigrants and the small San Francisco Korean community with which she was familiar. In a quest that combined both professional and personal interests, Dora decided to visit Korea to "see where these Koreans were coming from" as well as explore her Korean heritage. By her reasoning, she was "doing what had to be done," this time to enhance the quality of services she could provide for her brethren, the Korean immigrants.

While Dora realized the younger Korean immigrants' situations were new to her, the older Korean immigrants, particularly the women, continued to remind her of her mother, who died before ever really achieving "old age," thus denying Dora the opportunity to care for her. Dora focused on immigrant Korean seniors, and she assumed the directorship of the Senior Center located in the first Korean Community Center that she cofounded in 1976. Years of working at the state

Department of Employment had given her the background to launch that project. The social services provided by the center were crucial for the adjustment of the first wave of Korean immigrants to the San Francisco Bay Area after the 1965 Immigration Act. However, the continuing flow of immigrants eventually transformed the San Francisco Korean community, and the very condition that had contributed to the founding of the Korean community center also led to its downfall. As immigrant Koreans established themselves in San Francisco, the community began to take on the trappings of the Korean middle class, to which the majority of the immigrants had belonged. The service center that had helped them adjust to the United States was no longer seen as adequate for the community. Immigrant Koreans started their own social organization and service centers that more adequately reflected the class background of the new immigrants. This, however, has not diminished her work with older immigrant Koreans. Her primary interest is, and has always been, centered in service—"doing what has to be done."

MOTHERING A FEMALE LINEAGE

The women that Hang Shin Kim nurtured have averted the fate of the Confucian Yi society ideal of the "nameless woman."[20] *Although girls are named at birth, nameless women are so called because a woman's name is never used. Women are identified in relation to their men as "some man's daughter," "some man's wife," or "some boy or man's mother." The calling of a woman as a man's adjunct reflects the ideology that a woman's existence should be totally immersed in her men. For a virtuous woman there is no self, only self-abnegation.*[21] *Hang Shin Kim undermined that Confucian Yi society ideal for herself. While she may have been referred to as some man's daughter, wife, and mother in her lifetime, her descendants do not remember her that way. In raising her daughter differently, Hang Shin Kim gave herself voice through her daughter and through me.*

Dora has followed her mother's example in raising her children, paying particular care to her daughters. She encouraged her surviving daughter to make choices for herself, and to do whatever she wanted. That her daughter did not decide on her career in child welfare until her mid-thirties did not bother Dora; Darlyne had a husband and son to care for. Unlike her mother, Dora did not discourage Darlyne from her responsibilities as a mother, and did not tell Darlyne that she would be a bad mother. She did not have to. Dora's was the last generation to embrace large families. Like my mother, Dora believes that having children is an important experience for women and worries about women who may not experience motherhood. She has even commented to me, "I know motherhood may not be your bag. It really wasn't mine either. Women like us aren't meant to sit at home. Still, you really should have children. I know the husband thing is a lot of trouble, but children need fathers. And having your own children, at least one, is an experience that shouldn't be missed. There's nothing quite like it."

For Dora and Darlyne, as for other second- and third-generation Americans who must mediate dual or multiple cultural and social systems, the adaptation of existing narratives into new forms is essential for self-construction. It is under the auspices of obedience, compliance, and duty to parents that Hang Shin Kim made the space for Dora to shape her own life beyond cultural limitations. In following her mother's recommendations, Dora's form of obedience subverted the patriarchal text that constrained women to the private realm. Since men held all the positions of authority, prestige, and power within the Korean American community, Hang Shin encouraged Dora to find herself a place outside the community. Not surprisingly, community members initially attributed her success in her job to her mother's management of her domestic affairs. Later, when Dora began to work with immigrant Koreans in the late 1960s and early 1970s, her success was attributed to her commitment and self-sacrifice. Commitment and self-sacrifice, attributes valued in Korean women, proved helpful in her work with Koreans immigrants. It was only after the hwan'gap, when all vestiges of a woman as a reproductive commodity were shed, that Dora received the accolades that she deserves for her work with the Korean immigrant community.

In terms of finding a place in the world, Dora asserts that women eventually "just decide to do something." But this depends, in large measure, on the ways in which work can be reconstructed as womanly. The requisite qualities for social service are remarkably similar to those that figure in alternative Korean women's narratives. In Korean society, the shamanistic healing arts are one place that spirited, unruly, or defiant women can make a place for themselves. The legend of Princess Pari (Pari kongju), one of the mythical founders of Korean shamanism, celebrates the spirited woman. The legend tells of a king who wants an heir (son). When his seventh daughter is born, the king orders Princess Pari to be thrown into the water. As she is about to drown, a turtle rescues her and delivers her to heaven. Princess Pari, a pure and generous soul, lives gracefully in heaven. Many years later, Princess Pari hears that her parents have died of old age. Wanting to rescue them from death, she goes through indescribable efforts to return to earth and resurrect her dead parents. When her father is revived, he asks Princess Pari to return to the family and live with them in the palace. Instead of returning to her rightful place, Princess Pari refuses. She has learned that she prefers to heal the sick and protect people from evil. Despite the ferocious, warriorlike manner with which Princess Pari comes to her parents' rescue, the qualities exemplified in this legend are still self-abnegatory: selfless healing, and giving to and acting for others.[22]

In order to be effective, both the shaman and the social worker must be strong guardians of the weak, helping and protecting others from harm. While social *service does not require healing bodies per se, a social worker is often called upon to access care for the sick and the vulnerable. So while Dora and her daughter have found places in the world, as Hang Shin Kim would have wanted, theirs is a place that fits into the narratives available to Korean women. Each successive generation of women has taken Hang Shin Kim's selfless devotion and obedience (albeit subversive) to another level—Dora has broadened it and applied it to the interface between Korean Americans and American society. Darlyne has further expanded the cause to which she is committed—underprivileged American children.*

In the United States, social work, like teaching, public relations, and other occupations, can be reconfigured as "womanly" professions, and attracts many women of Korean descent. It is interesting to note that in the late twentieth century, these women are more likely than not to disregard as folly Korean women's shamanistic rituals of empowerment and resistance.²³ This is in spite of the fact that these rituals carry underlying messages that empower women to resist patrilocal practices.²⁴ While some shamanistic patterns have been integrated into Christian practice, since the Korean American communities of the first half of the twentieth century were predominantly Christian, there was no venue for such activities. However, with the influx of Korean immigrants after 1965, shamanistic practices have filtered into the lives of second- and third-generation Korean American women. Still, social workers and other women of Korean ancestry who have learned to be warriors in the workplace are resistant to these practices. It is not that the work of these "feminized" arenas is antithetical to Korean shamanistic practices. Rather, these feminized occupations are functional equivalents of shamanism in the Korean American context.

EVERYDAY FORMS OF RESISTANCE—WEAPONS OF THE WEAK?

The most significant break from Korean practice that Hang Shin was able to craft for Dora was her resistance to the conventional Korean patrilocal custom of severing ties with her daughter at marriage. Instead of giving up claims to their daughter, she maintained a fierce bond with Dora, encouraging and assisting her in seeking her place in American society. Under the guise of obedience to filial authority, Hang Shin created an alternative to the Korean male lineage— the start of a line of Korean women who would achieve beyond social and cultural expectations, and be recognized for their accomplishments outside conventional daughter/wife/mother designations.

In its outward compliance to conventional but contrary purposes, subversive obedience could be categorized as a form "of disguised, undisclosed resistance to material domination."²⁵ Although Hang Shin embraced American egalitarian notions as a liberation ideology, she lived her live within the confines of a male-dominated, Confucian-influenced Korean immigrant enclave, without access to mainstream society. Nonetheless, Hang Shin persisted in reshaping her possibilities in terms of American ideology, even though the only uncontested avenue available for her to express her new sense of being in the world was Dora. Hang Shin's encouraging her daughter to earn her own living counters the more conventional ideal of Korean womanhood in the early twentieth century, and could be constructed as an "everyday form of resistance," [26] *a strategy of disguised and undisclosed resistance, a "weapon of the weak," if strength is measured in terms of material and social capital.* [27]

Although Dora heard Hang Shin's repeated admonitions about duty to self and her encouragement to assert herself in the world, Dora discovered that subversive obedience was also a more effective survival strategy for herself. Located at the intersections of multiple, overlapping spheres of cultural authority, [28] *Dora traversed between the often contradictory ethos of various milieus. However, she did not experience these systems as closed. Rather, definitions of virtue within each sphere became interrogative and subversive in the matrix of multiculturalism, and she learned to selectively play the standards of one cultural system against another, evoking affiliation and nonaffiliation to each system, as circumstances required. For instance, as being Korean did not enhance her social standing among her peers, Dora evoked the authority and vernacular of American mainstream society, crafting herself as an Oriental in Chinatown. However, when it was convenient, Dora purposely used her Koreanness as an excuse, as she did when she did not want to join her girlfriend in playing mahjong. And when she wanted to go against her parents' wishes, as she did when she dated non-Korean men, Dora evoked Americanness as the rationale for her actions. While these actions could have been viewed as resistant to one or another system, by carefully selecting the cultural system to which she would abide, Dora could always position herself as an obedient subordinate.*

In contrast to her position in her youth, Dora's place in the world changed in her midlife. Not only had the social context of subordination altered, she had the resources and social standing to command attention without subversion. Additionally, by the end of World War II, the material restrictions placed on Orientals had diminished. While there is still economic and ideological discrimination against immigrants from Asia, particularly those without material or cultural capital, this is not the case for Dora. With her career earnings, the property her father left her, and the investments she made, Dora was and is by no means materially oppressed. Nonetheless, Dora continued to defer to her husband and played a role similar to her mother's—she took charge of household finances and the raising of the children. But Dora was neither the conventional wife nor mother. She continued to earn her own income, and her idea of managing her home and children was to employ a full-time baby-sitter to cook, clean, and look after her children.

The cultural cachet she carries in her later life, as a prominent San Francis-can, is also not small—her community involvement and her work with immi-grant Koreans from the late 1960s to the late 1980s has given her a voice with which to influence public policy. However, for the most part, Dora continued to present herself as a lucky subordinate who just happened to be at the right place at the right time. And when Dora established a room of her own outside the house in 1983, a decision that her husband did not censure or even oppose, she insisted on maintaining the semblance of cohabitation with her husband in a single residence for non–family members—as if knowledge of this arrangement could diminish her effectiveness in the community. Even the process of telling this life story, a narrative Dora was ready to share, was framed in such a way that she could maintain the stance of the passive and compliant giver. And de-spite disclosures in her life story that may suggest that she could do otherwise, Dora continues to engage in forms of subversive obedience.

Dora grew up a minority within a minority and was raised on the resistance movement against Japanese occupation in Korea. She also struggled against ra-cial and sexual discrimination in the United States throughout her life. Now, as a member of the relatively small cohort of Koreans descended from the first wave of Koreans, she sees her Korean American cohort becoming increasingly margin-alized within the predominantly immigrant community. For Dora, subversive obedience is not just a survival strategy tied to her subordinate position in the first half of her life. Defined more by what she is not, rather than what she is, resistance in and of itself emerges as a life theme. According to Scott, resistance is comprised of "survival strategies that deny or mitigate claims from appropri-ating classes."[29] Operating from the margins of multiple spheres of cultural au-thority, Dora's continued use of subversive obedience is one way that she has resisted the various identities foisted upon her by the different groups she has encountered throughout her life. As a subject, agent, and object, Dora's resistance emerges from her inability to comply with any one cultural system. Dora found her niche as a community activist, as one whose existence calls into question the values and beliefs of any mainstream. She thrives on causes and situations that destabilize the very idea of normative.

The creation of meaning in Dora's life is, and has been, in locating and resisting successive practices and embodiments of the dominant other. Her con-struction of the dominating group, however, does not bear upon her personal associations. While she has experienced discrimination, Dora has made strong alliances with people of all backgrounds and does not conflate her causes with people she knows personally. From childhood the oppressive other has been name-less and faceless, and over her lifetime the oppressing other has shifted.

Whether the oppressors are "those Japanese who occupied Korea" or "those white people" or "white men," they are distant and faceless; neither Dora nor the people she tries to protect have directly confronted them. Indeed, Dora's continued use of subversive obedience seems tied to the continual construction of some dominant other that she must resist. With resistance as a core value and way of being, Dora has developed the reputation of being something of a folk hero like Robin Hood, a righteous shaman or a good social worker, championing the rights of the weak. Although such forms of resistance seem to avoid confrontation, they are not weapons of the weak. Dora's success has depended upon her ability to assess complex power relations in continually changing sites of power and oppression, while struggling against complacency. Dora was able to apply the moral imperative of filial piety to other situations, showing remarkable virtuosity. What Dora was able to accomplish in her lifetime certainly speaks to a ferocious commitment and strength of spirit.

THE MAKING OF A CULTURAL HEROINE

While Dora is aware of her stature in the Korean community, her construction of her hwan'gap *reveals a lack of understanding of the cumulative effect of her life's work. Although she has an understanding of the number of lives she has touched, until the* hwan'gap *celebration, neither she nor community members saw Dora as a part of the community. Positioned as marginal to the community when she was actively involved with providing services for the immigrant Koreans, Dora was delighted when she heard that the Korean seniors, as well as community and family members, were planning a retirement party for her. Initiated by Korean immigrant seniors, the celebration took on a momentum of its own as various individuals and groups vied to participate in the planning of the event. Through careful negotiations between multiple spheres of cultural authority, Dora's life in the margins was repositioned to the center.*

It was the Korean immigrant seniors who initiated the hwan'gap/*retirement celebration. In the United States it has only been since the mid-1970s that adult children sent for their aging parents in Korea, and it was not until the late 1970s and early 1980s that the older constituency of the immigrant Korean community became more visible in active roles in church organizations as well as mobilizing and forming their own senior citizens' groups.[30] Despite the formation of community bases, older immigrant Koreans feel the dislocation of being cut off from their country of birth. For them, the discontinuities of living in the United States are sharp. In the San Francisco Bay Area immigrant Koreans do not live in close geographic proximity to one another. While family members within the area still maintain regular contact, in the new setting many miss the close contact that they once shared with extended and lifelong friends. Additionally, shifts in language and education threaten cultural continuity between generations of the same family.*

Older Koreans who have few witnesses to validate their individual claims to have lived a worthy life seek situations in which they can publicly dramatize and ritually display versions of themselves and their disrupted histories.[31] *That many expect cultural extinction because their Americanized progeny will be unable to carry forth their traditions further fuels this desire. Of particular significance at such events is the inclusion of age peers so they can validate their lives within the context of a collective experience. Groups of Korean seniors in San Francisco meet weekly under the auspices of senior citizens' associations and mark every occasion possible, whether it's a Korean observance of the liberation from Japanese rule, a Christian Christmas party, the anniversary of a senior citizens' group, a group member's seventieth, eightieth, or ninetieth birthday, or a sixtieth wedding anniversary.*[32] *Drawing upon their repertoire of Korean rituals and symbols to construct such events, these celebratory occasions are deemed "Korean" in some fashion. While there is often disagreement over form, ritual enactments invoke the primacy of being Korean, attesting to the strong need among older immigrants for circumstances in which their often outdated or obsolete versions of Koreanness can be articulated. The seniors who initiated Dora's celebration conceived of her retirement as an opportune occasion for such a gathering, and in planning Dora's retirement party, Korean seniors drew upon their repertoire of ritual and decided to called it a* hwan'gap *celebration.*

The hwan'gap *denotes retirement from activity into a more contemplative life stage. As a historically established practice, the protocol for the* hwan'gap, *the first in a series of many family rites of longevity, is written up in Korean manuals of etiquette and form.*[33] *The* hwan'gap, *as with other rites of passage, incorporates a three-part progression of separation, liminality, and reaggregation that marks transformations in the initiate's status and age.*[34] *First, introductions to the celebrant, usually an oral life narrative of the celebrant's accomplishments, identifies and separates the initiate. Liminality is then established through an honoring rite that echoes the Confucian practice of ancestor memorial services. The ceremonial core, in which junior family and community members offer wine to the initiate and then bow, signifies the filial duty of descendants to honor, respect, and care for an elder in her first step toward becoming an ancestor—a family deity.*[35] *Finally reintegration as a full member of society is established through the sharing of food and testimonials that corroborate the virtue of the initiate's life. Testimonials not only validate the qualities of a life well lived within the context of community, they also then objectify and externalize the same qualities as a traditionally constituted version of a life well lived.*

Actual practice, however, has always diverged from the protocols for celebration. Since the hwan'gap *incorporates the accomplishments and life circumstances of the celebrant, gatherings have always integrated differential scopes and sizes of social worlds, as well as varying positions within the social order without transgressing convention. Additionally, since increased life expectancy has pushed back the onset of old age and the rite of passage into that stage of life until age seventy, the* hwan'gap *has evolved into primarily a celebration of a person's life accomplishments.*[36] *As such, there is considerably greater latitude as to what is acceptable for* hwan'gap *celebrations. Seniors certainly took this creative license to fit Dora's retirement into the* hwan'gap *format, resurrecting and highlighting the retirement feature of the* hwan'gap *for the purpose of this particular celebration.*[37] *This adaptation was considered particularly appropriate for Dora since she had not been given one at age sixty. While Korean seniors felt that the cumulative loss of three close family members warranted a long mourning period that precluded celebration, since the inauspicious circumstances were behind her, they felt that a special celebration for the retirement of a woman of her accomplishment was warranted.*

While the seniors initiated plans for this celebration, they felt they did not have the power to follow through because of the critical importance of children's involvement in the planning and enactment of a hwan'gap *party.*[38] *As a family-based production, they needed family members to cosponsor the event. Hence, they sought support from her son Tom, who enthusiastically agreed to participate in organizing an event to honor his mother. Tom and the seniors decided that the Korean Community Service Center of which he is director would be the best venue for the event since his mother cofounded it. Since the center can accommodate hundreds of people, Tom and the seniors decided to expand the guest list to the all members of the Korean community, escalating the scale of the celebration beyond a gathering of family and senior citizens. While the planners wanted to honor Dora, each also had their own reasons for supporting the expanded audience for the event. The seniors were pleased because they would have an opportunity to validate their position before a much larger cross-section of the Korean community than just age peers. Tom also had another agenda; as director of one of many Korean community service organizations in the area, he also took this as an opportunity to promote the center since Korean community members would visit the center and familiarize themselves with its functions.*

The seniors agreed to integrate Tom's vision of the event into the planning and were pleased with themselves for having appropriated a family ritual for Dora's retirement party; they proceeded to manipulate the activity to give it the appearance of an untampered act of filial piety. According to Korean seniors, her son was unaware of the premium placed on the filial nature of this occasion, and wanted to share credit with the seniors for organizing the event. The seniors, however, adamantly insisted that they were "just helping," and insisted that Tom act as the nominal head of planning. The seniors understood their ability to carry off this event in terms of a fourfold message: first, by couching the retirement in terms of a hwan'gap, *it demonstrated and differentiated practices* for Korean elders from non-Korean old people in the United States; secondly, admitting a prominent figure like Dora into the ranks of elders gave them an opportunity to advance the position of the elder before a Korean constituency; thirdly, that a third-generation Korean American would celebrate his mother's hwan'gap sent the message of the persistence of Korean practices; finally, as an American-born director of a center serving a constituency increasingly dominated by immigrant Koreans, Tom's involvement would deploy a message of filial duty, a message many immigrant Koreans could interpret as a sign of Tom's Koreanness and his ability to serve the immigrant community.

Together Tom and the Korean seniors targeted prominent members of the Korean American community from whom Tom sought support. Both the seniors and the staff of the Korean Community Service spread the work among Korean constituents. Aware of Dora's service and contributions to the Korean American community, dignitaries of the Korean community such as the Korean consul and various Korean American organizations leaders such as the president of the Korean Residents' Association, the reverends of various Korean churches, as well as directors of other community centers were quick to offer support for the celebration. Leaders of competing senior citizens' centers coordinated with members of the Korean Community Center to delegate different areas of responsibility from food preparation and service, music and entertainment, ritual accouterments and decorations, to the celebration agenda. Finally, announcements were placed in Korean language newspapers as well as publicized at the Korean senior citizens' centers meetings and other public venues.

In the meantime, Tom and staff members of the Korean Community Center consulted Dora to construct an appropriate life narrative to include in a program designed for the occasion and surreptitiously sent out a photographer to take pictures of her for the cover of the program. Tom also contacted family members, such as his siblings and various younger relatives such as grandchildren, nieces and nephews, and invited them to commemorate her hwan'gap. Being third- and fourth-generation Korean American, most of them framed this event as a retirement/birthday party. In thinking about the hwan'gap as a birthday party, family members urged Tommy to invite non-Korean friends and colleagues from various times and areas of Dora's life.

When the seniors heard of the inclusion of non-Koreans on the guest list, some did not appreciate what they perceived to be an invasion of outsiders; they had not envisioned an event for anything but a Korean constituency, which had its own diverse and competing factions. Concerned with their need to make statements about themselves as older immigrant Koreans, they had planned for the event to highlight issues of old age within the Korean community. In talking about the way plans for Dora's celebration evolved, many seniors felt that it was only at exclusively Korean events that participants could freely assert and nego-

tiate the often conflicting multiplicities of Korean ethnicity, identity, and society. According to Korean seniors, the inclusion of non-Koreans foregrounds the need for a simple, more rudimentary symbolic statement about the position of Koreans in the broader American context. And indeed, given the increasingly diverse ritual constituencies invited to celebrate Dora's hwan'gap, one of the primary tasks of the event was persuasion that the ritual was not made up.[39] *To accommodate this diversity, the Korean cultural symbols employed referred to the most basic common denominators of belief and experience such as ambiance and accouterments, allowing participants their own interpretations.*

Despite initial dissent, since the hwan'gap *ultimately honors the life of the celebrant, the seniors understood the inclusion of non-Koreans as essential and reframed their inclusion as a sign of prestige. The presence of a relatively large contingent of non-Korean Asian Americans had a particularly interesting affect on Korean American community leaders. While Japanese and Chinese American community leaders acknowledge high levels of discord within their own communities, their historical experience of racist policies in the United States has taught them that it is essential to appear united in the face of a hostile society. Not only is the appearance of an ethnic group as a united body helpful in seeking public resources, among most Asian American groups, collective harmony is highly valued and maintained at group assemblies.*

The immigrant Korean community is perceived by other Asian community leaders as one that is unable to contain internal conflict for the collective good, and Korean community leaders have come under criticism for their inability to control their immigrant constituency. Aware of the allegations made against them, and the importance of countering this impression of immigrant Koreans, community leaders negotiated with their respective constituencies to present a harmonious ethnic front for outsiders. The event was orchestrated to leave a convincing impression of a cohesive cultural group through the demonstration of social connections and the symbolic identification with Korean culture. However, associative patterns among Korean guests revealed that cohesive behavior was understood as the appropriate action at public, plural ethnic gatherings. Conforming to the frictions and factions that exist in the San Francisco ethnic community, American-born Koreans and immigrant Koreans interacted minimally, and members of various warring factions were careful not to speak with one another to avoid disagreement at the ritual event.

While the inclusion of non-Korean participants encouraged a type of "good behavior" unlike other such occasions I attended in Seoul or San Francisco which were restricted to Korean constituents,[40] *like other* hwan'gap *rituals, there was much strategic negotiation in the planning and enactment. Although organizers rely on guests' foreknowledge of gift giving and reciprocity when plan-*

ning such events, events that are deemed successful are those in which guests or participants are apprised of both minor and major changes that are often made to protocol. Often those who are left out of the planning process seem unable or unwilling to appropriate the changes to form; not only are they likely to compare the activities to rigid interpretations of historical practice, they feel free to make claims that rituals are "not believable" and "inauthentic"[41] Although assaults to "tradition" and "authenticity" are the language of dissent, efficacy does not result from a predefined criteria of ceremonial components or the ritual agenda per se. Rather, it is the ability to hold open lines of communication with participants throughout the planning of the event which provides judgments of "authenticity."

Organizers of Dora's hwan'gap sought and took counsel from community leaders in the planning of the event, and informed them of plans for the event. Since prominent community members can disseminate information rapidly to their respective constituencies, guests were informed about the inclusion of outsiders and made aware of possible changes to practice. Advance notice empowers even the most casual participant because it constitutes informed consent, and prepares guests to attribute some sort of cultural logic to the proceedings. In actuality most public hwan'gap practices in urban America can be deemed "inauthentic" when measured against those in urban Korea. The very idea of an older Korean having a community function in the United States rings false because most are recent immigrants who do not have enduring ties to community.[42] Given that Korean definitions of community include extended family and lifelong friends and associates, it is only the rare celebrant who has sustained lifelong contact with ritual participants outside family members. In fact, only a deeply entrenched American-born person, such as Dora, could have the family and community base for an "authentic" celebration.

Despite the presence of an "authentic" body of ritual constituents at the gathering, the ceremonial core of the hwan'gap, the offering of wine and bowing to the celebrant by younger family members and commemorators, was conspicuously absent. The omission of the ceremony, an unusual departure, was not contested. One senior simply stated that "it was a concession to the fact that Dora is American-born." Another senior mentioned, "It would have been embarrassing for Dora, her family, and the Korean participants if her children attempted to bow and got the form wrong." Additionally, because this event included non-Korean participants who could grossly misinterpret both the form and function of the ceremony, there was a tension among Koreans that the honoring ceremony might be perceived as quaint or backward. As one teenaged Korean girl noted of Dora's function, "I'm glad they didn't do all that bowing stuff." Overlooking the obvious changes to practice, most Korean guests gener-

ated some cultural rationale for the proceedings. For the immigrant Korean constituency, the efficacy and authenticity of Dora's hwan'gap *was negotiated well in advance, in the planning of the event.*

While the various reasons given for the exclusion of the honoring ceremony are accurate, the omission is also embedded in reasons other than those stated. For immigrant Korean participants who are primarily Christian and Catholic[43] there were religious grounds for discarding the ceremonial component of the hwan'gap. The parallel between ancestor memorial services and the honoring ceremony is an obvious one. Ancestor memorial services are viewed by churches as the honoring of false gods and are forbidden, and Christian Koreans have eliminated the honoring ceremony in family rituals because of the association with ancestor worship. The practice of offering wine is further complicated because of clashes in symbolic meaning. In Christianity and Catholicism drinking wine is associated with drinking the blood of Christ, not the honoring of an elder. The elimination of the honoring ceremony is part of the religious transformation of cultural practices.

Given Korean media attendance and the number of guests who wanted to capture the moment on camera, a formal photo opportunity and the singing of "Happy Birthday" replaced the honoring ceremony as the central ceremonial activity of the hwan'gap. The taking of photographs and videos to capture ritualized activities for personal and public viewing has become an integral part of such events, and Dora posed with family members and friends expressly for this purpose. It was during the photo session of the family that her husband's absence became apparent. According to Dora, his absence was fitting because from his perspective, as a second-generation Korean who integrated into the larger society and not the Korean immigrant community by choice, Dora's commitment to the community had detracted from his life. When Dora started working with Korean immigrants, she found it impossible to limit their access to her, and the Kim household received emergency calls at all hours of the night and day, interrupting the household. According to Dora, her husband felt that she had sacrificed the personal for the public.

However, her husband's absence was not noted as unusual by most participants since most had never had occasion to meet or hear of him. Instead, guests remarked on the large family presence at the occasion as commemorative family photos were taken. Not only do visual reproductions become part of family memorabilia, in this particular event it was also the medium through which the event would be represented to a more general public. As video and camera crews took footage throughout the event, guests became increasingly aware that this event might broadcast nationally on Korean television, and might even be picked up by news networks in Korea as a social interest story. This gave added incentive for guests to make a display of "good behavior" throughout the event, not only for outsiders, but to put on a cohesive front for Koreans in other American locales, as well as friends and acquaintances in the United States and Korea. The success of Dora's celebration speaks to the importance of purposes. Dora's hwan'gap was a rite of passage into old age that celebrated retirement from her life's work. It marked her transition from coordinator of the senior center, or chip chu in,[44] to volunteer coordinator. However, the efficacy of any ritual event always go beyond fulfilling stated purposes; there is also the long-term impact on the celebrant and ritual participants, as well as its impact outside actual practice. On the personal level, this event was a rite of passage into the community of Korean elders. While her relationship with the immigrant community is ambivalent, and she often speaks of "those Koreans" with exasperation, the hwan'gap opened up an alternative way of being old for her.

Dora is acutely aware of the model of the old person who, in the larger American context, is devalued, and she addressed this issue: "It's difficult when you grow old here. In the last ten years I've had my purse ripped off twice, and while crime is getting worse, I also think it's because as an older woman, I am more vulnerable. As an older woman you become invisible to those who used to offer help, and a target for opportunistic people." As part of the Korean community she is valued not only for her contributions to the community, but simply because of her age. Younger people automatically behave deferentially, and the language is structured in a way such that the oldest are awarded the most honorific speech. Additionally, while older Koreans are the economic leaders of the community, older immigrant Koreans are viewed as cultural symbols because of their knowledge of Korean cultural practices. While Dora is not seen as a symbol of Korea, as an older second-generation Korean American, she is viewed as the symbolic bridge between Korea and America.

Dora's personal tragedies added another dimension to the participants' responses to the event. Public knowledge that she had experienced personal tragedy tapped into a common Korean sensibility that life is difficult and has to be survived. The loss of a child holds symbolic meaning for older members of immigrant communities. Intergenerational differences between Korean parents and their Americanized children often result in the loss of children, emotionally and culturally. Dora's continued commitment to the Korean immigrant community despite personal difficulties elevated her life to exemplary status, a symbol of transcendence of the personal for the group. Her disregard for "petty politics," a position that marginalized Dora from various factions within the community during her twenty-four years of community work, was also reinterpreted as proof of commitment to a larger cause. Dora's hwan'gap negotiated this collective definition of a social example, a life well lived, and Dora was objectified as an embodiment of a cultural example. This ritualization constructed new Korean visions of a life well lived, a life of social and moral significance.

Participants believed that the dominant messages that had been negotiated in Dora's hwan'gap were homage to Korean culture and a celebration of Dora's life. Both immigrant and American-born Koreans who participated in this event attempted to evoke "traditional form" to the best of their abilities. However, in tailoring the event to Dora's life circumstances, participants conveyed a different message. They participated in an event that was neither Korean nor American. Age sixty-five is significant by American standards of retirement, while fifty-five is the age of retirement in Korea. However, the choice of age sixty-five for a hwan'gap is fitting because in negotiating cultural meanings, American-born Koreans must deal with both the influence of the culture of origin, be it real, reinterpreted, or mythical, as well as the demands of the larger society. Dora's hwan'gap addressed this dilemma, and created new forms and meanings within the loose parameters of a traditional ritual. This ritual was the first of this scale in San Francisco that paid homage to Korean American culture as separate from Korean or American culture.

The impact of messages negotiated in the celebration extended beyond its practice. Most participants learned the full range of Dora's accomplishments at this event. In addition to learning about the numerous awards she had received, participants learned of the courage it took to achieve what she had over her life. Not only did she marry and raise five children, Dora was one of the first Korean women to attend the University of California at Berkeley, one of the first Asian woman to get a California Real Estate License, as well as the first Asian woman to work on a career track at the California Department of Employment. Widespread knowledge of the full range of Dora's accomplishments was a by-product of this event. And in 1987, Dora was further honored with the Woman Warrior Award from the Pacific Asian Women's Bay Area Coalition, an award that was named for Maxine Hong Kingston and given to accomplished Asian American women in various fields. Additionally, the extensive Korean media coverage that focused not only on Dora's contributions but also on the number of people who came to honor Dora from multiple service areas in and out of the Korean American community brought Dora's accomplishments to the attention of South Korean government officials. Shortly thereafter, Dora Kim was nominated for the South Korean President's Medal for her efforts on behalf of Korean immigrants, the highest award given a Korean civilian. In 1989, Dora Kim became the first noncitizen woman to win the award, gaining formal recognition from Korea for Korean American womanhood.

Loose Ends

THE epilogue is a compilation of outtakes from various inter-
views and conversations that we had between 1986 and 1995. Dora often intro-
duced what I understood to be loose ends into our conversations—stories and
comments unrelated to the themes we were exploring in the particular interview.
These outtakes provide valuable insights into the issues she was grappling with
at the time of the telling. Topics covered include the high rates of intermarriage
among her descendants, growing old, the legacy she hopes to leave for her family,
and the business she hopes to take care of before she dies. The outtakes are
organized dialogically into a final narrative entitled "Loose Ends," a phrase she
uses to describe the things in her life to which she still needs to attend.

You often speak of your life as a response to external influences, in terms of
"doing what has to be done." Were there things you sacrificed in order to do
what had to be done?

I don't know that I would call it sacrifice. When you call it sacrifice, it
sounds pretty bad. There were plenty of compromises, but I think I did
the best that I could and made the only choices I could live with.

And in spite of the hardships, I feel like I've had tremendous opportunity in my life. You have to experience life, and I feel I have. It's only after
you've experienced things that you can speak about them. For example,
I'm a pro-choice person because I've seen the terrible consequences of
unwanted children. I don't understand how people can be otherwise if
they seriously consider the effort it takes to raise an unwanted child. It's
such a waste of everything—energy, time, money. But I also wonder
about some of the so-called feminists who are pro-choice. Some have
never had children, and I wonder how much contact they have with the

real situation. I'm a bit suspicious of people who come out so strong. I think it's one thing to believe in something or understand things through reading, but it's another to know something through experience.

Are you saying that we can't learn except through experience?

No, there are many ways to learn things, but for me experience is the best teacher. And I feel fortunate that I've been able to do so many things in my life. It's taught me to do a range of things competently although I'm not an expert in any one area. When I think of myself, I feel like I'm a Jack-of-all-trades, master of none. I can cook, I can sew, I enjoy playing the piano. I never wanted to be an expert and I've gotten by fine.

I don't know about that. You seem to be an expert in living. . . .

You know, going through my life and telling you about it has been an experience for me. The past seems so close to me—my childhood, my youth. And I'm a great-grandmother now. Time really flies. It blows my mind so I don't think about it too much. I find that hard to believe. I think, "Gee am I living that long? I must be old to be a great-grandmother." But some of my girlfriends don't even have grandchildren yet.

I'm in my seventies. Sometimes, I shake my head at that. Years ago that was considered so old. But I don't feel that old. When I was younger, I thought it was old, but I don't feel that way now that I've gotten here.

I still look through the want ads in the paper sometimes, and I want to apply for some of the jobs. Then I catch myself and think, "Hey, they're not going to hire you at 70-something." I also see the school catalogues and the new majors they have and think, "I want to major in everything." I still want to go to school and study the things I haven't had a chance to, just for interest. I would love to take some Asian American Studies classes.

While you lived through more constrained times, you've had quite a few opportunities.

I realize that, in many ways, I've had more opportunity than many women of my generation. That was my mother's influence. She really pushed me to go to work because she wanted me to have the opportunities she didn't have. She used to say that I needed to be able to work in case something happened to my husband or if I left him. But I was a product of my times, and over my life, I never seriously thought about leaving Tom. It simply wasn't an option. But since I worked, I am now aware that if something did happen to him at this point, I have my own social security and pension. That does provide a security that I would not have pursued had my mother not pressed me into it. She really was far ahead of her time in terms of thinking.

I wish I had the kind of vision for my grandchildren and great-grandchildren that my mother had for me. I sometimes wonder how they'll manage in the world, especially in terms of finding life partners. When I was younger I did not even imagine all the different combinations of ethnic backgrounds for marriage. I didn't even think about it, because there was no choice. During the time of the war, one of my mother's friends used to complain to her, "I have chop suey in my family." My parents didn't want that, so I had to marry a Korean or not at all.

As I've said, I don't feel one way or another about who my children marry. But I remember once my daughter came home and told us, "A black guy asked me out. What do you think?" I believe her father told her, "If you go out with him, nobody else will ask you out." At that time this was true. Both the Asian and Caucasian boys would have stopped asking her out. So we let her know what the consequences of that might be so she could make her own choice. She didn't go out with him, because, at that time it would have been difficult.

But when Tommy's son—my grandson—got married, his best man was black. He grew up with this kid, and they're still best friends. There were a lot of Koreans at his wedding but he didn't care. Your best friend is supposed to be your best man. I have to give him credit for his convictions. I think it's good. But you know how the Koreans think. They think it's terrible. But that's how it goes.

When it gets down to it, I really don't care who my children marry, as long as they know what they're up against. I guess my children figured that out, because not one of my children or grandchildren married a Korean. My great-grandchildren are even more racially mixed than their parents. Why, if you want to get technical, my great-granddaughter is a fourth Japanese, a fourth Korean, a fourth unidentified European American—her mother was adopted—an eighth Scottish, a sixteenth Chinese, and a sixteenth Filipino. What does that make her?

Actually, in some ways, it might be easier for them than it was for me because they're so obviously mixed it will be hard to stereotype them. That they're different is really of no surprise to people who meet them. It could be a real advantage if people can't make certain assumptions about you.

And despite discrimination and difficulties, I've always been fortunate in that I've had choices. If you feel like you've chosen your life, it's a lot easier to be accepting of yourself as well as those around you. In fact, one of the more remarkable things in my life is that I started to have a lot more choices as I've gotten older. And while it isn't conventional wisdom, there are advantages to being older. I remember the first family picture we took when we first got married, and there were maybe a dozen people from my family and my husband commented, "I came from Korea all alone and look at how large the family is." Well, in the last picture that we took, there were dozens of us, and that is just the immediate family, children, their wives and husbands, and their children. That's the good part about being older. There's a sense of being part of something much larger than yourself, and that's rewarding.

But your attitude—it's so refreshing.

Sometimes. My attitude goes up and down. I think my attitude is better now than it was when I was younger. That's because I know myself better now. But I wasn't brought up that way. I didn't think to do anything for myself until after sixty. I felt a lot of fear. Like many women, I was afraid that the man was going to say something. And the fact is that neither my father nor my husband have ever said anything to encourage me. So I didn't come into my own until I was older.

For me, having that studio apartment for myself was a turning point. It was there that I finally had the chance to know myself better, and set limits for myself. At home, on Dewey Boulevard, I have to consider everyone else. And that's usually okay, but it can also wear me out. It's really helpful to have a place of my own. Sometimes I just have to go home, to my own place, to rest and recuperate. I'm really comfortable there. Then I'm ready to handle whatever comes my way.

Many people fret about getting old. So, are there other advantages to being older?

I think the greatest advantage I've had, and I've been fortunate in this way, is that as I've gotten older I've been able to go back and take care of loose ends.

What kinds of loose ends are you talking about?

As I mentioned, when we were younger, we were so busy just managing our lives that we were just going from one thing to another. We didn't really have the time or energy to consider what we wanted to do. Well, when I started living on my own in 1983, I decided I wanted to go back to school and get my B.A. School was one of those things that I had always meant to finish, and with the children all grown, I finally decided to go back and do it.

When I started back again they had new rules for graduation that hadn't existed when I was going to school. You had to pass a math test and an English test. The English test wasn't a problem, but the math test . . . The younger kids can pass that math test, but it's been too long since I took algebra, geometry, trigonometry and all that. I can't pass. I started out as liberal arts. Liberal studies, it's called at State. And then I got up to 135 units. You only need 120 to graduate. And so every counselor I see, they tell me a different story.

Once they said, "Oh you need American History and so you can go to City College and take it."

So I went to City College and I took American history and passed it.

I went back to State the next semester and they said, "You don't need this."

And after many years of this back and forth I finally gave up. I also didn't think I could pass the math requirement. I looked at the questions and I say, "Hey, what is this?"

I was so good at geometry. I used to love to work that out. And I look at it now, and it doesn't really make sense any more. That was over fifty years ago. So I said I gotta find a college that doesn't have so many requirements. I took history, which I don't like. I even took geology, which I don't like. You know to me some of the educational requirements seem pretty silly, but I got everything in. And then in the summer they had a travel industry course that I wanted to take because I'm into travel now. But with all those units behind me already, I just want to get that degree and be finished.

Then in 1988, the people at San Francisco State told me I had completed all the requirements for graduation so they had me come down, get pictures taken, and go through the ceremony. Then they asked me to write something about what I would do with my B.A. And I wrote that I didn't want to do anything with it. I've already done it. There's nothing for me to do anymore except get the B.A.

Then after all that, they said I didn't finish all the requirements. Apparently, the requirements for graduation had changed since I started back. It's a different story every time. So now I'm not sure that I'm going to get that piece of paper.

Of course I could pay somebody seven thousand dollars for a degree, but I don't want to do that. I've completed 135 units now. That's 15 more than required. I just want that piece of paper because I've done the work.

I think it's great that you went back and finished up the coursework for your B.A.

Well, it would be nice to get that piece of paper. But even if I don't, I know I've done all the work. And for me, that's enough. I feel fortunate to have had the chance to take care of that piece of unfinished business.

Are there other bits of unfinished business you want to attend to?

When you get to be my age, the idea of dying becomes a pressing issue. Sometimes I wonder, "Why am I living this long?" I'm the only one. My mother died at fifty-five, my brother George at fifty-seven, and my brother Henry at fifty-three. They all died in their fifties, and I've already reached the seventies.

What about your father? Didn't he live into his seventies?

Yes, but I'm now older than he was when he died. It really makes me feel strange.

Some people tell me, "Well, you have a purpose in life." But that just makes me wonder, "What can that be?" Maybe it was to arrange everyone else's funeral. When my mother died, it was up to me to make the arrangements although my father paid for it. When my father died, I arranged for his funeral. When my two brothers died, I arrange for theirs. I also arranged for my daughter's funeral. No one else in my family has had to deal with it so I don't think they'd have known what to do. I don't know what's going to happen when I die. So I've made some arrangements. That's the reason I bought spaces in the mausoleum for my husband and myself.

I'm afraid of death. I don't know why we have to die. But I know we have to. I sometimes wonder what's going to happen to me when I die. I'm not into furs and jewelry, but on my fiftieth anniversary my husband gave me a beautiful jade piece which is worth two thousand dollars. Then when he went to Hong Kong, he got me custom-made earrings. When I went to Japan I bought myself a pearl necklace. In Thailand, the visit when Tom and I met your parents, I bought a sapphire ring because that's what Thailand is known for. So I have a small fortune in jewelry, although I'm not really into it. I don't know why I bought it except that people said that was the thing to do.

I thought I would keep the jade set because that's sort of dressy for when I go out dressy. I'll give the pearl set to my daughter because she can wear that. When I gave it to her, I told her, "I'm not contemplating suicide." You know they say when you start giving things away it's a sign of contemplating suicide. She laughed. I told her, 'I just want to give this to you to be sure that you got it.'

When my mother died I was in mourning, so I didn't pay attention to material things. Well, my two sisters-in-law came over and took all my mother's jewelry. She had some really expensive jewelry too. I only have one daughter, and I don't want the same thing to happen to her. I tell her, "You can borrow any of this anytime you want." I've gradually started giving things away. I figure after I die, I won't have any say in where it goes. If my son comes and cleans up after I'm gone, he might just throw everything away. I kind of hope that people will leave some of the pictures on the wall even after I die.

Sometimes I wonder what's going to happen after I go. There are so many loose ends to take care of. Who's going to pay all the bills? I wonder if my husband can do it. I've been paying the bills all the fifty-some-odd years we've been married. I used to just put them in my purse, and deal with them when I had time. But lately, I've been telling my family, "Look, in case I'm gone, these bills are in the cabinet in the dining room. These are monthly bills, and these are incidentals." At my age, it's important to make sure that someone can take care of the loose ends when you go. And that's what I've been doing. It's satisfying to know that I won't leave too much of a mess when I go. And you just don't know when you're going to die. That's why death is kind of scary. My stroke was just part of the aging process, and a warning that I should be taking care of business. I suppose I've been fortunate to have that reminder, and the chance to take care of loose ends.

I worry, but life goes on. I guess somebody will take over. I thought my husband could never deal with the details of life, but he's taken over the cooking and shopping, and he does it better than I ever did. Maybe if he had to deal with the other details like the household budget and stuff, he would. Everybody said I would go down after my mother died, but I didn't. In the end, you just have to keep doing what has to be done.

The one thing I have left to complete is my life story. I can write proposals and reports, but I can't write a life story. I'm not a writer. I don't know how to put it together. But I have you, and you want to do it, so everything that needs to get done will get done. I do hope that it can be finished before I go, but even if it isn't, I know you'll get it done.

CHRONOLOGY

1883   Dora's father, Man Suk Yum, is born in Kangwon province, Korea.

1898   Dora's mother, Hang Shin Kim, is born in Pyongyang, Korea.

1903   Korean immigration to the Americas begins.

1904   Man Suk Yum arrives in the United States.

1905   All Korean emigration stops.

1908   Gentlemen's Agreement between Japan and the United States prohibiting immigration of Japanese laborers to the United States

1910   Japanese occupation of Korea begins.

1913   California Alien Land Law passes. Aliens ineligible for citizenship can not own or purchase land.

1920   Hang Shin Kim arrives in San Francisco as a picture bride. She and Man Suk Yum move to Dinuba, California.
California Alien Land Law amended so that land cannot be bought in the name of native-born children.

1921   Dora is born on March 16 in Manteca, California, while her parents are making the move from Dinuba to Chinatown, San Francisco.

1923   Brother George is born in a Chinatown alley.
Dora's father opens cigar stand on the corner of Pacific and Kearny.
Dora's father works with Mr. Lee to open Lee's Lunch on Jackson and Kearny in Chinatown.

1924   Immigration Act barring all Asian immigration.

1927   Father moves cigar stand to corner of Jackson and Kearny.

1928   Dora's parents move to Oakland, California
Brother Henry is born in Oakland.

1929   Dora's father buys Lee's Lunch from Mr. Lee.
Family moves back to San Francisco's Chinatown.

1937   Dora's father buys a four-unit building on Mason Street in his lawyer's name.

1938   Dora graduates from San Francisco's Girls' Public High School.
        Kim family moves into Mason Street building.
1939   Dora begins college at the University of California, Berkeley.
1940   Dora leaves school.
1941   Lifting of land covenants in certain areas of San Francisco around China-
            town area.
        Father sells two units of the Mason Street building, and buys six-unit
            building on Jones.
        The United States enters World War II.
1942   Koreans participate in American Day Parade for the first time.
        Mason Street building deeded to Dora.
        Dora's marriage to Tom.
        Dora and Tom move into unit on Mason Street building.
        Father sells Lee's Lunch.
1943   Repeal of Chinese Exclusionary Act of 1882.
        Birth of first child, Tom Jr.
1943   Father sells building on Jones and buys a fourteen-unit building at Broad-
            way and Jones.
        Dora starts to work as clerk-typist at various insurance companies and
            goes to school part-time.
1945   World War II ends.
1946   Congress passes War Brides Act to ensure reunion of spouses and chil-
            dren of veterans.
        Land covenants officially deemed unconstitutional in San Francisco.
        Birth of second child, Darlyne.
        Dora passes California Real Estate Broker's Exam, one of the first Asian
            women to do so.
1948   Korean consulate opens in San Francisco.
1950   Dora's father buys two-hundred-room Golden Gate Hotel on Kearny.
        Tom and brother George take leaves from jobs to help operate hotel.
        Korean War begins.
1951   Birth of third child, Kyle.
        Dora receives Licensed Vocational Nurse's certificate.
        Father sells Golden Gate Hotel; Tom and brother George return to
            shipping.
1952   McCarran-Walters Act passes, ending exclusion of Asian immigrants and
            granting them naturalization rights.
1953   Dora starts working as a clerk-typist at the California State Department
            of Employment.
        Korean War ends, Korea divided along 38th parallel.
1954   Death of Dora's mother.
        Dora passes the entrance exam for Employment Service trainee at the
            California Department of Employment.
1955   Birth of fourth child, Kerry.

Death of Dora's father.

Dora becomes an Employment Security Officer.

Tom begins with Matson Co. on San Francisco to Honolulu line.

1956   Birth of fifth child, Debby.

1958   Dora buys a home on Dewey Boulevard in a "restricted area" of San Francisco.

Birth of Soo-Young Chin in Seoul, Korea.

1959   Dora takes ESO2 Exam for a promotion at the California State Department of Employment.

1961   Son Tom Jr. weds Arlene. Couple move in with Dora and the family at Dewey Boulevard house.

1962   Birth of Thomas, first grandchild, Tom Jr.'s first child. Tom Jr. and family move out.

1963   Soo-Young's family moves to Singapore.

1965   Passage of 1965 Immigration Act, which eliminated quota system in favor of preference system.

Birth of Eric, second grandchild, Tom Jr.'s second child.

Tom Jr. and Arlene separate.

Darlyne moves in with Tom Jr. to help with children.

Dora finally admitted as a licensed member of the San Francisco Real Estate Board.

1965   Tom retires from Maritime Service. Takes exam for stationary engineer and starts working for the city and county of San Francisco.

Soo-Young's family moves to Bangkok, Thailand.

1967   Darlyne weds Alan Rickard and couple gets an apartment

Birth of Marc, third grandchild, Darlyne's child.

1968   Dora buys a studio unit at the Fontana and rents it out.

Tom and Dora buy a house on Kensington Way and a condo on Pine Terrace.

Soo-Young visits Korea with her family.

1971   Dora visits Seoul, Korea, for the first time.

1973   Dora receives an Adult Teaching Credential from the San Francisco Community College.

1974   Dora visits Korea.

1975   Dora starts working with travel agency.

Soo-Young is sent to boarding school in the United States.

1976   Dora is cofounder of the Korean Community Service Center as coordinator of the Senior Center. Gets funding for Hot Meals Program.

Dora given Award of Merit from the International Association of Personnel Employment Security.

Soo-Young starts college.

1977   Dora becomes a Coro Foundation Trainee in Public Affairs for Women.

In July Dora retires from the State Department of Employment.

Dora starts keeping regular hours at Korean Center.

Dora also starts doing outside sales for a travel agency.

Dora visits Korea.

Soo-Young attends summer school at Ewha Women's University in Seoul, Korea.

1979   Dora becomes vice president of the San Francisco Business and Professional Women's Club.

Dora visits Korea.

1980   Son Kerry marries Nancy and couple live on Dewey Blvd.

Debby moves to her own apartment.

Soo-Young moves back to Bangkok, Thailand.

1981   Dora honored by the City and County of San Francisco for being one of the founders and president of the United Nationalities in San Francisco.

Elected as a delegate to the White House Conference on Aging.

Son Kerry and Nancy move out.

Debby moves into the Fontana condominium.

Death of brother Henry.

Death of brother George.

Death of daughter Debby.

1983   Dora moves into Fontana studio as a second residence.

1984   Soo-Young moves to the San Francisco Bay Area to work on a master's degree.

Soo-Young marries.

1985   Dora begins to do medical interpretations.

Soo-Young enters Ph.D. Program in Human Development and Aging at University of California, San Francisco.

Soo-Young divorces.

1986   Dora's husband, Tom, retires at age sixty-five as chief engineer of water pollution for city and county of San Francisco.

Senior Center loses funding for Senior Meal Program; Kimochi starts delivering meals to site.

Soo-Young starts volunteering at the Korean Community Center.

Dora and Soo-Young meet.

Dora's official retirement from Korean Community Service Center, and the occasion of her *hwan'gap*.

Dora continues to volunteer at the Senior Meal Program at the Center.

Birth of Kerry, Jr. fourth grandchild, Kerry's child.

1987   Kerry and Nancy split up.

Son Kerry and grandson Kerry Jr. move to Dewey Blvd.

Dora awarded Woman Warrior Award by Pacific Asian Women's Coalition.

1989   Dora awarded Korean President's Medal of Honor.

Dora and Tom go to the Asian Games in Seoul, Korea.

Dora and Tom travel to Southeast Asia, visit with Soo-Young's parents in Bangkok, Thailand.

Grandson Michael marries Nancy.
Soo-Young does fieldwork in Korea.
Dora has a stroke. Stops all activities temporarily.
Funding for meal site given to another Korean Center. Kimochi stops delivering meals to Korean Center.
Darlyne gets her master's in counseling.

1990   Dora resumes interpreting at U.C. Medical Center.
Soo-Young spends six months in Thailand writing dissertation, then returns to San Francisco.

1991   Son Kyle Jr. marries Anne.
Grandson Michael marries Nancy.
Grandson Eric marries Cindy.
Soo-Young starts teaching at San Jose State University.

1992   Dora and Soo-Young begin to systematically tape-record Dora's life story.
Birth of Shina, Dora's first great-grandchild, Eric's child.

1993   Narrative takes shape.

1994   Soo-Young moves to Chicago for a one-year postdoctorate fellowship to work on Dora's life story.
Soo-Young's brother is in serious bicycling accident.
Great-grandson Thomas Jordan Kim born.

1995   Soo-Young starts teaching at University of Southern California. Dora has another stroke, goes for rehabilitation, and then starts working again.
Dora given Certificate of Recognition by the City and County of San Francisco for work with Korean immigrants.
Dora given Certificate of Honor from the Board of Supervisors for public service.
Dora designated a "Living Treasure" by a California Assembly Legislature for lifetime achievements in the Asian American Community.
Soo-Young accompanies Dora to the KAM pioneer reunion in Los Angeles.

1996   Yum Family is included in *ReViewing the Past: Finding Family Stories,* a Korean American Museum Exhibit, July 1996–December 1997.
Soo-Young's parents immigrate to the United States to take care of their youngest son.

NOTES

Introduction

1. The General was an older Korean woman who frequented the Korean Community Service Center. Staff, volunteers, and clients of the Senior Meal Program affectionately referred to her as the General because of her authoritative ways.

2. See narratives of seven other second-generation Korean Americans of pioneer families from "Reviewing the Past: Tracing Family Stories" (June–December 1996) in the Korean American Museum, Los Angeles holdings.

3. See Richard R. Shweder, *Thinking Through Cultures* (Cambridge: Harvard University Press, 1991), for a discussion on cultural context of morality.

4. I am indebted to Jon Haidt and Rick Shweder for providing insights on issues of life stage as they relate to ethics of morality.

5. Shweder refers to this type of moral reasoning as falling into the ethics of divinity. See "In Defense of Moral Realism," *Child Development* 61 (1990): 2060–67, in which Shweder counters the developmental notion that issues of autonomy make up the one true natural moral order and asserts the notion of three codes of moral reasoning (ethics of autonomy, community, and divinity) that coexist.

6. See Shweder et al., "The 'Big Three' of Morality (Autonomy, Community, Divinity), and the 'Big Three' Explanations of Suffering, in *Morality and Health,* edited by Allan M. Brandt and Paul Rozin (New York: Routledge, 1997), for an elaboration on the ways in which discourses coexist.

7. I, like James L. Peacock and Dorothy C. Holland ("The Narrated Self: Life Stories in Process, *Ethos* 21, no. 4 [1993]: 367–83) and others, prefer the term *life story* as opposed to *life history* for the purposes of this project because the term *life story* does not make claims to historical accuracy per se. Life stories are constructed and reconstructed through the telling, and again reconstituted in textualization. Since we are dealing with text and not social reality, accuracy is not

of the same import to this writer as is the presentation and interpretation of events and life experiences from Dora's perspective.

8. See L. L. Langness and Gelya Frank's *Lives* (Novato: Chandler & Sharp Publishers, 1981) and Lawrence C. Watson and Maria-Barbara Watson-Franke's *Interpreting Life Histories* (New Brunswick, N.J.: Rutgers University Press, 1985) for expanded discussions on the history of anthropological life research and writing, as well as an elaboration of the problems and methods involved.

9. In 1920 Paul Radin first put forth this notion that if the narrator is carefully chosen, a life story moves beyond the particulars of a life to reveal that which is typical of a member of a cultural group in "The Autobiography of a Winnebago Indian," *University of California Publications in American Archaeology and Ethnology* 16, no. 7, 381–473. Clyde Kluckhohn took up this issue in "The Personal Document in Anthropological Science" (in Louis Gottchalk et al., "The Use of Personal Documents in History, Anthropology, and Sociology," *Social Science Bulletin* 53 [1945]: 178–193) where he critiqued life history method for lacking sampling rigor. The assumption he made was that with larger sample size, validity and reliability of life stories could be ascertained, and elements that constitute a "typical" or representative respondent could be discerned. More recently Stanley H. Brandes, in "Ethnographic Autobiographies in American Anthropology," *Crisis in Anthropology: View from Spring Hill,* edited by F. Adamson Hoebul, Richard Curner, and Susan Kaiser (New York: Garland Publishers, 1982), also dealt with the methodological issue of informant selection in discussing the collection and presentation of life history materials.

10. The issue of anthropologists' impact on the production of a life story was first taken up by anthropologists in the late 1970s. To cite a few examples, Renato Rosaldo wrote about it in "The Story of Tukbaw: 'They Listen as He Orates,'" in Reynolds and Capps, *The Biographical Process: Studies in the History of Psychology of Religions* (The Hague: Mouton, 1976), 121–51. Vincent Crapanzano addressed the issue in numerous works, such as the introduction to *Case Studies in Spirit Possession* (New York: John Wiley, 1977) 1–40, which he coedited with Vivian Garrison, and his life story *Tuhami: Portrait of a Moroccan* (Chicago: University of Chicago Press, 1980), as well as his essay "Life Histories" in *American Anthropologist* 86, no. 4, 953–60. James M. Freeman wrote about the impact of the anthropologist on the life production in the conclusion to *Untouchable: An Indian Life History* (Stanford, Calif.: Stanford University Press, 1979).

11. James M. Freeman and David L. Krantz address the issue of authority in "The Unfulfilled Promise of Life Histories," *Biography* 3, 1–13. Barbara Myerhoff and Jay Ruby also addressed the ethnographer-subject relation as an issue to consider in "The Journal as Activity and Genre," *Semiotica* 30 (1/2) 1980, 97–114, and in the introduction to *A Crack in the Mirror* (Philadelphia: University of Pennsylvania Press, 1982) under the guise of reflexivity. James Clifford takes up the issue in "On Ethnographic Allegory," *Writing Culture: The Poetics and Politics of Ethnography* (Berkeley: University of California Press, 1986) under the rubric of postmodern theory, as do George E. Marcus and Michael M. J. Fischer in *Anthro-*

pology as Cultural Critique: An Experiment in the Human Sciences (Chicago: University of Chicago Press, 1986). In *Works and Lives: The Anthropologist as Author* (Stanford, Calif.: Stanford University Press, 1988), Clifford Geertz also calls into question the authority of the anthropologist to speak for and of their informants, as does Sally Cole in "Anthropological Lives" in *Essays on Life Writing,* edited by Marlene Kadar (Toronto: University of Toronto Press, 1992), 13–127.

12. The term "ethnographies of the particular" was put forth by Lila Abu-Lughod in "Writing Against Culture" in *Recapturing Anthropology,* edited by Richard G. Fox (Sante Fe: SAR Press, 1991), as a strategy against inaccurate and unwarranted generalizations that anthropologists often make about the other from the position of authority. "Clinical ethnography," asserted by Gilbert Herdt and Robert J. Stoller in *Intimate Communications: Erotics and the Study of Culture* (New York: Columbia University Press, 1990) to refer to the full complex of subjectivities in ethnographic experience, also addresses the issue of anthropological authority. Herdt and Stoller caution that the kinds of statements that a researcher can make about a culture is tied to the subjectivity of the researcher, the subjectivity of those that inform her, and data that emerges in that interplay between the two.

13. Crapanzano, *Tuhami: Portrait of a Moroccan* (Chicago: University of Chicago Press, 1980).

14. Laurel Kendall, *Life and Hard Times of a Korean Shaman* (Honolulu: University of Hawaii Press, 1988).

15. Ruth Behar, *Translated Woman* (Boston: Beacon Press, 1993).

16. See Peacock and Holland, "The Narrated Self: Life Stories in Process" for a discussion of the process approach as a way to reconcile the oppositionally situated life-focused and story-focused approaches to life story.

17. See, for example, James Freeman, *Hearts of Sorrow: Vietnamese American Lives* (Stanford, Calif.: Stanford University Press, 1989); Usha Welaratna, *Beyond the Killing Fields: Voices of Nine Cambodian Survivors in America* (Stanford, Calif.: Stanford University Press, 1993); Sucheng Chan, *Hmong Means Free: Life in Laos and America* (Philadelphia: Temple University Press, 1994); Yen Espiritu, *Filipino American Lives* (Philadelphia: Temple University Press, 1995); Elaine H. Kim & Eui-Young Yu, *East to America: Korean American Life Stories* (New York: The New Press, 1996).

18. Akemi Kikumura's *Through Harsh Winters: The Life of a Japanese Immigrant Woman* (Novato: Chandler & Sharp) mainly covers the years after Mrs. Tanaka (psuedonym for the subject) immigrated to the United States as an adult. Sucheng Chan's edited rendition of Mary Lee Paik's autobiography, *Quiet Odyssey: A Pioneer Korean Woman In America* (Seattle: University of Washington Press, 1990), spans Ms. Paiks's entire life, but the subject is an immigrant Korean, not American-born.

19. Brian T. Niiya, "Open-Minded Conservatives: A Survey of Autobiographies by Asian Americans." Master's thesis, University of California, Los Angeles, 1990, 2.

20. Ibid., 24.

21. In-sob Song, in *An Introduction to Korean Literature* (Seoul: Sam Young Printing Co., Ltd, 1970), attributes this to Korea's turbulent history which promoted autobiographical writings of political activists as early as the seventeenth century such as the novel *The Story of Gil-dong Hong* by revolutionary and writer Gyun Ho. He was beheaded for writing the book.

22. Clifford Geertz, "On the Nature of Anthropological Understanding." *American Scientist* 63 (1975): 47–53.

23. Hazel Rose Markus and Shinobu Kitayama, "Culture and the Self: Implications for Cognition, Emotion, and Motivation," *Psychological Review* 98, no. 2 (1991): 227.

24. Marie Ann Wunsch, "Walls of Jade: Images of Men, Women and Family in Second Generation Asian-American Fiction and Autobiography" (Ph.D. diss., University of Hawaii, 1977).

25. While there are autobiographical accounts of Asians written in English, such as Lee Yan Phou's *When I Was a Boy in China* (Boston: Lothrop, Lee, & Shepard Company, 1887), published earlier, Yun Wing's *My Life in China and America* (New York: Henry Holt & Company, 1909), is the first account that grapples with life in both the country of origin and the United States, and marks the emergence of an Asian American autobiographical genre.

26. A list of known titles follows: Etsu Inagaki Sugimoto, *A Daughter of a Samurai* (New York: Doubleday, Doran & Company, Inc., 1925); Kathleen Tamagawa, *Holy Prayers in a Horse's Ear* (New York: Ray Long & Richard R. Smith, Inc., 1932); Sugimoto's youngest daughter, Chiyono Sugimoto Kiyooka, *Chiyo's Return* (New York: Doubleday, Doran & Co., Inc., 1932); Shidzue Ishimoto, *Facing Two Ways: The Story of My Life* (New York: Farrar & Rinehart, 1935); Haru Matsui, *Restless Wave: An Autobiography* (New York: Modern Age Books, 1940); and Sumi Seo Mishima *My Narrow Isle: The Story of a Modern Woman in Japan* (New York: John Day Company, 1941). Wong Su-Ling and Earl Herbert Cressy coauthored *Daughter of Confucius: A Personal History* (London: Victor Gollancz Ltd, 1953).

27. This notion of biographies as illustrative of a cultural or psychological process is grounded in popular readings of biography as well as earlier uses of life story. Elsie Clews Parson, in her anthology *American Indian Life* (1922), used life story as illustrations of Native American culture, as did Paul Radin (1926) in *Crashing Thunder,* who stated that his purpose was to describe a representative middle-aged individual, a life in relation to the social group.

28. Brian T. Niiya, "Open Minded Conservatives: A Survey of Autobiographies by Asian Americans" (master's thesis, UCLA, 1990), 5–7.

29. That *uri* is the preferred and proper possessive pronoun is the linguistic reflective of the importance of relational referents in self-construction.

30. I would like to thank Eunshil Kim, who helped me sort this issue through by discussing Korean translations of Dora's text to see if the problems were linguistic.

31. I would like to acknowledge Melanie Han, a reviewer for the manuscript who permitted Temple University Press to share her identity with me, for this insight.

32. According to Sidney Mintz, "The Sensation of Moving, While Standing Still," in *American Ethnologist* 16 (1989):786–96, life story differs from other forms of ethnographic information gathering in that the owner of the story, in some way, solicits the writer.

33. In *Getting Married in Korea: Of Gender, Morality, and Modernity* (Berkeley: University of California Press, 1996) Laurel Kendall writes that Korean ceremonial events, assessed in Confucian terms, foster the morality and well-being of the people in the context of weddings. It is commonly believed that *hwan'gap* ritual serve similar purposes. Kendall asserts that for Koreans of upper middle class standing, ceremonial events are critical for maintaining status.

34. See Soo-Young Chin, "A Comparative Study of Korean Late Life Rituals: Seoul and San Francisco," (Ph.D. diss., University of California, San Francisco, 1990), for discussion of the *hwan'gap* in a comparative perspective.

35. One of the strongholds of the Korean Independence Movement was located among Korean exiles in the United States, and local Koreans unanimously supported this movement.

36. R. Bellah et al., *Habits of the Heart* (New York: Harper & Row, 1985), 152–55.

37. Sucheng Chan and Mary Lee Paik's *Quiet Odyssey*, Monica Sone's *Nisei Daughter*, Akemi Kikamura's *Through Harsh Winters*, Jade Snow Wong's *Fifth Chinese Daughter*, and Maxine Hong Kingston's *Woman Warrior* are but a few we discussed as models for this project.

38. The list included Shostak's *Nisa*, Freeman's *Untouchable*, Crapanzano's *Tuhami*, Myerhoff's *Number Our Days*, and Behar's *Translated Woman*.

39. Gelya Frank, "Finding the Common Denominator: A Phenomenological Critique of Life History Method," *Ethos* 7(Spring 1979): 68–94.

40. See Frank's review, "Ruth Behar's Biography in the Shadows: A Review of Reviews," *American Anthropologist* 2 (1995): 357–74 for a discussion of the controversy that Behar's final chapter sparked.

Part 1, Introduction

1. Biologistic notions of race have been put forth ever since European explorers brought back stories of strange, dark-skinned peoples from their travels around the world. Biological determinism ran through the scientific research in the 1800s. Racial hierarchy placed Europeans at the top and Africans at the bottom, with Asians in the middle. There was an assumption that "pure" races existed. These notions also permeated social sciences, and found their way into popular notions about race.

2. For a more detailed example, see Lawrence W. Crissman's treatment of overseas Chinese urban structure and its relationship to social organization of

cities in China in "The Segmentary Structure of Urban Overseas Chinese Communities," *Man* 2 (1967).

3. According to Dora, various ministers in the church would evoke the comparison between Korean immigrants in America and Western Christian missionaries in Korea during sermons when addressing issues of discrimination. Also see Mary Lee Paik, *Quiet Odyssey: A Pioneer Korean Woman in America,* edited with an introduction by Suchen Chan (Seattle: Washington University Press, 1990), 12–14.

4. See Michael Omi and Howard Winant, *Racial Formation in the United States: From the 1960s to the 1980s* (New York: Routledge & Kegan Paul, 1986) for a discussion of the foregrounding of race to ethnicity in the United States; Yen Le Espiritu, *Asian American Panethnicity* (Philadelphia: Temple University Press, 1992) for discussions of the development of a pan-Asian identity; and Yasuko I. Takezawa, *Breaking the Silence: Redress and Japanese American Ethnicity* (Ithaca: Cornell University Press, 1995) for analysis of ethnographic data regarding panethnicity.

5. Dora was born just ten months after her parents married, and their marriage is a prelude to Dora's own *myth of creation,* her story of American origins and birth. Gelya Frank rightly asserts that "it is axiomatic that considerable construction of the self has taken place by the time a narrative of childhood is written by an adult" and that "stories of birth and infancy accentuate the possibilities for self-construction and self-creation"(p.1) See "Myth of Creation: The Construction of Self in an Autobiographical Account of Birth and Infancy," in *Imagined Childhoods: Constructions of Childhood in Autobiographical Accounts,* edited by Marianne Gullestad (Oslo: Scandinavian Press, 1995) for further elaboration.

6. See Maxine Hong Kingston's *Woman Warrior* (New York: Vintage Books, 1977) and *China Men* (New York: Ballantine, 1981) for but two of many examples of the reconstructive process among second-generation Asian Americans who seek to construct possible scenarios for their parents' lives.

7. Bong-Youn Choy, *Koreans in America* (Chicago: Nelson Hall, 1979), 72.

8. For additional readings on Korean migration to Hawaii and the United States, see Wayne Patterson's *The Korean Frontier in America* (Honolulu: University of Hawaii Press, 1988). Also refer to Bong-Youn Choy, *Koreans in America,* and Won Moo Hurh and Kwang Chung Kim, *Korean Immigrants in America* (Toronto: Associated University Presses, 1984).

9. There are a few Koreans who did come to the United States after that point, but they are difficult to track as they traveled on Japanese papers and were categorized as Japanese subjects.

10. Refer to Bong-Youn Choy's *Koreans in America* and Hurh and Kim's *Korean Immigrants in American* for additional reading on the history of the Korean church in San Francisco.

11. Choy, *Koreans in America,* chapter 6.

12. Ibid.

13. Sucheng Chan, *Asian Americans: An Interpretive History* (Boston: Twayne Publishers, 1991), 109.

14. See Edward Said, "Reflexions On Exile," *Granta* 13 (1984): 159–72.

15. Victor G. and Brett de Bary Nee, *Longtime Californ': A Documentary Study of an American Chinatown* (New York: Pantheon Books, 1972).

Chapter One

1. This is a reference to the 1965 Immigration Act, which eliminated national quotas and shifted the criteria for immigration to a preference system that favored the reunion of families.

2. It is possible that Mr. Yum came to California as a ginseng salesman, as they were among the small number of Korean merchants who migrated to California.

3. Dora's speculation that her father must have come over with the Chinese is contradicted by the immigration restrictions that prevailed in 1904. The 1882 Chinese Exclusion Act stopped all migration from China, with the exception of merchants, students, diplomats, and their wives. According to his obituary in the Korean paper, the *Kongnip Hyop Hoe,* Man Suk Yum arrived in San Francisco via Hawaii in February 2, 1904. Given Dora's belief that her father never actually lived in Hawaii and Mr. Yum's involvement with peddling ginseng, it is probable that he came to the United States on a ship that only made a stopover in Hawaii, with one of the few visas issued to ginseng merchants from Korea. Mr. Yum might have worked as a section hand on the trunkline in Washington alongside other Koreans recruited by railroad companies (steadier and better-paying work than selling ginseng).

4. When Japan annexed Korea in 1910, Ahn Ch'ang Ho fled to the United States. In 1913, he organized the *hungsadan* in San Francisco, calling for the unification of the Korean people in the belief that spiritual and military preparation would be essential for Korea's liberation. Ahn Ch'ang Ho was the primary organizer of the independence movement in San Francisco, the *kungmin hoe* [the Korean National Association], around which the community was organized. In 1919 he was elected as a cabinet minister for the Korean Provisional Government located in Shanghai, but he tired of the infighting and returned to the United States to work with the *hungsadan.*

5. *Peyang* is the way Pyongyang is pronounced by people from that region. Pyongyang was the largest city in the northern portion of Korea before Korea was divided. It is presently the capital of North Korea.

6. Dora fixes the age difference between men and their picture brides based upon the age difference between her parents. However, since the Korean community in San Francisco was small, Dora used photographs from her childhood to recall each couple's names and their ages.

7. In 1907 the Gentlemen's Agreement between the governments of Japan

and the United States stopped the migration of laborers from Japan. After 1907 the phenomenon of getting married to women via proxy in Japan started so that laborers could bring their "wives" to the United States. This practice continued until 1924 when all migration from Asia (the Philippines excepted, as it was a protectorate of the United States) was stopped. In the meantime, Japan had established Korea as a protectorate in 1905, taking over her foreign policy. In 1907 the Japanese had seized the country after King Kojong abdicated and stopped all legal emigration of Koreans. The Korean migrants, with no land to return to, began to utilize the picture bride avenue of courtship so that they could start families and have some semblance of a normal life until they could return home.

8. In Chinese medicine, curative herbs fall into a continuum between hot and cold, used to balance the energy in the body, which also ranges from hot to cold. Ginseng is a warm ingredient often used with other herbs as a remedy for ailments ranging from digestive disorders, impotence, and other sexual difficulties to memory problems. Korean, or red, ginseng, in particular, is the warmest ginseng variant most frequently used to tone up energy and blood to improve sex gland functions.

9. Scholars of Korean American history contradict Dora's version of the history of the Korean Methodist Church in San Francisco. According to Dora, the Korean constituency commissioned the building of the Korean Methodist Church on Powell Street in 1928.

10. The Methodist Church was the center of community life for the Korean community in San Francisco. One's church affiliation still remains one of the main anchors of the Korean American community in San Francisco although the proliferation of Korean churches in the San Francisco Bay Area has also created cleavages within the community.

11. Euphemistic reference to the Japanese practice during the occupation of kidnapping Korean women to use them as "Comfort Women," or sex slaves in "Hospitality Centers" for Japanese troops in Asia. It is estimated that 90 percent of "Comfort Women" were Korean.

12. The Irish did not retain their language after the Isles were taken over by the English; however, the parallel to the Irish is one that Dora drew upon to explain the tenacity of the Korean people under Japanese occupation.

13. The March First Movement was a national and international event in which tens of thousands of Koreans joined together to read copies of a declaration of independence and marched through the streets of Seoul and other cities throughout the country singing the "Song of Patriotism" and waving the Korean flag, both of which were banned by the Japanese.

14. The Tongji Hoe was a splinter organization from the Kungmin Hoe, the initial Korean National Association in the United States, which Syngman Rhee helped to established in 1910.

15. Dora's inability to reach more than an octave might have prevented her from continuing piano, but there might also have been other kinds of pressure; at that time, Orientals could not become concert pianists.

16. There were generally three shifts of workers in Chinatown who worked twenty-four hours a day, which allowed for laborers to share housing since they slept in separate shifts. This work schedule created a demand for services, especially food, twenty-four hours a day.

17. Dora differentiates Filipinos from Orientals, as was common for Northern Asians to do when she was growing up. Accordingly, when the term *Asian* came into popular usage, she simply substituted it for *Oriental*. The term *Oriental* has its roots in the European discovery of Northern Asia, specifically China, Japan, and by geography, Korea. The Philippines is geographically part of Southeast Asia, an area of Asia that was not commonly known of in the 1930s. According to Dora, "When you say *Asia*, per se, it means China, Japan, and Korea. That's the way it has always been known. And Southeast Asians are below— closer to the equator. So there we have the Vietnamese, Cambodians, Thais, Laotians, Burmese, Filipinos. They're in a different part of the world." I believe this construction of the world has to do with the ethnocentrism of Northern Asians, as well as the way in which world geography was taught (or mistaught) in the United States in the 1920s and 1930s.

18. After the Gentlemen's Agreement in 1907, Japanese laborers could no longer enter the United States, and there was a labor shortage in the West. Filipino men started to come into the United States to fill the labor shortage. Because the Philippines became a protectorate of the United States in the 1898 Treaty of Paris after the Spanish American War, Filipinos were considered U.S. nationals. Although nationals did not have the rights and privileges of citizens, as nationals of the Untied States, Filipino men could travel freely to the United States between 1989 and 1934. Hence, many single men came to the United States to seek adventure and their fortunes. They came alone as sojourners hoping to accumulate enough wealth in a short period of time so that they could return home, buy land, find a wife, and start a family. The reality of saving money, however, differed dramatically from their overblown hopes.

19. The bulk of the early immigrants were male sojourners who came to the United States with the hopes of making their fortunes and returning home with enough money so they could afford a comfortable home and support a wife and family.

20. Dora's mother's concern with the bachelors stems, in part, from Korean notions that being without family is being without bearing in the world. Without family, one is disconnected and to be pitied.

21. The 1790 Naturalization Act stipulated that "only white persons" were eligible for naturalized citizenship. In 1913 the California legislature passed the alien land law, which stipulated that the ownership of land by aliens ineligible for citizenship was unlawful.

22. In 1913 the practice of purchasing land in their children's names became common among immigrant Asians, particularly among the Japanese. In order to prevent Japanese and other Asians from gaining access to land, in 1920 the land law was amended to exclude the purchase of land in the name of citizen minors.

23. While this is accurate for many Asian groups, in fact, anti-Asian immigration laws were appealed on a nation-by-nation basis, and the Chinese were granted the right of naturalization in 1943 with the repeal of the Chinese exclusion laws. At this time, 105 Chinese were permitted to immigrate per annum.

24. Restrictive covenants prevented Orientals from leasing or buying property outside areas that were designated for them. Laws regarding "Restricted Areas" in the city and county of San Francisco were lifted in 1947.

Chapter Two

1. See Charles M. Wollenberg, *All Deliberate Speed: Segregation and Exclusion in California Schools, 1855–1975* (Berkeley: University of California Press, 1977); and Victor Low, *The Unimpressive Race: A Century of Educational Struggle by the Chinese in San Francisco* (San Francisco: East/West, 1982).

2. Sucheng Chan, *Asian Americans: An Interpretive History* (Boston: Twayne Publishers, 1991), 57–60.

3. Ibid., xxv.

4. The Omnibus act of 1924 brought a complete closure of immigration from Asian nations. Missionaries and students were not immigrants, and were permitted to enter the United States.

5. Presently Benjamin Franklin Middle School.

6. Dora's use of race in this context is embedded in the Korean construction of race whereby all non-Koreans are thought to be racially different.

7. The Top of the Mark refers to the top of the Mark Hopkins Hotel at the top of Nob Hill.

8. *Joe* is a pseudonym.

9. It is not clear if this is her mother's wishes, or some Korean practice with which I am unfamiliar. In the past, Korean infants were kept secluded until they reached the age of one hundred days, and many still observe the hundred-day mark for an infant's first public appearance for a child. However, this is and was not the case for peasant or working-class women who must continue to work despite their postnatal condition.

Chapter Three

1. Dora does not elaborate on the reasons for her father's diminished role in Korean community affairs. While it may not have been significant for Dora, without continued Korean immigration to California through San Francisco, the city had stopped serving as the nexus of the Korean community. The size of the Korean community in Los Angeles quickly exceeded the numbers in San Francisco, and in 1936 the Korean National Association (KNA) decided to construct a building to house its headquarters in Los Angeles. In December of 1937 the KNA moved to the new building on Jefferson Boulevard, a move that limited her father's ability to participate in Korean community affairs.

2. The 1952 McCarran-Walter Act permitted Korean and Japanese alien residents to become naturalized.

3. *Mangneh* is a term used for the youngest child. This word carried connotations of spoiled and most loved, as is considered usual for youngest children in Korea.

4. Korean practice is to bury the dead, ideally facing west on a mountain clearing with a view. Mr. Yum may have objected on the cultural grounds.

Part 2, Introduction

1. Sucheng Chan, *Asian Americans: An Interpretive History* (Boston: Twayne Publishers, 1991), 139–40.

2. After the war the resettlement pattern for younger Japanese Americans from internment camps also mirrored the trend toward integration into previously restricted areas.

3. The Boy Scouts, Lions Club, and Rotary Club are a few that encouraged the creation of ethnic chapters.

4. See chapter 3 of Lon Yuki Kurashige's doctoral dissertation, "Made in Little Tokyo: Politics of Ethnic Identity and Festival in Southern California, 1934–1994" (University of Wisconsin–Madison, 1994), for an analysis of the Japanese American "integration," such as it was, in the postwar period.

Chapter Four

1. Despite the fact that the restrictive covenants were struck down in 1947, for practical purposes, certain neighborhoods remained restricted to Orientals.

2. There are three degrees of membership in the Masonic Order. After a man is sponsored by a member into the Masonic Order, he can then join the York or Scottish Rite. After joining one of those two organizations, he can then become a Shriner, if he so chooses. Wives of Masons have separate organizations, which the women refer to as auxiliary groups. The Eastern Stars, Job's Daughters, and the Daughters of the Nile are three such organizations (personal communication with Shrine Recorder in Los Angeles, August 16, 1996).

3. Arlene is Chinese American.

Chapter Five

1. This estimate is a composite of U.S. Bureau of Census figures for Hawaii, and immigration figures from the U.S. Commissioner of Immigration and Naturalization between 1952 and 1965.

2. Figures from Bill Ong Hing, *Making and Remaking Asian America Through Immigration Policy, 1850–1990* (Stanford, Calif.: Stanford University Press), 1993, 66.

3. U.S. Bureau of the Census.

4. Alex Haley, *Roots* (New York: Doubleday, 1976).

5. Gina is a pseudonym.

6. Panmunjom is the town in the demilitarized zone on the thirty-eighth parallel where talks between North and South Korea are conducted.

7. Minsukchon, located one hour outside of Seoul in Suwon.

Chapter Six

1. Sucheng Chan, *Asian Americans: An Interpretive History* (Boston: Twayne Publishers, 1991), 174–75.

2. Asian American ethnicity is necessarily four-tiered and tends to be divided conceptually and functionally along pan-Asian, particular Asian ethnic, as well as gender- and class-specific lines. In fact, although there are gender differences, the notion of a pan-Asian consciousness is often one that native-born, American-educated, and middle-class Asians embrace. Those confined to ethnic enclaves, immigrant or otherwise, are far less likely to participate in pan-Asian organizations.

3. A new Korean center that initially opened for employment training for multicultural usage opened up about two miles away from the Korean Community Service Center. In the mid-1980s the other center started catering to the needs of the elderly as well, becoming more of a full-service center.

4. See *Hanguk Ilbo*, December 4, 1993, for the article on the growth of Korean churches in Northern California.

5. There is a lot of controversy around the Korean Methodist Church. It is alleged to be the first Korean church established in the United States mainland, and the present congregation wants to sell the building and move the location because the space does not meet the needs of the congregation. However, there is a faction that is trying to halt the sale of the building because they feel that it should be saved as a historical landmark, given its history.

Part 3, Introduction

1. While it was historically awarded at age sixty, in Korea, as in other industrialized contexts, age sixty is no longer viewed as old. In the past twenty years, the seventieth birthday has become celebrated as the more appropriate occasion to mark retirement from active life. As such, sixty now serves as the age to mark lifelong accomplishments.

2. 1990 census data indicate that the Korean population in the San Francisco Bay Area (San Francisco, Oakland, San Jose) was 39,459. That figure was considered a gross undercount by Korean community workers. By their estimates the figure was closer to 60,000. In 1996 Korean language publications fix the estimated population for Koreans the San Francisco Bay Area between 80,000 to 100,000.

3. Los Angeles, New York City, and Chicago are but three urban areas in which Koreatowns have flourished.

4. For reading in the growth of Korean entrepreneurs, see Ivan Light and Edna Bonacich's *Immigrant Entrepreneurs: Koreans in Los Angeles 1965–1982* (Los Angeles: University of California Press, 1988); and Ilsoo Kim's *New Urban Immigrants: The Korean Community in New York* (Princeton: Princeton University Press, 1981).

5. According to the *Hanguk Ilbo,* December 4, 1993, there were 120 Korean churches in northern California. (Northern California designation in this case includes the Sacramento area.) The significance of Christian churches in Korean American communities is well documented. For a few sources on the topic see Hyung-chan Kim, "The History and Role of the Church in the Korean American Community" in *The Korean Diaspora* (Santa Barbara: Clio Press, 1977); Won Moo Hurh and Kwang Chung Kim, "Religious Participation: Ethnic Roles of the Korean Church" in *Korean Immigrants in America;* and Ai Ra Kim, *Women Struggling for a New Life: The Role of Religion in the Cultural Passage from Korea to America* (Albany: State University of New York Press, 1996).

6. See Chin, "A Comparative Study of Late Life Ritual" (Ph.D. diss., University of California, San Francisco, 1990); and Keum Young Chung Pang, *Korean Elderly Women in America: Everyday Life, Health, and Illness* (New York: AMS Press, 1991).

7. Terms often utilized by Koreans in America to differentiate American-born and Korean-born community members.

Chapter Seven

1. In *The Essential Other* (New York: Basic Books, 1993), Bertram Cohler asserts that while grief is universal, there is enormous cultural variation in "appropriate" expression.

2. The idea that loss "should" lead to recovery and a zest for new challenges is one interpretation of Freud's discussion of mourning on inevitable inconsolable loss in "The Future of Illusion" in *The Standard Edition of the Complete Psychological Works of Sigmund Freud,* edited and translated by J. Strachey, vol. 21 (London: Hogarth Press, 1927 [1961]), 5–58. See Elizabeth Kubler-Ross, *On Death and Dying* (New York: Macmillan, 1969); George H. Pollock, *The Mourning-Liberation Process,* vols. 1 and 2 (Madison, Conn.: International Universities Press, 1989); and Catherine M. Sanders, *Grief: The Mourning After* (New York: Wiley, 1989), for perspectives that can be understood as proponents of the "recovery" model. While this paradigm may reflect one response to loss and resolution, according to Cohler (1993), the notion that mourning leads to a readiness to move on, unencumbered by prior life experiences, is dismissive of the enormous cultural variation in grief and mourning, and the complex circumstances affecting the meaning of bereavement. He notes that this "is the American tale of conquest of adversity in psychological rather than economic terms, a Horatio Alger story of the psyche" and cautions that painful feelings often continue for life.

Conclusion

1. Since Dora had no Korean agemates, the girlfriends to whom she refers are Chinese and Japanese.

2. S. Farnham-Diggory, "Self, future, and time: A developmental study of concepts of psychotic, brain injured and normal children," *Monographs of the Society for Research in Child Development* 33 (Monograph 103), 1966.

3. Bertram Cohler, *The Essential Other*, 325–26.

4. In "The life review article: an interpretation of reminiscence in the aged" *Psychiatry* 26, 1968, 65–76, R. Butler focuses on Eric Erikson's concept of integrity in later life from *Childhood and Society* (New York: Norton, 1963), to assert the importance of life review to older persons.

5. The internal coherence of narrative probably varies according to culturally defined perspectives of time since time perspectives do impact narrative. See Janet Hoskins, *The Play of Time: Kodi Perspectives on Calendars, History, and Exchange* (Berkeley: University of California Press, 1993), for example.

6. See Chin, "A Comparative Study of Korean Late Life Rituals" (Ph.D. diss., University of California, San Francisco, 1990).

7. There are other reasons for the tendency to celebrate men's life passages in the United States. See Chin, "A Comparative Study," for more.

8. This statement is made relative to the numbers of Koreans in the United States today, which renders the first wave of immigrants to minority status within the community.

9. Barbara Myerhoff, in *Life History Among the Elderly: Performance, Visibility, and Re-Membering* (Berkeley: University of California Press, 1985), 152–55, indicates that "cultural performances are reflective in the sense of showing ourselves to ourselves." While Myerhoff referred specifically to the telling of life history as cultural performance, the writing of life story is similar in that it is a reflexive cultural product. Myerhoff also wrote extensively about the transformation of ethnicity in the United States, focusing on Jewish elderly.

10. With their underlying emphasis on the equality of all people before God, Protestant churches had served as a center for oppositional movements to class domination during the late 1800s and continued to serve as the headquarters for the Korean Independence Movement during the Japanese occupation.

11. Ai Ra Kim, *Women Struggling for a New Life: The Role of Religion in the Cultural Passage from Korea to America* (Albany: SUNY Press, 1996), 31.

12. Men held all the public positions of authority, prestige, and power within the Korean American church, the nexus of the community. The concession to egalitarian ideology was that women were allowed active roles in the church, serving as Sunday School teachers, managing Korean language schools, raising scholarship funds, acting as deaconesses, stewardesses, and choir members in the church. While these roles enhanced women's visibility in public life, they were also deemed acceptable as they were public roles commensurate with the conventional Korean woman's role of household manager whose responsibilities included managing household affairs and raising children.

13. There is no evidence among Korean picture brides that fathers or brothers sold their daughters or sisters into marriage. However, the agency of picture brides is unknown. What is known about Korean marriage practices in 1920 is that marriages, by and large, were arranged by older family members.

14. This information was ascertained from detailed reconstructions of Korean immigrant families in San Francisco as well as a sampling of family genealogies mapped for the *ReViewing the Past: Tracing Family Stories* exhibit (July 1996–January 1997) at the Korean American Museum in Los Angeles.

15. In interviewing seven other families for *ReViewing the Past: Tracing Family Stories* (Korean American Museum, July 1996–January 1997), it is evident that in the 1930s and 1940s sons were encouraged to go to college. Daughters were not encouraged to go to college, and it is the rare woman who had the will, resources, and family support to acquire a B.A.

16. From Family Story interview by Yoon Cho for *ReViewing the Past: Tracing Family Stories,* exhibit at the Korean American Museum, July 1996–January 1997. Examples of this can also be found in Ai Ri Kim's *Women Struggling for a New Life: The Role of Religion in the Cultural Passage from Korea to America* (Albany: SUNY Press, 1996).

17. This is the case for picture brides who came from the northern provinces of Korea. Travel to and from Korea was difficult during the Japanese Occupation. After the Occupation the Korean peninsula was divided, and North Korea closed itself off from what was then the noncommunist world. Americans have not been able to travel to North Korea until the last decade. After she left Korea Hang Shin Kim never saw any of her agnatic kin again. There are, however, documented instances in Hawaii of Korean picture brides from the south returning home and bringing back their sisters as picture brides for other men. (For example, Hom family history, *ReViewing the Past: Tracing Family Histories,* Korean American Museum, Los Angeles. July 1996–January 1995.) This, however, is the exception rather than the rule. Travel fare to Korea was restrictive for most Korean laborers in Hawaii, and absolutely prohibitive from the U.S. mainland.

18. Of European ancestry.

19. Robert W. Gardner, Bryant Robey, and Peter C. Smith, "Asian Americans: Growth, Change, and Diversity," *Population Bulletin* 40, no. 4 (October 1985): 3–43.

20. In *Women of Korea: A History from Ancient Time to 1945* (Seoul: Ewha Womans University Press, 1976), Yung-Chung Kim defines the "nameless woman" as one of two social ideals of women.

21. Kim, *Women Struggling for a New Life,* 25.

22. Indeed, when examining the role of Korean shaman, both Youngsook Kim in *Six Korean Women: The Socialization of Shamans* (St. Paul: West Publishing Co., 1979) and Laurel Kendall in *Shamans, Housewives, and Other Restless Spirits: Women in Korean Ritual Life* (Honolulu: University of Hawaii Press, 1986) and *The Life and Hard Times of a Korean Shaman: Of Tales and the Telling of Tales* (Honolulu: University of Hawaii Press, 1988) discuss the personal sacrifices that a shaman must make in order to pursue her calling in the service of healing. Like house-

wives who sacrifice their lives for their families, shamans too give up their lives. They do not give up their lives for corporeal others but to spirits who must be appeased. Additionally, there is tremendous social stigma associated with being a shaman.

23. Mary Chun Lee Shon, a prominent Los Angeles social worker and educator commented, "The shamanistic stuff that many of these Korean women go in for . . . I don't know about that. When you work in social service you can't afford to indulge in stuff like that. We social workers deal with the here and now, not spirits and ghosts. There are quite a few Korean women in social work today. And you know, you don't find many Korean women in social work who go in for that stuff. We have our own share of miracles to perform" (Personal communication, July 1996).

24. See, in particular, Laurel Kendall's *Shamans, Housewives, and Other Restless Spirits: Women in Korean ritual Life* (Honolulu: University of Hawaii Press, 1986) and *The Life and Hard Times of a Korean Shaman: Of Tales and the Telling of Tales* (Honolulu: University of Hawaii Press, 1988) for the ways in which shamanistic practice empower women in male-dominated Korean society.

25. See James C. Scott, *Domination and the Arts of Resistence: Hidden Transcripts* (New Haven, Conn.: Yale University Press, 1990).

26. James C. Scott, in *Weapons of the Weak: Everyday Forms of Peasant Resistance* (New Haven, Conn.: Yale University Press, 1985), discusses "hidden" forms of struggle against domination in the daily lives of the peasants in Sedaka, a Malaysian village. Challenging Gramscian notions of hegemony, Scott uses the term "weapons of the weak" to refer to disguised forms of resistance that are often mistaken for compliance. Scott is but one of many scholars who writes of resistance in terms subversion, dissidence, counterdiscourse and counterhegemony in the study of subordinated groups. See, particularly, Michel Foucault's *Power/ Knowledge: Selected Interviews and Other Writings, 1972–1997*, edited and translated by Colin Gordon, as well as Foucault's other works, for intellectual antecedents. Work produced in the 1980s for the origins of this discourse applied to specific groups include Aiwa Ong's *Spirits of Resistance and Capitalist Discipline: Factory Women in Malaysia;* Michael Taussig's *The Devil and Commodity Fetishism in South America* (Chapel Hill: University of North Carolina Press, 1980); Lila Abu-Lughod in *Veiled Sentiments: Honor and Poetry in a Bedouin Society* (Berkeley: University of California Press, 1986); and Emily Martin in *The Woman in the Body: A Cultural Analysis of Reproduction* (Boston: Beacon Press, 1987), a short list of examples of such work.

27. The range of behaviors that Scott allows for dominant classes includes acts of resistance. However, since subversion is not necessary, particularly in dealings with the dominated, this is not an avenue he fully explores.

28. Shirley Geok-lin Lim, in "Asians in Anglo-American Feminism" in *Changing Subjects: The Making of Feminist Literary Criticism* (London: Routledge, 1993), 244, edited by Gayle Greene and Coppelia Kahn, refers to the "intersections of

overlapping . . . circles of authority" to describe the margins between multiple cultures.

29. Scott, *Weapons of the Weak*, 302.

30. See Chin, "A Comparative Study," for discussion of the function of Korean senior citizens' groups in the United States.

31. Barbara Myerhoff discussed the need for older people, particularly those with disrupted histories, to seek public validation of their lives in "Life History Among the Elderly: Performance, Visibility, and Re-Membering," in *A Crack in the Mirror: Reflexive Perspectives in Anthropology,* edited by Jay Ruby (Philadelphia: University of Pennsylvania Press, 1982).

32. See Chin, "A Comparative Study."

33. See Kim, Yi, Yi, and Ha, eds., *Suyon* [Celebrations of Longevity] in *Kajong Uirye Taebaekkwa* [The Encyclopedia of Family Ritual] (Seoul: Hando Munhwa Sa, 1983), 235–41 for one of many examples of manuals of form.

34. Arnold Van Gennep first outlined this three-part progression of separation, liminality, and reaggregation in his now-classic study *Rites of Passage,* translated by M. B. Vizedon and G. L. Caffee (Chicago: University of Chicago Press, 1908).

35. Embedded in the language and cultural logic of ancestor worship, Robert L. and Dawnhee Yim Janelli note in *Ancestor Worship and Korean Society* (Stanford, Calif.: Stanford University Press, 1982) that many refer to the *hwan'gap* as the *san chesa,* or living ancestor, memorial service.

36. Although this is true in both Korea and the United States, reasons for celebrating a person's accomplishments at the *hwan'gap* differ. In Korea the *hwan'gap* has become a particularly important marker of accomplishment among middle class men since many must retire from their first and official careers at age fifty-five, the official retirement age in Korea. With many taking on second, less prestigious careers in later life, the *hwan'gap* serves to remind others of the celebrant's past accomplishments. In the United States, with retirement age being sixty-five, the celebration of the *hwan'gap* does not indicate retirement from active life. The *hwan'gap* celebration more often serves as an ethnic marker, where contributions to the Korean immigrant community are highlighted.

37. In the three years I spent in San Francisco and the year I spent in Seoul examining late life rituals (1986–1989), not only was Dora the only American-born Korean given a public *hwan'gap* celebration, hers was also the only *hwan'gap* celebration that was awarded at age sixty-five.

38. Soo-Young Chin, "Korean Birthday Rituals," *Cross Cultural Journal of Gerontology* 6 (1991): 145–52.

39. For a discussion of persuasion as one of the special tasks of ritual, see Barbara Myerhoff, "We Don't Wrap Herring in a Printed Page: Fusion, Fictions, and Continuity in Secular Ritual," in *Secular Ritual: Forms and Meanings,* edited Sally Falk Moore and Barbara Myerhoff (Assen: Royal Van Gorcum Press, 1977), 199–224.

40. In San Francisco between 1986 and 1988 and in Seoul in 1989.

41. See Soo-Young Chin, "The Role of Ritual for Korean American Elderly," in *Frontiers of Asian American Studies,* edited by Gail Nomura, Stephen H. Sumida, Russell C. Long, and Russell Endo (Pullman, Wash.: Washington State University Press, 1989). Also see Chin, "A Comparative Study."

42. See Chin, "A Comparative Study."

43. See Bong-Youn Choy's *Koreans in America* and Hurh and Kim's *Korean Immigrants in American* for additional readings on the religious composition of Korean American immigrants.

44. Korean term for house manager or head of household.

INDEX

Abortion, 101–102, 193–194
Abu-Lughod, Lila, 209n, 222n
Adolescence, 46–52
Ahn, Ch'ang Ho, 10, 22, 29, 33, 34, 109, 128, 213n
Allen, Horace N., 21
Asian American movement, 91–92, 97, 110, 140–141, 178; activism in, 112–113
Asian American Studies, 6, 194
Autobiographical narrative: cultural influence on, 6–8; examples of, 210n, 211n, generalizability of, 7–8, 210n

Bachelors: Korean, 33; Oriental, 35; Filipino, 35
Behar, Ruth, 5, 14, 15, 209n, 211n
Bellah, Robert, 211
Bonacich, Edna, 219n
Brandese, Stanley H., 208n
Business and Professional Women's Club, 166
Butler, R., 170, 171

California State Department of Employment, 3, 10, 80–81, 88, 93–96, 98–99, 101, 114, 115, 166
Ch'ama, 11, 152
Childbirth, 31, 59–60, 148; as final crossing into adulthood, 61, 179–180
Childrearing, 62, 80–86, 87, 177–178; with baby sitter, 70–71; Dora's beliefs about, 73–74, 79; and grandparents, 87–88, 89, 158
Childhood, 17–18; 31–39, 41–46, 60–61

Ch'ima chogori, 165
Chan, Sucheng, 209n, 212n, 213n, 216n, 217n, 218n
Chin, Soo-Young, 211n, 219n, 220n, 223n, 224n
Chinatown, 22, 23, 31, 32, 34–38, 41, 44, 45, 70, 71, 73, 169, 170; economy in, 38; Koreans in, 11, 17–19
Chinmok Hoe [Friendship Society], 22
Chip chu in, 191
Chong, 8
Choy, Bong-Youn, 212n, 224n
Christian missionaries, 20–22
Chungmae, 53, 122
Clifford, James, 208n
Cohler, Bertram, 170, 219n, 220n
Cole, Sally, 209n
Comfort women, 214n
Confucian influences, 61, 173–174, 179, 181; subverting Yi society ideal, 179, 211n
Courtship, 52–57
Crapanzano, Vincent, 5, 208n, 209n, 211n
Cressy, Earl Herbert, 210n
Crissman, Lawrence, 211n, 212n
Cultural crossings (journeying), 2–3, 4, 60, 110, 111, 114, 180, 182, 183, 222n–223n
Curner, Richard, 208n

Death, 67–70, 148, 155–156; child, 139, 141, 145–146, 149, 153; Dora's attitude toward her own, 198–199; sibling, 139, 141, 143–143, 149

Desegregation, 73; San Francisco, 75–76, 216n
Discrimination, 17–18, 43, 62, 75–79, 82–83, 120, 183–184, 195, 214n; age, 135, 191; California Alien Land Law, 37–38; employment, 63, 64, 88 114; endured by Koreans, 20, 212n; housing, 77–78; impact on social life (youth), 48–49; in military, 66; legislation 37–38; race, 78–79, 82–83; and post-1965 immigrants, 124; race and gender, 3, 170, 183
Divorce, 87, 122, 144–145, 158

Education: continuing, 63, 64, 65, 95, 196–197; discrimination in, 45, 51; Dora's, 42–52; Dora's children, 153; girls' school, 46–50; Korean language, 44; segregation in, 41; University of California, Berkeley, 51–52
Elderly, Korean, 115, 116–119, 163–164, 170–173, 184–188, 191
Espiritu, Yen, 209n, 212n
Ethnic identity: cultural practice of, 163, 165 185–190; Dora's understanding, 172; as expressed in hwan'gap, 187–188, 190; formation of, 43, 177–178; intergenerational, 81–82, 84; and interpersonal relationships in late life, 149–160; pan-Asian, 212n; reformulation of, 103–109, 136–138; reformation in late life, 149–161, 191
Ethnic Studies, 6
Ethnographic collaboration, 6, 13–15, 207n–208n, 209n, 211n

Family structure (Korean), 61, 173–174, 179–181
Family-run business (Korean), 219n; Yum family, 34–37, 215n
Farnham-Diggory, S., 220n
Feminism, 43, 160
Filial piety, 156; as expressed in hwan'gap, 63–64, 186–187; and immigration, 90, 184; obedience, 173; as parent care 90, 140, 162, 184; role of elder, 170–178; transference of, 113–114, 172, 178
Filial relations: guise thereof, 182–183; mother-daughter, 170; parental roles,

174; mother's obligation to children, 175, 177; women's position 174–175
Fischer, Michael M. J., 208n
Foucault, Michel, 222n
Frank, Gelya, 15, 208n, 211n, 212n
Freeman, James M., 208n, 209n
Freud, Sigmund, 219n
Funeral, 68–69; arrangements, 68, 139;

Gardner, Robert W., 221n
Garrison, Vivian, 208n
Gay and Lesbian Studies, 6
Geertz, Clifford, 209n, 210n
Gentlemen's Agreement, 213n, 214n
Grandparents, 81, 84; and childcare, 87–88, 89, 158

Ha, Hyogil, 223n
Haley, Alex, 91, 217n
Han In Hwe [Korean Residents' Association], 129
Hanbok, 164
Hanguk Ilbo, 218n, 219n
Hawaiian Sugar Planters' Association, 21
Health, 125
Herdt, Gilbert, 209n
Hing, Bill Ong, 217n
Hoebul, F. Adamson, 208n
Holland, Dorothy, 207n, 209n
Hoskins, Janet, 220n
Hungsadan, 10, 29, 159, 213n
Hurh, Won Moo, 212n, 219n
Hwan'gap, 1–2, 170–172, 184–192, 218n, 219n, 223n, 224n; as birthday party, 163, 165; celebrant as cultural exemplar, 185, 191; ceremonial clothing, 164–165; ceremonial core, 185; Christian influence, 190; Dora's, 2, 3, 9, 11, 139, 142, 163–168, 184–192, 223n; contemporary reasons for, 223n; as expression of ethnic identity, 187–188, 189, 223n; filial nature of, 186–187; issues of authenticity, 188–190; as living ancestor memorial, 185; 223n, Man Suk Yum's, 63–64; meaning for women, 171; media influence, 190–191; mediated by celebrant's life and accomplishments, 185–186, 188; practice of 186–190; public narrative for, 9–10, 187; as retirement party, 163,

184; as rite of passage into community elder, 191, strategic negotiation of, 188–190
Hwang, Sa Sun, 35

Ilse, 173
Immigration (Korean): and English as a Second Language 95–97; and filial imperative, 184; first wave, 21–23; impact of post-1965 immigrants on Korean American community 102–103; narratives of, 98–101; older, 184–185; post-1965, 91–93; post-1965 and language barriers, 94–95; post-1965 political orientation, 97; vocational training, 98
Immigration laws: U.S., 74, 75, 91, 179, 213n, 214n, 215n, 216n, 217n; 1790 Naturalization Act, 215n; 1898 Treaty of Paris, 215n; 1907 Gentlemen's Agreement, 213n–214n; 1924 Omnibus Act, 216n; 1943 repeal of Chinese exclusion laws, 216n; impact of 1965 Immigration Act, 27–28
Insam (ginseng), 29, 30, 214n
Integration, 74, 80, 158, 177, 217n
Interracial relationships, 132–135, 195; children born from, 195; marriage, 83–84, 152–153, 195
Ishimoto, Shidzue, 210n

Janelli, Dawn Hee Yim, 223n
Janelli, Robert L., 223n
Japanese American Internment, 66
Japanese Occupation, 20; stories of, 32–34; 110, 221n

Kaiser, Susan, 208n
Kendall, Laurel, 5, 209n, 211n, 221n, 222n
Kikumura, Akemi, 209n, 211n
Kim, Ai Ra, 219n, 220n, 221n
Kim, Elaine H., 209n
Kim, Hang Shin, 22, 67–69, 174–176, 179, 181, 182; immigration story, 29–30
Kim, Hyung-chan, 219n
Kim, Ilsoo, 219n
Kim, Kwangon, 223n
Kim, Yung-Chung, 221n
Kimchi, 114, 152
Kingston, Maxine Hong, 211n, 212n

Kitayama, Shinobu, 7, 210n
Kiyooka, Chyono Sugimoto, 210n
Kluckholn, Clyde, 208n
Kongnip Hyop Hoe [Mutual Assistance Society], 22
Korean American Community (San Francisco), 2–3; coming of age in, 58–59; conflicts within first wave community, 130–131; integration, 76; inter-racial relations, 134–135; living conditions, 31–32; second generation and marriage, 52–54, 56–57
Korean American Community: American Day Parade, 58; cohorts of, 4, 74, 92–93, 119–123, 178; as community of memory, 185; community service industry, 123–124, 125–127, 140–141, 179; demographics of, 91, 140, 173, 218n; divisions within, 127–128, 132, 188; historical influences on identity, 19–20, 22; inter-racial relations, 132–134; rituals, 185
Korean American History, 173, 212n–213n; conflicting versions, 214; revision of, 128–130, 172–173, 218n
Korean American Museum [KAM], 138, 207n, 221n, 214n
Korean Christian Church(es), 21–22, 127–130, 173–174, 190, 214n; women's (first wave) participation in, 173–174, 219n, 220n
Korean Community Service Center [Han Il Bong Sa], 1, 9, 112–126, 186, 187; co-founding of, 98; funding of, 115, 124, 135, 163; seniors, 115, 116–119, 163–164
Korean culture, and class, 103–109, 110, 119–120; changes with modernization, 121–123
Korean Independence Movement, 10, 18, 23, 32–34, 73, 108, 211n, 213n, 214n
Korean Methodist Church, San Francisco, 29, 32, 33, 35, 44, 127, 129–130, 214n
Korean Senior Citizens' Association [Group], 1, 127, 137
Korean shamanism, 221n; influence of, 180–181, 183–184, 222n
Korean War, 66–69
Krantz, David L., 208n

Kübler-Ross, Elizabeth, 219n
Kungmin Hoe [National Korean Association], 33, 38
Kurashige, Lon Yuki, 217n
Kwang, Chung Kim, 212n

Langness, L. L., 208n
Lee, Dae Wi, 32, 128
Lee, Tai-Young, 107–109
Lee, Yan Phou, 210n
Legislation: 1790 Naturalization Act, 215n; 1898 Treaty of Paris, 215n; 1907 Gentlemen's Agreement, 213n-214n, 215n; 1920 Amendment to 1913 Alien Land Law, 215n; 1924 Omnibus Act, 216n; 1943 repeal of Chinese exclusion laws, 216n; 1965 Immigration Act, 27–28, 213n; California Alien Land Law, 37–38; McCarren-Walters Act, 67
Life narrative (life story): collective rendering, 171; construction of, 170–171, 220n; definition, 5–6, 207n; about Dora's, 2, 28; Dora's understanding of, 6, 8–9, 199; examples of, 14–15, 209n, 211n; generalizability of, 7–8, 208n, 210n; life review, 171, 220; logic of, 3–4, 76, 142, 171, 177–178, 182, 207n; "myth of creation," 20–21, 212n; in old age, 171–172, 223n; in other disciplines, 6; personal, 170; public, 187; public versus private, 9–13, 171–172; time orientation, 170–171, 220n
Light, Ivan, 219n
Lim, Shirley Geok-lin, 222n
Loss and mourning, 139, 143–148, 198–199, 219n
Low, Victor, 216n

Marcus, George E., 208n
Markus, Hazel, 7, 210n
Marriage, 57–58, 148, 174, 175; children, 83–84, 135, 152; and compromise, 152, 156–156; 160, 161–162; conflict in, 149–154; 156; first wave, 29–30, 173, 213n; grandchildren, 152, 195; as marker of adulthood, 58–59, 61; post-1965 Korean immigrants, 122; second generation (first wave), 53
Martin, Emily, 222n

Mashima, Sumi Seo, 210n
Matsui, Haru, 210n
Menstruation, 47
Methodological considerations, 6, 208n; ethnographic collaboration, 5–6, 9, 12–13, 207n–208n, 209n, 211n; ethics, 13–15, 208n–209n; ethnographer effect, 4–5, 208n–209n
Mintz, Sidney, 211n
Myerhoff, Barbara, 173, 211n, 220n, 223n
Myerhoff, Barbara, 208n

Nee, Brett de Bary, 213n
Nee, Victor G., 213n
Niiya, Brian T., 8, 209n, 210n

Omi, Michael, 212n
Ong, Aiwa, 222n

Paik, Mary Lee, 211n
Pang, Keum Young Chung, 219n
Panmunjom, 104, 218n
Parson, Elsie Clews, 210n
Patterson, Wayne, 212n
Peacock, James L., 207n, 209n
Picture brides, 22, 221n; stories of, 29–30, 175, 176
Pollock, George H., 219n
Pregnancy, 62, 64, 65
Princess Pari, 180
Pyongyang, 29, 213n

Race, 211
Racialization, 19, 211n, 212n, 215n; in education, 42; and identity, 35
Radin, Paul, 208n, 210n
Reflexivity, 220n
Resistance, subversive (subversive obedience), 169–184, 222n; as duty to husband and children, 182–183; as duty to superiors, 178–179; as everyday forms of resistance, 170, 181–182, 222n–223n; as filial obligation to children, 177–179; as of filial duty to parent, 174–177; inculcation of, 174, 180
Retirement, 86, 114–115, 117, 157
ReViewing the Past: Finding Family Stories, 207n

Rhee, Syngman, 33, 214n
Rosaldo, Ronato, 208n
Ruby, James, 208n

Said, Edward, 213n
Sanders, Catherine M., 219n
Scott, James C., 183, 222n, 223n
Segregation, 17, 19; 45–51, 75, 76; in edu-
    cation, 41
Self, constructions of, Dora's, 11–12
Servicemen's wives, 99–101; parents of,
    100–101
Shon, Mary Chun Lee, 222n
Shostak, Marjorie, 211n
Sibling care, 90
Singmo, 30
Smith, Peter C., 221n
Social life, 45–50, 74; mainstream organi-
    zations, 80, 158
Socio-economic mobility, 73–75, 85, 89
Sone, Monica, 211n
Song, In-sob, 210n
Stoller, Robert J., 209n
Subjectivity, 5, 6
Subversive obedience (see Resistance,
    subversive)
Sugimoto, Etsu Inagaki, 210n
Sweder, Richard, 207n

Takezawa, Yasuko, 212n
Tamagawa, Kathleen, 210n
Taussig, Michael, 222n

Time orientation, 170–171, 194, 220n
Tongji Hoe, 33

Union Pacific Railroad, 28
United Nationalities, 139
Uri, 8

Van Gennep, Arnold, 223n

Watson, Lawrence C., 208n
Watson-Franke, Maria Barbara, 208n
Welaratna, Usha, 209n
White House Conference on Aging,
    128, 140
Winant, Howard, 212n
Wing, Youn, 210n
Wollenberg, Charles M., 216n
Women's Studies, 6
Wong, Jade Snow, 211n
Wong, Su-Ling, 210n
World War II: impact on employment of
    Asian women, 66; impact on social life
    54–59; social impact of 23, 54–59, 75
Wunsch, Marie Ann, 210n

Yi, Hyonsun, 223n
Yi, Kwanggyu, 223n
Young, Ryan, 221n
Yu, Eui-Young, 209n
Yum, Man Suk, 69–70, 173–176, 213n;
    business acumen, 37, 65; immigration
    story 21, 28–29